CHERYL ROBSON

Australian-born, Cheryl worked at the BBC in London for several years then developed and produced new writing for theatre before working as an editor and publishing over 200 writers, winning numerous awards. As a playwright, she won the Croydon Warehouse International Playwriting Competition, was longlisted for the Bruntwood Prize and has had several stage plays produced. Her co-translation of *David's Story* by Stig Dalager was shortlisted for the Marsh Award for Children's Literature in Translation and her co-edited book *Silent Women:Pioneers of Cinema* (Supernova) was voted best book on silent film in 2017. As a director, her film *Rock 'n' Roll Island* won four awards at US film festivals and was nominated at Raindance London. She initiated *Sight/Unseen* a conference on Asian Drama to coincide with the launch of this collection at Goldsmiths and Tara Arts in London.

AMANDA ROGERS

Associate Professor in Human Geography and the Geohumanities at Swansea University, her research focuses on Asian American, British East Asian and South East Asian theatres. Her book *Performing Asian Transnationalisms: theatre, identity and the geographies of performance* (Routledge, 2015) examines the geographical interconnections between these three spheres of creative practice. She has published peer-reviewed articles in journals, including *Progress in Human Geography*, *Annals of the Association of American Geographers*, *Cultural Geographies*, *Social and Cultural Geography*, *The Journal of Intercultural Studies* and *Contemporary Theatre Review*, the latter being a co-edited special issue on the Royal Shakespeare Company's 2012–2013 production of *The Orphan of Zhao*.

ASHLEY THORPE

Senior Lecturer in Theatre at Royal Holloway, University of London. Books include *Performing China on the London Stage: Chinese opera and global power, 1759–2008* (Palgrave, 2016) and *The Role of the Chou ("clown") in Traditional Chinese Drama: comedy, criticism and cosmology on the Chinese stage* (Edwin Mellen Press, 2007). He is co-editor of the book *Contesting British Chinese Culture* (Palgrave, 2018) and has published peer-reviewed articles in journals, including in *Asian Theatre Journal*, *Studies in Theatre & Performance*, *Theatre Dance and Performance Training*, *TRI*, *TDR*, and *Contemporary Theatre Review*, the latter being a co-edited special issue on the Royal Shakespeare Company's 2012–2013 production of *The Orphan of Zhao*. He has directed the annual Noh Training Project UK since 2011, and has written and performed in his own English-language Noh play, *Emily*, based on Emily Wilding Davison, the suffragette killed at the Epsom Derby in 1913.

First published in the UK in 2018 by Aurora Metro Publications Ltd.
67 Grove Avenue, Twickenham, TW1 4HX

www.aurorametro.com   info@aurorametro.com

Bound Feet Blues – A Life Told in Shoes copyright © 2015 Yang-May Ooi
The Last Days of Limehouse copyright © 2018 Jeremy Tiang
Jamaica Boy copyright © 2018 Stephen Hoo
Special Occasions copyright © 2016 Amy Ng
Conversations With My Unknown Mother copyright © 2018 Lucy Chau Lai-Tuen
Tango copyright © 2017 Joel Tan
The Fu Manchu Complex copyright © 2018 Daniel York Loh

Cover photo credits, top to bottom:

The Last Days of Limehouse, photograph by Robert Workman. www.robertworkman.co.uk
Tango, original production, Pangdemonium Theatre Company, Singapore, May 2017. Ruzaini Mazani and Benjamin Chow. Photograph by Crispian Chan.
The Fu Manchu Complex, photograph by Ikin Yum. www.ikinyum.com

Production: Simon Smith

With thanks to: Marina Tuffier, Harry Read, Ana Rice-Wallace, Abi Silverthorne, Madeleine Cuckson and Laura Mackenzie.

All rights are strictly reserved. For rights enquiries including performing rights please contact the publisher: rights@aurorametro.com

For *Tango*, inquiries concerning staging rights may be addressed to Tracie Pang, Artistic Director, Pangdemonium at admin@pangdemonium.com

No part of this publication may be reproduced, stored in or introduced into a retrieval system, or transmitted in any form, or by any means (electronic, mechanical, photocopying, recording or otherwise without the prior permission of the publisher. Any person who does any unauthorised act in relation to this publication may be liable to criminal prosecution and civil claims for damages.

This paperback is sold subject to the condition that it shall not, by way of trade or otherwise, be lent, resold, hired out, or otherwise circulated without the publisher's prior consent in any form of binding or cover other than that in which it is published and without a similar condition being imposed on the subsequent purchaser.

Printed in the UK by 4edge Limited.

ISBN: 978-1-912430-08-6 (print)
ISBN: 978-1-912430-07-9 (ebook)

BRITISH EAST ASIAN PLAYS

EDS. CHERYL ROBSON, AMANDA ROGERS AND ASHLEY THORPE

AURORA METRO BOOKS

CONTENTS

INTRODUCTION 6
Amanda Rogers and Ashley Thorpe

***BOUND FEET BLUES
– A LIFE TOLD IN SHOES*** 15
Yang-May Ooi

THE LAST DAYS OF LIMEHOUSE 35
Jeremy Tiang

JAMAICA BOY 87
Stephen Hoo

SPECIAL OCCASIONS 149
Amy Ng

CONVERSATIONS WITH MY UNKNOWN MOTHER 157
Lucy Chau Lai-Tuen

TANGO 201
Joel Tan

THE FU MANCHU COMPLEX 291
Daniel York Loh

INTRODUCTION

This volume brings together contemporary plays from British East Asians: a diverse and creatively vibrant group whose growing presence is making its mark on British cultural life. This community of practice has long participated in British theatre but has been under-represented in nearly all areas of the profession. However, after years on the fringes, BEAs are now taking ownership of the ways they are represented in British theatre. In the process they are advancing their presence and visibility with increased dynamism. In collecting this volume of material, we bring together a group of writers who reflect the range of work being produced by BEAs and their manifold creative approaches. It forcefully demonstrates that there is a wealth of BEA playwriting in this country and challenges any assumption that erasure from British theatre stemmed from a lack of BEA creativity, talent, or interest in writing for the stage.

What, then, is British East Asian? The descriptor 'British East Asian' has been widely adopted by practitioners as an umbrella term that holds together a diverse and complex range of experiences. Many of these assert a belonging to contemporary British life, contributing to narratives of British multiculturalism. However, the ethnic heritages of BEAs also move beyond Britain to encompass geographies in East Asia (China and associated territories, Korea and Japan), South East Asia (e.g. Singapore, Malaysia, Thailand and Vietnam), and across the globe (including the Caribbean, West and South Africa, and other parts of Western Europe). Some BEA practitioners are mixed-race, and identify with Black, South Asian, or Malay racial backgrounds, rather than those of East Asian descent (e.g. Chinese, Japanese or Korean). Although many BEA theatre makers were born and grew up in Britain, some migrated here when younger, whilst others may be living and working here in the medium to long term. Indeed, some practitioners, including those within this volume, have international profiles that allow them to produce and create work that speaks to multiple locations of culture, identity and belonging.

As a term, 'BEA' has facilitated greater cultural visibility for theatre makers of East and South East Asian descent in the wider landscape of British theatre. This is because it has brought together diverse experiences in a way that enables identification and inclusion into wider debates about Black and Minority Ethnic (BAME) representation. In the late 1970s and 1980s, all BAME groups in Britain were placed together under the single analytical category of 'Black' as a marker of multicultural difference from a supposedly 'White' universal norm. Indeed, the 1989 collection *The*

Colour Black: Black images in British television, included a discussion of the landmark British Chinese television series, *The Chinese Detective*. As discourses of multiculturalism evolved and an understanding of Britain's racial-ethnic communities grew, a differentiation became necessary between Black British and British Asian experiences, arts and cultural formations. However, as a direct legacy of the British Empire, British Asian refers solely to those from, or with ancestral connections to, the Indian subcontinent. It excluded those from East and South East Asia, who historically were labelled as 'Oriental' or placed under the broader racial category of 'Chinese'. Those from, or who can claim, East and South East Asian descent have rejected the terms 'Oriental' or 'Far East' owing to their colonial and exotic associations. Indeed, the persistence of imaginary notions linked to Britain's colonial past in East and South East Asia has led to depictions of BEAs as irrevocably 'different' and constantly 'foreign', which has sustained stereotypes such as the 'sly wily Chinese', the sexually charged 'lotus flower woman', the 'heathen Chinee' and the criminal mastermind Fu Manchu invented by the British author Sax Rohmer in 1913. The writers here implicitly or explicitly challenge these depictions, offering a more nuanced account of BEA experiences and identities. In so doing, they challenge two-dimensional stereotypes and claim representational territory for themselves.

BEA theatre has a long history. Chinese plays first appeared on the British stage as early as 1759, when Arthur Murphy's *The Orphan of China* was performed at Drury Lane starring David Garrick. The play was an adaptation of Voltaire's 1755 play *L'Orphéline de la Chine*, itself based upon a French translation of the thirteenth century Chinese classic *The Orphan of Zhao* (*Zhaoshi Gu'er*) published in 1735. Whilst this production brought East Asian literature to the British stage – albeit in a highly adapted form – it also introduced the possibility of the European depiction of China without involving practitioners of East Asian descent, a trope that was sustained into the early twenty-first century, and is only now being dismantled. Yet the narrative is not wholly one of exclusion. By the early twentieth century, Asian American, Asian Australian and BEA practitioners were beginning to assert limited ownership over stage representations of East Asia. Anna May Wong and Rose Quong appeared opposite a young Lawrence Olivier in *The Circle of Chalk* (1929) – an adaptation of the Chinese classical play *Huilanji*, which was also adapted by Bertolt Brecht into *The Caucasian Chalk Circle* (*Der kaukasische Kreidekreis*) in 1944. More significant was Hsiung Shih-yi's *Lady Precious Stream* (1934), a spoken drama adaptation of a Chinese opera and the first West End play written and co-directed by a Chinese practitioner. Although the play can be critiqued for its deployment of cultural stereotypes that pander to British ideas of exoticism, it did give its author a degree of visibility in British society at a time when London and Liverpool Chinatowns were in decline, and anti-Chinese xenophobia was rampant. The commercial success of the play, and its print circulation into the 1960s as a play for young people, makes it the most successful BEA play to date.

In the contemporary period, the first BEA theatre company was the award-winning Mu-Lan founded in 1988. The company pioneered original new work that directly challenged stereotypical depictions of British Chinese, such as Chay Yew's *Porcelain* (1992) which was a sell-out success at the Royal Court, and Anna Chen's solo show *Suzy Wrong Human Cannon* (1995). The company also led the development of work with mixed-race BEA lead characters, most notably Matt Wilkinson's *Sun is Shining* (2002). However, despite the high calibre of its artistic work, funding decisions made by Arts Council England in 2002 forced the company to close in 2004. Other companies operating during this period include Tripitaka Theatre Company (1993–1998) which created productions offering an Asian point of view to both UK and global audiences, notably Ivan Heng's autobiographical show *Journey West* (1995), as well as Chowee Leow's solo show (co-authored with Heng) called *An Occasional Orchid* (1996), which challenged exotic stereotypes by exploring the intersections between race, gender and sexuality. In addition, True Heart Theatre, established in 2006, assisted with the development of some BEA plays, including *In the Mirror* (2011), which featured Lucy Chau Lai-Tuen's *There Are Two Perfectly Good Me(s): One Dead, the Other Unborn*, Anna Chen's *Anna May Wong Must Die!*, and a full production of Veronica Needa's *Face*, the latter having been developed in both Hong Kong and the UK. Another BEA theatre company established during these years was Yellow Earth Theatre, seeded in 1993 and formally founded in 1995. The company has explored various Asian movement and performance aesthetics (from Kung Fu to Beijing Opera) such as in Philippe Cherbonnier's adaptation of *Rashomon* (2001) and Paul Sirett's *Running the Silk Road* (2008), as well as developing works addressing a range of issues such as criminal gangs (David Tse's *Play to Win*, 2000), migration histories and inter-generational family relationships (Sung Rno's *wAve*, 2009, and In-Sook Chappell's *Mountains: The Dreams of Lily Kwok*, 2018) as well as producing Shakespearean plays and adaptations (*Lear's Daughters*, 2003, and *King Lear*, 2006). In 2011, Yellow Earth Theatre lost its revenue funding from Arts Council England after a change of leadership and a loss of creative direction, funding that has subsequently been reinstated for the period 2018–2022. In the interim, a number of BEA companies have emerged that focus on developing and producing new plays, for example, Moongate Productions (who have produced Daniel York

Loh's *The Fu Manchu Complex* (2013) and *Forgotten*遗忘 (2018) – which is a co-production with Yellow Earth Theatre) Papergang Theatre (who co-produced Francis Turnly's *Harajuku Girls* with Nicholas Goh, China Doll Productions and The Finborough Theatre in 2015), and Trikhon Theatre (who produced Anna Nguyen's *A Dream from a Bombshell* (2014) and Nguyen and Mingyu Lin's piece *Rice Paper Tales* (2016) which was inspired by the storyteller Tiet Van Nguyen). Despite having lost its revenue funding, Amy Ng's *Shangri-La* at the Finborough Theatre in 2016 was also produced in association with Yellow Earth Theatre.

A major shift in participation for BEAs has recently been initiated through a string of protests about Yellowface, the practice whereby White actors perform as East Asian (specifically Chinese). Of particular importance here was the international protest against The Royal Shakespeare Company's adaptation of the Chinese classic *The Orphan of Zhao* in 2012–2013. Cast with only three BEA actors, all of whom played minor and/or stereotypical roles, the production embodied the exclusion of BEA practitioners (including writers) from British theatre. The use of White actors to perform East Asian characters highlighted the unequal playing field in which BEA practitioners participated and their exclusion from employment opportunities across the theatre profession. The protest was led by the advocacy group British East Asian Artists who continue to raise the visibility of BEA practitioners, and who have increased awareness of the creative needs of this community of practice. The impact of the RSC protest has been undeniably significant for BEA theatre-makers and has successfully led to major theatre institutions providing training, development and employment opportunities for BEA practitioners.

For writers, this has meant a greater degree of participation in the wider landscape of British theatre. Key here was the Royal Court's *Unheard Voices* programme, which aims to cultivate and highlight previously hidden writing talent. The programme has sought out writers from a wide variety of groups, including Muslims, Somalis and Romani, and in one of its rotations, the programme included writers from East and South East Asian backgrounds. From this, Tuyen Do, Amber Hsu, Daniel York Loh, Clare Mason and Francis Turnly were then invited into the Royal Court's racially non-specific, and prestigious, Studio Group for further development. In 2015, the Royal Court also commissioned BEA writers to "create short plays with British East Asian experiences at the centre of their stories" for *Live Lunch: Hidden*, which featured work by Lucy Chau Lai-Tuen, Daniel York Loh, Kathryn Golding and Amber Hsu, as well as two White writers, Vivienne Franzmann and Chris Thompson. A number of BEA writers have been members of other Royal Court writing groups (such as the Young Writers' Programme or the

Critical Mass Writers' Programme), including Rebecca Boey, Ming Ho, Amy Ng and Jingan Young, but BEA playwrights have also been selected for writing groups elsewhere such as The Orange Tree Writers Collective and SoHo Theatre's Young Company Writers' Lab. These schemes have been vitally important in raising the profile and abilities of BEA writers, and in allowing BEA writers to fully explore, embrace and express their own stories, adding further nuance to our understanding of what it means to be British and to the politics of contemporary multiculturalism.

Indeed, BEA playwrights can now be found working across both racially specific and non-racially specific spheres of practice in increasing numbers, often making BEA experiences and/or characters visible to wide-ranging audiences. For example, In-Sook Chappell won the Verity Bargate Award for *This Isn't Romance* (2009), which was then adapted for BBC Radio 3 and then turned into a screenplay for Film Four. Her plays *Tales of the Harrow Road* (2010), *Absence* (2016) and *P'yongyang* (2016) have all been produced, and she is currently under commission to the National Theatre Connections programme. Amber Hsu has adapted *Tales of Ovid* (2017) for the Royal Shakespeare Company, and was commissioned for *The Big Idea (Hangman)* at The Royal Court Theatre (2015), Amy Ng is under commission to the Royal Shakespeare Company and Belgrade Theatre Coventry, whilst Francis Turnly has also been Playwright-in-Residence at The Tricycle Theatre. There are historical antecedents to such writers, such as Simon Wu (*Pilgrimage of the Heart*, 2008) and Benjamin Yeoh, whose stage plays *Lemon Love* (2001), *Lost in Peru* (2003) and *Yellow Gentlemen* (2006) were produced by The Finborough Theatre, Camden People's Theatre and Ovalhouse Theatre respectively. However, in the contemporary moment it is evident that there is a dynamism, presence and reach among BEA writers that has not previously been experienced, and this is also reflected in the increased interest in producing their work.

In addition to the production of plays and the staging of play-readings at established venues for new writing like the Finborough Theatre, as this collection goes to print there are at least three plays by BEA playwrights on Britain's stages, namely In-Sook Chappell's *Mountains: The Dreams of Lily Kwok* playing in a sold out run at Manchester Royal Exchange before touring nationally as part of Black Theatre Live, Amy Ng's college drama *Acceptance* has received a hard-hitting production in the Hampstead Theatre Studio while Francis Turnly's epic *The Great Wave*, which explores North Korean abductions of Japanese citizens, is being co-produced by The Tricycle and the National Theatre in the 450 seater NT Dorfman Theatre on London's South Bank. These productions represent significant, positive, progress in BEA participation in British theatre.

What, therefore, is a BEA play? This collection, quite simply, comprises contemporary plays by BEA writers. This is with the awareness that non-BEA writers have successfully produced plays with BEA leads (for example, Philippe Cherbonnier, Anders Lustgarten and Matt Wilkinson), and that BEA writers are from highly varied backgrounds. Some playwrights choose to engage with specific BEA experiences or stories that may also speak to broader universal themes, whilst others choose to make no explicit reference to BEA issues in their work. The plays included in this volume address, or are informed by, questions of racial and ethnic identity but they also open up the multiplicity of that experience and its intersection with other dimensions of identity such as gender and sexuality.

Nearly all of the contemporary plays selected have been produced, whereas some, such as Stephen Hoo's *Jamaica Boy* and Lucy Chau Lai-Tuen's *Conversations With My Unknown Mother* are 'production ready' and have received development work from theatres such as Theatre Royal Stratford East. They collectively explore ideas of memory, nostalgia, community, identity and identity politics that resonate with contemporary BEA experiences – and beyond. They also provide a range of characters, of all ages and persuasions, which challenge the stereotypical representation of BEA people that persists in the media.

The Plays

Bound Feet Blues – A Life Told in Shoes by Yang-May Ooi uses the practice of foot-binding (experienced by her Chinese great-grandmother) as a way to explore female sexuality and empowerment across three generations of her family. The piece traces the tensions experienced by women in both 'East' and 'West' between conformity and tradition, between desire and being desired. It highlights how physical and psychological restrictions have been placed on women in the service of male heterosexual desire and patriarchy, but the play loosens these restrictive bindings to positively reconcile the past and the future.

Themes of nostalgia and memory are picked up in Jeremy Tiang's *The Last Days of Limehouse*. The play documents the end of London's first Chinatown, detailing the attempts of a 'Eurasian-American' woman, Eileen, seeking to preserve the gritty reality of the London Chinatown before it is bulldozed by developers. However, in her attempts to stir up a protest against the area's demolition, she encounters resistance from local British Chinese communities, who want different opportunities, experiences and all mod cons. The play opens up questions of heritage and loss, what is deemed culturally valuable (and by whom), and highlights the complex dynamics of nationality in relation to BEA experiences.

Jamaica Boy by Stephen Hoo similarly exposes the varied migratory histories of the Chinese diaspora, only this time through the less recognised route of the Caribbean. The play centres on the relationship between a young British Chinese offender and the Afro-Caribbean woman, Ophelia, he helps as part of his Community Service order. As the story unfolds and their relationship develops, we see the inter-racial tensions between black and Chinese communities, specifically in terms of hyper-masculinity, male pride, and heterosexuality. The play questions what it is to seek love across racial and sexual norms, and how new forms of communication might overcome isolation bred by division.

Under-represented stories of migration and the wider challenges of divided relationships are also explored in *Special Occasions*, this time through the relationship of Nina to her Viennese Jewish mother. The play presents snapshots of an awkward relationship during special occasions marked by the purchase of a Sachertorte. Nina's mother makes over-bearing demands on her daughter, yet we are left questioning whether she was right all along. A bullish parent who wants to do the best for her child, and the need for children to rebel and find their own way, are hardly themes specific to BEAs, and this is a strength of the play. Yet, there is the suggestion that the mother was part of the Jewish presence in Shanghai (it is not stated whether she was based in the Shanghai Ghetto during World War II, but the mother's anti-Japanese sentiment hints that she might have been), enabling the exploration of the themes of survival, matriarchy and the wisdom of age to be explored alongside the Confucian expectation that children obey their parents.

Similarly, *Conversations With My Unknown Mother* explores the relationship between mother and daughter, but this time through abandonment, dislocation and loss. The central character, Michelle, was born in Hong Kong, but abandoned by her mother who had run out of hope. Raised in Britain by adoptive parents, Michelle confronts her feelings towards her recently deceased adoptive mother (Mary) and the ghost of her real mother (Fei Yen). The play is unique for taking the experiences of Hong Kong adoptees, whose history is largely unknown, as its starting point, but it explores the wider universal themes of relationships between mothers and their daughters, and the nature of family bonds. Whilst there is a bleak undercurrent to the play, it proffers a message of hope and reconciliation, to live life to the best of one's abilities and accept who we are, and just as importantly, who we are not.

Acceptance is also at the heart of *Tango*, where the central family unit in the play consists of two men and their son. Set in Singapore, where homosexuality and LGBTQQ adoption remain illegal, the play narrates what happens when the family are discriminated against and refused service in a restaurant on the basis of their sexuality. The ensuing fracas is captured on video and posted online, sparking intense viral debate, and later street protests. Politically, the play is a direct challenge to Singaporean law (specifically sections 377A, 354 and 294A) that prohibit 'outrages on decency', 'outrages on modesty' and 'obscene acts'. The play asks where are the outrages on decency, and who commits obscene acts, when there is open discrimination? For the characters, this question causes a tussle between British and Singaporean identity, between experiencing racial discrimination in Britain and sexual discrimination in Singapore. The ambiguous ending of the play suggests that only through open and honest dialogue, and by listening to the concerns of the other side, might these issues be resolved.

The final play in the volume also represents a political challenge, this time, to representations of BEAs in British culture. *The Fu Manchu Complex* is a satirical comedy that ridicules any colonial longing for Victorian Empire, and the imagined security of race, gender and sexuality the period supposedly invokes amongst White Britons. The play is written for actors in Whiteface – East Asian actors presenting themselves as Caucasians, thereby subverting the Yellowface tradition that has been endemic to British theatre for the last 250 years. It also addresses Sinophobia, the fear of China taking over the world, which was endemic to Sax Rohmer's early twentieth century Fu Manchu novels, but also finds expression in the present as China commands greater influence economically and politically. A singular and direct challenge to British theatrical representations of China, and of wider xenophobia, the play offers a robust articulation and rebuttal of the discrimination that BEAs have faced.

As a selection of the many contemporary plays that are now being produced, we hope that this collection challenges dominant narratives about BEAs, and encourages a greater recognition of the diverse experiences, agendas and aesthetics of the voices that exist in this theatrical community.

Amanda Rogers
Associate Professor in Human Geography and the Geohumanities
Swansea University

Ashley Thorpe
Senior Lecturer in Theatre
Royal Holloway, University of London.

BOUND FEET BLUES – A LIFE TOLD IN SHOES

Bound Feet Blues – A Life Told in Shoes began as an idea for a book ten years ago. I wanted to re-tell the oral stories passed down by the generations of women in my family. However, the stories only came to life when I tried them out loud live in front of an audience, leading me to develop the script as a storytelling piece. Working with director Jessica Higgs, we created a full theatrical performance from it while retaining the feel of traditional storytelling. Wearing a simple black costume and with a minimalist set, both inspired by East / West elements, I created the range of characters and locations without costume changes, set embellishments or props.

The play was performed barefoot. For a piece about shoes to feature no actual shoes emphasised their power as a metaphor – and bare feet underscored the brutality of footbinding. My left hand stood in for a foot in the footbinding sequences, transforming into a twisted mutilated shape before the audience's horrified eyes.

A Malaysian accent was used for the childhood scenes, evoking my Malaysian childhood and the voice of my mother. The rest of the play was performed in RP English.

The first full production of the play was performed at the Tristan Bates Theatre, London in November / December 2015 for a three week run as part of the South East Asian Arts Festival, following development at the Centre for Solo Performance and a showcase performance in 2014. It was performed by me, Yang-May Ooi, directed by Jessica Higgs and produced by Eldarin Yeong Studio. The production was supported by Arts Council England, The Housing Finance Corporation and Maclay Murray Spens.

More information, including a video of the complete one hour play, can be found at www.BoundFeetBlues.co.uk.

Yang-May Ooi is a multimedia author of Chinese-Malaysian heritage. Her creative works include novels *The Flame Tree* and *Mindgame*, live storytelling performances and online multimedia projects. *Bound Feet Blues – A Life Told in Shoes* is her first theatre piece. She lives in London with her partner.

www.TigerSpirit.co.uk

BOUND FEET BLUES
– A LIFE TOLD IN SHOES

YANG-MAY OOI

Final performance version as developed in rehearsal with Jessica Higgs.

01 – CHINA DOLL

It's a beautiful summer evening in Oxford in 1983. I'm twenty and I'm walking arm in arm with Josh. He's tall and tanned and looks gorgeous in his dinner jacket. We're going to a ball and there's a gang of us strolling up the High Street – the young men in black tie and us girls in our beautiful ball dresses.

I'm wearing a blood red *cheongsam* – that's Chinese for long dress. It's that traditional dress with a high collar and buttons down the side. It was made for me by our family tailor in Malaysia to fit my every curve all the way down to the ground. There are slits up either side, stopping just short of obscene high on my upper thighs.

I'm wearing silk stockings and lacy suspenders. As I walk, the dress moves and there – can you see it? – a hint of that delicate strap, high up on my thigh.

I'm wearing a pair of Kurt Geiger stilettoes – black patent leather with three inch heels.

There's a shiny black triangle at their tip, where my toes are. There's a thin leather strap that runs up the middle of my foot like a thong to meet another strap that goes around my ankle like a bondage collar. The shape of the shoe makes my foot arch back like a woman in ecstasy.

And I swish along. The stilettoes make me walk in a delicate, swaying manner and I'm taking tiny baby steps. I feel a class above the other girls in their flouncy ball dresses, walking arm in arm with their young men.

Because the men – they are all looking at me.

02 – HELPLESS

And every step is an agony. All my weight is on the balls of my feet and my toes are jammed into the tips of the shoes – crushed up against each other, overlapping, crooked.

The arches of my feet feel contorted. And every time the sharp piercing heel slams down on to the pavement, my ankles wobble, threaten to snap over.

Josh has swagger in his walk; he loves having his China doll on his arm. He's picking up the pace, with his long masculine stride. I'm tottering along beside him with my tiny baby steps.

I say, Josh, please, slow down. And he does, but absently, not really understanding why I need him to slow down. Soon, he's picking up the pace again. And I struggle along beside him.

I look up at the High Street stretching out ahead of me. There's such a long, long way to go. How many tiny painful steps is it going to take to walk that long, long way to the ball? I envy Josh his strong sturdy shoes, his long manly stride, that sense that he owns the world.

Whereas my world is so tiny, shrunken to the next painful little step.

03 – SOME ENCHANTED EVENING

I'm eight years old. It's after dinner time in Malaysia. My sister is five and my brother is four. We run into my parents' bedroom and jump on the bed. My Dad is reading a book and my Mum is doing a crossword.

We say, *Mum, mum, mum, tell us a story*.

And they both put their books down.

I say, *Tell us how you and Dad met*.

MUM Well, I was a student at London University and one Saturday night, my friends and me, we all went to a dance. It was at Malaya Hall which is near Marble Arch.

I didn't know anybody so I was sitting by myself. And I felt like a wallflower. The other girls, they were looking so modern – in their 1960s outfits. I was only half modern – I had pointy glasses and my hair was up in the latest fashion like this, they call it the beehive.

But your Mama, your grandma, my mum used to say to me that whenever I go to this kind of formal dance I must wear traditional dress. So I was wearing a *cheongsam* and I felt like an old maid.

But then, across the room, I saw this young man. He was so good looking, in his DJ.

And he was also looking at me.

Waah, it was so romantic, just like in that song in that film, South Pacific.

KIDS Mum, mum, mum, sing the song.

MUM Well... okay– 'Some enchanted evening, you may see a stranger, you may see a stranger, across a crowded room...'

We listen to her and we stare at her. I think: this is what it is going to be like when I am a grown up woman.

My Dad says, *Ya, I saw this kampong girl, this village girl, so old fashioned. I took pity on her, lah.*

MUM Haiya, you are so rude!

But I see they are beaming at each other.

MUM So then he came over to me, lah, and we talked, lah.

Then afterwards, we went for a walk through the London streets, late at night, it was so romantic with all the lights shining brightly. We walked from Marble Arch to Piccadilly – do you know how far that is? It's a long, long way – me in my *cheongsam* and high heel shoes, tick tock tick tock like that – my feet were so painful! Aiyo, I thought I would die, my feet hurt so much.

But I didn't care – because I was with your Dad.

04 – SMALL FEET

It's the day after the ball in Oxford – Josh and me and our friends are hanging out in our student house. We're wearing T-shirts and jeans.

I am barefoot and I am so relieved. I can feel the carpet under my feet. I love being able to wiggle my toes. It's such a freedom. But a part of me feels ashamed.

I think of those women last night laughing and dancing in their high heels. They didn't seem to care that their feet hurt. Or maybe their feet didn't hurt. Maybe it's just me.

What's wrong with me? Why can't I endure the pain?

I feel bad that being with Josh is not enough to make me forget the pain. I feel like a fraud.

I walk across the room to get another drink. My feet are size 3½ which is quite small by Western standards.

Josh follows me with his eyes. He says, almost to himself but loud enough for everyone else to hear – "Mmm, I do like small feet."

And I'm so embarrassed in front of all my friends.

But, secretly, I'm rather pleased. Because I'm quite proud of my small feet.

05 – THE CONCUBINE

Once upon a time, in China, a thousand years ago – there lived an Emperor. He had many concubines. One of them was a pretty dancer. She was his favourite.

She had small delicate feet and one day, she bound them up and danced on point, like modern ballerinas do, and her feet looked even smaller and more delicate.

And the Emperor said, "Mmm, I do like small feet."

All the other concubines flew into a jealous rage – they wanted small feet too. So they began to bind their feet.

Everyone could see how dainty and delicate small feet could be. And the dukes and princes and courtiers all said, "Mmm, we do like small feet."

These women with bound feet were considered feminine and desirable. They walked in a swaying, delicate manner which all the men in the kingdom found charming. They couldn't move fast and had to take tiny baby steps. These women were considered a class above those dirty, ugly, vulgar peasants with their big, horrible, masculine feet.

These women with baby feet were the ones who found the best and richest husbands.

So more and more women began to bind their feet.

And their daughters' feet.

Till all the women in the land had small, dainty, delicate feet. These bound feet became known as Lotus Feet. Little Lotus Feet like the bud of the lotus flower.

But when all the women have small feet, how do you distinguish yourself, be the special one that the prince or duke or rich man will notice – like Cinderella – and take to be his wife?

You make your feet even smaller.

So the greatest prize of all, the most treasured perfect foot was a foot that was three inches long, the tiniest that a human foot could possibly be. And this was known as The Golden Lotus.

06 – A MOTHER'S LOVE

As a mother, you want the best for your daughter, don't you? You want her to have a good life and to be chosen by the best and richest husband. You look out there and see all those women with small feet and you know it's a competitive market.

So you call your daughter to you. She is four years old, the best age to start. You explain to her what you need to do and why you need to do it.

You start gently at first. You bend her toes over and tie them loosely with ribbons. It hurts her but only a little. And she must learn to go about her daily life with her toes curled over.

She used to be able to run and play. Now she can't. She is so small as you watch her.

She hobbles like an old woman; but when she wants to go somewhere fast, she crawls.

And you think, she is so resourceful.

Then she tries to pull the ribbons off so you chide her and remind her this is so she can find a good husband. She listens to you and learns what it is to be an obedient girl.

But her feet keep growing. So you make the bandages tighter. And her feet keep growing, as she grows taller.

She is five years old. You slice the bottom of her foot, cutting through muscle and tendon.

And you fold her foot over and tie the bandages tight.

She screams. And you weep.

And you remember what it was like for you at that age. How you screamed and struggled and tried to run away. But how could you with your feet cut in two?

You're not angry with your Mama, no, no you're not – you are grateful to her – because look – you have this good life, this good husband and you know your children will never go hungry.

But your daughter's feet keep growing.

She is six years old. And you break her toes.

And still her feet keep growing.

She is seven now. And you break the bones in her foot.

And still her feet keep growing. So you keep breaking the bones and tying the bandages tighter and tighter.

She is ten years old and after six years of this ritual every week, every month, she doesn't try to run away. She can't. She submits. She knows the value of having tiny feet – yes, she does. After six years of this ritual every week, every month, she is obedient, she is passive, she endures – all these are good qualities that a desirable Chinese wife should have. However her husband treats her, she will endure. And you feel so proud of her.

And you break the bones again and tie the bandages tighter and tighter till there is nothing left but two tiny little stumps.

That are three inches long.

The same size as your feet.

The prized Golden Lotus.

07 – THE POWER OF THE GOLDEN LOTUS

That night, you're lying in bed, naked, your feet unbound. Your husband is kneeling at the end of the bed, holding your tiny foot in his hand.

He is naked, ecstatic, erect. He is gazing at your Golden Lotus, adoring its delicate beauty. And suddenly you know it's all been worth it.

You may not be able to stand in this moment because without the tight bandages, your feet would just collapse under your weight. But you don't need to stand, you are where you should be, your husband at your feet, worshipping their soft, contorted shape.

You're aware that some people – Westerners – think these feet ugly and deformed. Their missionary women come to your country and want to stop footbinding because they say it's cruel. These big Western women with their big bosoms and big masculine feet – they dare to tell you that natural feet can be beautiful!

But look at their own culture. Their women will do anything to be more feminine and desirable. If they had the skills to do it, what cutting and slicing would they endure to tie up their intestines, enlarge their breasts, break their teeth, break their nose, break their faces and reshape them according to their standard of beauty?

So you make no apology for the Chinese standard of beauty, which has been endured for a thousand years and will endure for a thousand more.

As a wife – with your tiny feet and your beautiful embroidered gowns – you don't need to walk about freely, you stay where you belong, bound to the house, bound to your husband.

A woman who moves about freely like a man – with natural feet – is an abomination. She knows nothing of obedience or submission and cannot be controlled. Men may use her as a servant. Or they may use her as they please but they would never marry her.

It makes you angry to think of the ruined lives of these women. It's their mothers who are to blame. Their mothers were weak and pitied their pain and did not break their feet enough.

But You – with your obedience and submission and endurance – you achieved the three inch Golden Lotus. It is You who deserve this man.

This man – so powerful, who could have any woman he chooses, chose you to be his wife.

And he is here kneeling naked at your feet, caressing them, kissing them, loving them.

This is your only power. This power makes sense of everything that you have endured from the first moment your mother curled your toes over.

This was the only power your mother had, and your mother's mother before her, going back forty generations.

So the next morning, you take out a fresh set of bindings and call your beloved daughter to you again.

08 – TOMBOY

I'm ten years old in Malaysia.

At home, I don't like to wear shoes. I love to feel the wooden floor in the bedroom, the cold tiles in the hallway and the prickle of grass in the garden.

I have short hair. I like to play soldiers. I have a green helmet and a canteen and I love my toy gun

I'm Bruce Lee…

I'm John Steed with his bowler hat and brolly.

There's Emma Peel – with her long hair and her catsuit and knee high boots.

But I don't want to be Emma Peel.

I don't want to be a girl.

I want to be a boy.

I should have been a boy.

There's a story in my family that everyone knows. This is how my Aunty Diana tells it:

AUNTY DIANA So, May-May, in Chinese tradition, when a man and woman get married and they want to have a son – and every Chinese family wants a son, right? – they must take a young boy on the wedding night and roll him on the marital bed. That way, his boy essence goes inside the bed and when the newly married couple go to lie down on the bed to, you know – the boy essence passes from the bed inside them and that is how you make a son.

You don't believe me? It's true, one!

So on the night of your parents' wedding, there is a big party at your grandparents' house. I am nine years old and your Aunty Leng is eleven and we are so excited to be at the party with all the grown ups. Then the party comes to an end, late at night and it is the job of your Great Aunt No.3 – your Sahm Koo – to be responsible for this significant ritual. She goes to find a baby boy, one of the nephews – he is all sleepy – and she picks him up and carries him upstairs to the marital bedroom. All the guests follow, lah, because they also want to witness this significant ritual.

We follow also, lah. We are so excited to be part of this ritual. We push through the legs and we pop out in the bedroom, in front of Sahm Koo.

There is the bed, big and empty and waiting for something to happen.

So we jump onto the bed – we are giggling and laughing and rolling around.

But the grown ups are like: "Aiyo-yo, you naughty girls! This ritual is not for girls! You spoil the ritual, you spoil it all! So shameful girls to be on the bed. You are so naughty and disobedient." And we roll off the bed and we are crying. We don't want to be disobedient.

Sahm Koo puts the baby boy on the bed but it's too late. The ritual is already spoilt.

So I was born, eldest daughter instead of eldest son. When I am three years old, my sister is born. And then when I am four – yes, my parents had to wait four long years – my brother is born. He was the precious boy and he became the eldest son. Two girls, then a boy.

You see – the ritual does work!

But it's when I am four that I knew for the first time that I should have been a boy. I've got pigtails and I'm wearing this fluffy white dress and white socks and little white shoes with pearl buttons on the side. I look at myself and see this girl, this worthless girl. And I feel ashamed. I'm a disappointment. Everybody is over there fussing over my brother.

Nobody sees me.

But I know I'm not worthless. I can't be worthless. I can't be just a worthless girl.

I am the eldest son. I should be the eldest son. It's just that they can't see me because I'm dressed like this stupid girl.

So the next time my mother tries to make me wear a dress, I scream and struggle and try to run away. I want to be like a boy, with short hair and boy clothes and boy shoes. My mother is weak and she pities my pain. So she cuts my hair and lets me wear boy clothes and boy shoes.

I love my boy shoes, they are strong and sturdy. They have these fantastic laces and they go kok kok kok when I walk. Just like Grandpa's shoes. Everybody respects Grandpa, with his smart suit and pipe and kok kok shoes that give him power and glamour and authority.

But when the family – Grandpa, Grandma, my uncles and aunties – when they look at me, they are angry with me. So shameful for a girl to dress like a boy. You are so naughty and disobedient.

I don't understand. I thought they wanted an eldest son. Look, I want to say, I'm here, I'm your eldest son.

But I don't have the words.

09 – PONDAN

By the time I am ten, I'm wearing boy clothes at home.

But at school, I have to dress like a girl. I have this navy pinafore thing but it's okay because at least I don't have to wear girl shoes. I can wear my white rubber shoes – you know, like sports shoes.

There's a woman who works at the canteen at school. She is big and fat and has short hair. She wears man clothes and man shoes. We are having lunch, me and my school friends.

One of them says, *Eeee, look at the pondan – the queer – don't go near her. I hear stories – you go near her and she touch you down there.* We go, *Eeeey, so shameful.*

And the woman must know we are staring at her and laughing at her.

Another one says, *Geelllee – makes me sick, these women that wear man's clothes. There must be something wrong with her. They should put her in that mental hospital, Tanjong Rambutan, and never let her out.*

I don't know if what they are saying is true or not. But it doesn't matter. They think it's true.

But all I see are the woman's sad and lonely eyes.

I stay sitting with my friends. I listen to their laughter. I think about my family's disappointment and shame when they look at me. Is that me, there, that *pondan* with short hair and man's shoes?

And so over time, I give up my kok kok shoes – and all the power and glamour that they mean for me. I give up Bruce Lee and John Steed.

I hide my shame and I bind up my spirit of rebellion and defiance. With obedience, submission and endurance, I bind up my tomboy energy and I break its bones, cut down the eldest son and bind the bandages tighter and tighter till there is nothing left but a heart that is tiny and broken.

And over it all, I put on a beautiful, embroidered disguise. I'm 25. I'm in London. I'm a lawyer. It's the 80s. I have incredible, amazing power hair. I have beautiful clothes and beautiful tik-tok tik-tok shoes.

A pair of navy Gucci pumps, red wedges with a white trim, white wedges with a blue trim, delicate Italian slip-ons in a two toned black, tan sling backs with killer heels and – knee high boots like Emma Peel.

All the men in my social circle see a woman who is feminine and desirable.

And this is my power.

These lovely young men who are good looking and tall. They are lawyers and bankers, they have CVs that would make my family swoon. We go to the opera, we go to the theatre, we host dinners parties together. They can cook and keep house, they are sweet and they are kind. They would make such perfect husbands.

And every moment is an agony.

It's her they love, the China Doll – with her beautiful hair and beautiful clothes and beautiful little shoes.

I see my life stretching out ahead of me for so many long, long years. How many tiny painful moments does it take to make a long, long life?

How will I endure it?

I cannot scream or struggle or run away. My world is so tiny, bound up inside this disguise.

Looking out from this broken place, I wonder – will anyone ever see me?

Will I ever dare let anyone see me?

10 – CHOSEN

My great-grandmother was born into a good family in China in the late 1800s. She was the eldest daughter, and after her came two more girls. Three girls.

Her father was a physician but he became an opium addict and smoked away their fortune.

For a family left with nothing, having too many girls can be a disaster. Because for each girl to marry, you have to pay a dowry to each husband's family.

I imagine her mother looking at her three daughters and thinking about their future.

The eldest, Ah Mooi, is four, pretty with delicate features. The second one is sturdy and plain. The youngest is still a baby.

If all her daughters have small feet, they could marry well and escape this hard life.

There will never be enough money for three dowries.

So she must choose. If she cannot save all her daughters then at least she can save one of them.

She chooses Ah Mooi, the one who is pretty and delicate. It is Eldest Sister whose feet she binds. Ah Mooi, who would become my great-grandmother.

AH MOOI On the day of my wedding, there is great cause for celebration. I marry a man whose family is better off than my own, with land and servants and a good income.

My Mama made this happen: she chose my feet over my sister's feet. And my whole family, also, they made this happen – all of them working and saving, saving all their money for one dowry.

11 – RUNAWAY

It should have been a happily ever after for Ah Mooi after her wedding. She has married into a good family. She would be provided for and her children would never go hungry

But she cannot give her husband a child.

Then the family she marries into falls on hard times.

Ah Mooi is no use any more as a wife or mother. She's just another mouth to feed. She is worthless. So they put her to work.

MOTHER IN LAW Go till the fields. Clean up that mess. Fetch water.

And every step is an agony.

But she is resourceful – so she crawls. She harvests the big heavy pumpkins on her knees, she carries water on her knees. She lives her life on her knees.

AH MOOI This is not the life I was meant to have. My Mama promised me – if I was obedient, if I endured, I would have a good life, a good husband. And it has all come to nothing.

I cannot endure this. I will not endure this.

I have a cousin who owns a goldsmiths shop in Malaya. "Come", she says, "work in our shop. Life is good here. No-one cares about bound feet. This is the new frontier."

A new frontier. "Like that Gold Mountain in the America where so many people have gone to find a better life. Malaya is overflowing with the riches of tin and rubber". But I have heard it's a wild, dangerous place – it's hot and humid, it's a jungle and busy with so many people, it's a place of ruffians and loose women.

She imagines for the first time a place without shame. A place where women walk, and run, wherever they please.

I picture her crawling out of the fields and taking her first step onto the road. How long does it take to walk from her husband's village to the coast, to board a junk to Malaya?

How many days, how many nights? How many tiny baby steps does it take to make such a long, long journey?

That pain, that journey she can endure.

And this is her power.

This cry to the universe, I am not worthless, my hopes matter, my heart matters. I matter.

12 – THE CANYON

I'm twenty-six and I'm in Australia. I'm wearing my first pair of hiking boots. They are heavy duty grey leather with blood red laces. Strewth, mate, I'm Crocodile Dundee!

I'm visiting my best friend Susan. She is a rising star at a multi-national and she's on secondment in Sydney. We hire a car and drive into the Outback. We're going to Ayers Rock as it then was, Alice Springs, the Olgas and Kings Canyon.

After these few months apart, it feels good to be laughing and talking with her again.

I tell Susan about Andy. He is hunky and sporty and a great kisser. There's also Mark who's not so good with the kissing but he's a sensitive, intellectual type. They are both waiting for me back in London – which one should I choose? She teases me, You and all your men – do you even like any of them?

We drive for days through the red desert. There's only us in this vast landscape. We camp beneath the upside down stars. We watch the sun rise over Ayers Rock turning it into living fire.

Here, beyond the gaze of others, we let slip our disguises. Our voices turn soft, speaking only to each other. Our eyes become gentle, looking only at each other. I tell her about Bruce Lee and John Steed. And she tells me shyly about a secret agent caught behind enemy lines. I see the girl she used to be – turning cartwheels in the sand, laughing without shame, warm and affectionate without embarrassment.

And sometimes when our eyes meet, I feel as if she sees the girl in me.

We spend a long hot day hiking through Kings Canyon. My boots are stiff – I haven't worn them in enough. I have blisters and my toe nails feel sliced through. Every step is an agony. But I plod on, down the steep trails into the gorge and back up again. My feet feel torn and raw.

But I don't care. Because I'm with her.

13 – THE NIGHT

That night, I'm sitting on a bench at our campsite near the rim of the canyon. There's a single candle on the picnic table next to me. We've just had our evening meal.

Susan comes back from the washing up block. She has short hair and strong shoulders.

She seems so at ease here in the outdoors.

I'm sitting sideways on the bench, hugging one knee. My feet are bare and free. She comes up behind me and sits down, straddling the bench.

She takes me in her arms.

I can feel the warmth of her body against my back. I cross my arms over hers as she holds me. I can feel her cheek against mine. I can hardly breathe. My throat is dry. My heart feels like it will explode.

And it feels like the most natural thing in the world. Everything else disappears. My life in London. Andy. Mark. The world beyond this moment. There is only her.

We sit there and talk. The sky above is bright with stars. We talk about the places we have been. We plan the route back to Sydney. We talk about everything but this one thing right here, right now.

In the darkness, this moment seems to last forever. And it is over just like that.

We put out the candle, and crawl into our little tent, into our separate sleeping bags. We do not speak. Susan seems to sleep through the night. We do not touch. Bound up in the tight bag, I lie awake and stare into the darkness.

The next morning, she is cold and abrupt. She does not look at me.

I want to tell her how I feel.

But every time I move close to her, she moves away.

And I feel as if I'm back in the school canteen: *You don't go near that pondan. People like that, they should lock them up in the mental hospital.*

Before we leave, we stop by the canyon one last time.

They say this part of the canyon could be a mile deep, maybe more. It's a strange thing to stand right at its very edge. If we miss our footing, fell, how long would it take to reach the canyon floor?

Susan stands a few feet from me but it might as well be a hundred miles.

She heads back to the car.

It doesn't matter if what happened last night was no more than the gesture of a friend, soon to be forgotten. It doesn't matter if she can never love me.

All I know is – I feel alive, and I can never put on that disguise again.

I look down at the abyss – and I see infinity.

And it seems to me that in that moment I step off – into air.

14 – THE GARDEN

I'm awake in my old bedroom, the one I've had since I was four. It's 1990 and it's the recession. I'm twenty-seven and I've just lost my high flying law job. I am back home in my parents' house in Malaysia. It's dawn and I can't sleep.

I get up in my pyjamas and go and look for my mother. She is outside in the garden, hanging up the laundry. She is in her long night dress and the sun is just coming up over the palm trees.

Hello, my *noi* – my daughter – you're up, she says.

Yah, jet lag.

I had a dream. I dreamt I was in a dangerous place, like on a rocky ledge and if I took a wrong step, I could fall. Then I came to a cross roads and I had to choose. Which way should I go? And then I realized you were with me in the dream and everything would be okay.

MUM It's just a dream, darling. Of course, everything will be okay.

ME Mum, I'm gay.

And then I'm rambling, talking, it's all disconnected, words coming out of my mouth. Maybe the words will hold back the next moment because I don't know what she's going to say.

She puts down my father's shirt and holds me in her arms.

MUM Are you sure, darling?

I can see her thinking about all those lovely young men I've brought home over the years to show her.

I nod and we start to talk. We walk arm in arm, taking turn after turn round the garden.

The sun is brighter now behind the palm trees.

MUM Did I do something wrong? Is it my fault? Did I do something to make you this way?

ME No, no, mum, it's not your fault. It's just who I am. I've always been like this.

We take another turn round the garden. We are both wearing flip flops. My feet feel free as if I am a child again.

ME I tried so hard, Mum. I wanted to get married. I wanted to give you grandchildren. I wanted to have the life that everyone – the whole family – expected me to have. And now, I'm letting you down.

MUM You can never let me down. You are my *noi* and I will always love you. All I want is for you to be happy. I just worry that your life will be more difficult because you are gay.

ME But it was already difficult because I was trying not to be.

And suddenly, we are both laughing.

We walk on beneath the gaze of the arching sky. It's a beautiful morning.

15 – THE CROSSING

The crossing to Malaya will take three weeks with a fair wind. Ah Mooi – the woman who would become my great-grandmother – huddles with the other third class passengers on board the junk. They terrify her, these crowds of stinking bodies – the leering men, the jostling for food and water at meal times. The big sky terrifies her, the heaving of the boat terrifies her. She is so unsteady, so unable to fight for her rations.

Then one day, something draws her up onto the deck.

She stands up, clinging to a rope, holding her weight up with her arms.

She feels the power of the swells beneath the ship. She feels the sun on her face. The sea spray showers her in bursts as the boat skids onward. It is as if she is reborn.

She sees infinity in the vast endless horizon.

Everything in her old life was so certain, so uncompromising – going back for a thousand years. Everything ahead of her is an unknown. Out there beyond the horizon, is a new country where they don't care about bound feet – can that be real?

Is it possible to throw away tradition, just like that? To make your own life, your own choices, your own traditions?

She has never seen the world move past her so fast. The wind buffets her body. The sea swooshes by.

Her world is no longer shrunken, no longer defined by her tiny painful steps.

It is as if she has taken flight.

She looks up and gives herself over to the arching sky, laughing like she has never laughed before, a woman in ecstatic joy.

16 – ACCEPTANCE

In Chinese tradition, when you get married, you must bring your spouse to the family to be formally accepted. This is done through the tea carrying ceremony. The newly weds carry tea to the elders. If the elders do not drink the tea, that means they reject you and your beloved. But if they drink the tea, it means they accept you and your spouse into the family and the bonds between all of you become even stronger.

It's 2008. Angie and I have been together for fourteen years and it is the day after our civil partnership. Angie has eyes as blue as the arching sky and a shy, gentle manner that makes my heart take flight.

We're at my sister's house in London and the whole family is there – my parents, my sister, my brother and his family. We are all dressed casually and I'm wearing my biker boots. When my parents got married, they performed this same tea ceremony to their parents – as did my grandparents to theirs, going back innumerable generations.

Angie and I carry tea to my father. He sips from the cup and says, We all in the family cherish you both.

Then Angie and I carry tea to my mother. She too sips the tea. She says to me, I am so proud of you, my *noi*. She says to Angie, Ever since you came into Yang-May's life, we have seen how much happier she has become. The whole family is grateful to you.

Thank you, Angie, my Sum Po – my daughter-in-law.

Today, Angie and I have been together for twenty-one years. I see all of her. And she sees all of me.

She sees Bruce Lee and John Steed. She sees the sulky four year old in the fluffy white dress. She sees the mother who would do anything for her daughter's happiness, she sees the daughter who dares to live unbound. She sees the slinky young woman in the red *cheongsam*, she sees the *pondan*. She sees in me my mother and my great-grandmother. She sees the feminine and the masculine, the shameful and the desirable, she sees my endurance and my defiance. She sees the lover and partner always by her side, she sees me bound and she sees me free.

*

It's a beautiful September day in 2012. I'm almost fifty and I'm walking side by side with Angie. We are hiking the South Downs Way, a hundred miles along the Southern Coast of England from Winchester to Eastbourne – and there's a gang of us, all of us in our hiking gear.

We've walked ninety-five miles and we turn the corner. There stretching out ahead of us are the Seven Sisters, seven hills rolling out over the white chalk cliffs like the hem of an embroidered gown. To our right, the infinite sea glitters in the bright sun.

Looking up at the delicate beauty of the landscape I have a sense that I own the world – and I break into a wild, unfurling race: up the first hill, then the next, and the next. My feet leap up the steep slopes, instinctively finding the best path. I am wearing old battered hiking boots, sturdy on the outside and soft as bedding on the inside. It's like dancing on air.

On this bright day, here with my friends, here with Angie, I love the gift of this fragile body. I love to feel my heart pumping so hard. I love the stickiness of my sweat. I love the fire in my chest as my lungs gasp for breath. I love my small feet that have carried me this long, long way. I love my short chunky legs that have pistoned me up these hills, my muffin top that will always be there no matter how far I run. I love my smaller than average breasts, my crooked teeth, my squashed nose, my short sighted eyes, my grey hair.

I love the beauty of my imperfection.

And this is my power.

The end.

Themes

Gaze / looking / seeing
Beautiful
Mothers and daughters
Masculine v. feminine
Personal power / powerlessness
Control of women's movement = control of our sexuality

Part 1	Part 2
Binding	Free / fly
Cut / slice	Open / vast
Break	Sky / sky / wind
Tiny / shrunken	Nature / outside
Feminine = desirable / small	Unbind
Masculine = ugly / big	Heal / whole
Shame	Being seen
Queer	Acceptance
Obedience, submission, endurance	Taking off disguise
Rejection	Authentic self
Not being seen	Natural body
Stillness / trapped	Journey / escape
Hierarchy = class above / husband and wife / parent and child	Movement
	Rebellion / defiance
Put on disguise	Acceptance
Disguise / modified body	Gay
Inside house / bedroom – claustrophobic	Freedom / liberation / self directed
Oppressive tradition	Community / equality / togetherness
Marriage for protection / duty / social reason	Tradition that brings together
Power of fitting in	Romantic love
Controlling	Power of outsider

THE LAST DAYS OF LIMEHOUSE

As part of the research for *The Last Days of Limehouse*, Kumiko Mendl and I spent a great deal of time delving into records of this neighbourhood: old photographs, maps, oral histories, newspaper reports. We also walked the East End streets that once made up this Chinatown, around Limehouse Causeway and Pennyfields. I came away struck by a disparity: the archival materials we had found told of a vibrant, thriving community that had been an integral part of London's fabric, yet there was virtually nothing left of it. You had to look hard to spot vestigial signs, in names such as Ming Street. Otherwise, Limehouse Chinatown had completely vanished, to the point that many Londoners assume that the Chinatown in Soho is the only one we've ever had. How is it possible for a populace to be so completely erased?

The Last Days of Limehouse arose as a response to this disappearance. If the Chinatown had not survived in fact, we could at least tell the stories of its inhabitants. Yellow Earth produced the play in Limehouse Town Hall, transporting us back to the 1950s, just before the community was uprooted. (Kumiko had initially approached me about writing a play set in the 1920s, its heyday, but I find decline much more interesting.) Gratifyingly, a few older residents of the area came up to me afterwards, and shared their memories of the neighbourhood we'd depicted. For a moment, at least, we'd been able to bring this place back to life for the audience – before sending them out into the streets of Limehouse, where they could feel its loss all the more keenly as they made their way home.

Jeremy Tiang trained as an actor at Drama Centre, London. His plays include *The Last Days of Limehouse* (Yellow Earth), *Salesman*之死 (LPAC / Gung Ho Projects, NYC) and *A Dream of Red Pavilions* (Pan Asian Rep, NYC); his theatre translations include *A Son Soon* by Xu Nuo (Manchester Royal Exchange), *A Fable For Now* by Wei Yu-Chia (PEN World Voices 2018) and *Floating Bones* by Quah Sy Ren and Han Lao Da (Arts House, Singapore). Jeremy is also a novelist (*State of Emergency*, Epigram Books) and the translator of novelists including Zhang Yueran, Yeng Pway Ngon, Tianxia Bachang and Chan Ho-Kei. He has received an NEA Literary Translation Fellowship and a People's Literature Award Mao-Tai Cup for Translation. He was born in Singapore and lives in Brooklyn.

www.JeremyTiang.com

THE LAST DAYS OF LIMEHOUSE

JEREMY TIANG

The Last Days of Limehouse *was first produced by Yellow Earth Theatre at Limehouse Town Hall, London, 16 July to 3 August 2014, directed by Kumiko Mendl and Gary Merry.*

The cast was C. Amanda Maud, Gabby Wong, Matthew Leonhart, Sara Houghton, and Jonathan Chan. The ensemble was made up of members of the Yellow Earth Academy (Emiko Jane Ishii, Emma Chung Yi Lau, Rita Tsang, Jean Tan, Philip Law, Shihua Bai, William Kwan, Yiu Fai Choi, Zheng Chi and Lloyd Li). The part of Councillor Brinkman was played in rotation by Anthony Best, Nia Davies, Penelope Dimond, David McGillivray, Sean Patterson and Jeremy Todd.

Characters

EILEEN CUNNINGHAM	Eurasian-American, late 30s.
MARY CHEAH	British Eurasian, mid 30s.
STANLEY LIM	Chinese, late 40s.
JOHNNY WONG	British Eurasian, late 20s.
IRIS WONG	British Chinese, late 20s.

The actor playing Iris Wong also plays her mother (Frances Foong), her daughter (Frances Wong) and her granddaughter (Chloe Mann).

DANCE INSTRUCTOR	At Limehouse Town Hall.
MABEL MENG	Limehouse resident, 20s.
JENNY SZETO	Limehouse resident, 20s. Mabel's friend.
CHUANG	Jenny's cousin from China.
BAO	Chuang's friend from China.
ERIC BRINKMAN	Local Councillor.
COLIN	University lecturer, 30ish.
GERMAN SOLDIER	
NURSE	

OTHER LIMEHOUSE RESIDENTS
CHURCHGOERS ETC.

Setting

The play takes place in London in 1958, and then later.

SCENE ONE

A slide show: images from Limehouse Chinatown in its glory days, the 1920s and 30s. Children playing, Chinese laundries, Anna May Wong's visit. We pause on an image, and Eileen Cunningham appears.

EILEEN   Then Mrs Teoh said to my father, 'But I thought that was your hat!'

Perhaps some scattered laughter. She is a little too tense to be an effective teller of jokes.

EILEEN   That's how I remember it, anyway. I must have been about six. *(Click. Another photograph)* Ah, this is a special one. That's my mother holding me. This would have been in the yard of our house on Limehouse Causeway. We lived above my father's restaurant. Yee Leng's. Some of you might remember it? *(Click. Another photograph)* And that's the man himself. My father, Yong Yee Leng. Everyone called him Herman. He was a ship's cook – when he came on shore it took him a while to learn to cook with fresh vegetables. His restaurant was popular, he said, because he used such a big flame. It gave his food *'wok hei'* – the breath of the wok.

He decided we should leave London after my mother passed, but going back to Hong Kong wasn't an option. That's how we ended up in New York. So there was that Chinatown too. But Limehouse was my first home. *(Click. Another photograph)* This is Limehouse Causeway as I remember it, and I'm sure you recognize it too. 1925 or thereabouts. More than thirty years ago. Oh dear, showing my age.

Could someone put on the lights, please?

The lights come on. The slideshow is over. We see Eileen for the first time, an elegant Asian-American woman dressed slightly too well for the locale.

EILEEN   I presume you've all had the opportunity to look at the plans on display downstairs. If not, I urge you to do so on your way out. What the Council proposes to do to this area is nothing less than wholesale destruction. The area will look very neat indeed, straight roads and modern apartment blocks, all very laudable, but Limehouse is where the Chinese first lived in London. We can't allow all this history to be wiped out. My proposal is that we initially–

She is interrupted by a dance instructor in a jaunty outfit, striding forward from the back of the hall.

INSTRUCTOR Pardon me, I didn't want to interrupt but you do seem to be going on. We've booked the hall, I'm afraid.

EILEEN Well, so have I.

INSTRUCTOR I mean for now. Actually, we were due to start fifteen minutes ago.

EILEEN You're mistaken. I have it until– *(But she is drowned out by music. The dance instructor begins ushering in students)*

INSTRUCTOR That's it, chickadees, find a space on the floor.

EILEEN *(overlapping)* This is outrageous! I'll speak to management about this.

INSTRUCTOR Sorry, ladies and gentlemen, but we've got the hall now. If you just move aside–

EILEEN *(overlapping)* No, wait! Don't go yet, we're still – Can you hear me?

INSTRUCTOR Step to the right! And one-two-three-four, and left-two-three-and-four–

SCENE TWO

Immediately following. Eileen is waiting by the side of the road. A breathless (and very pregnant) Iris Wong runs up to her.

IRIS Mrs Cunningham.

EILEEN Gracious. Catch your breath, my dear. You shouldn't be running, in your condition.

IRIS You walk ever so fast.

EILEEN I wanted to get away from that place. I'm furious.

IRIS They were out of order.

EILEEN Yes, well. I shall be having stern words with the management tomorrow.

IRIS Probably just some confusion.

EILEEN   I don't expect confusion for what they were charging.

IRIS   It's a shame you didn't get to finish your meeting. It was good.

EILEEN   Well, how kind. Thank you, Mrs–

IRIS   Wong. Iris Wong. You looked so confident up there.

EILEEN   I've been on committees. Lots of committees. Let me tell you, Mrs Wong, there's very little a dedicated committee couldn't accomplish with the right woman to steer it.

IRIS   Why don't you set up a committee here?

EILEEN   I haven't been in this country long. I don't really know anyone yet.

IRIS   There were lots of people at the talk tonight.

EILEEN   You can't just let anyone onto a committee. They have to be the right sort.

IRIS   Oh.

EILEEN   What is it?

IRIS   I was going to say I could help, but you don't know anything about me.

EILEEN   Is urban preservation your area of interest?

IRIS   I don't know.

EILEEN   But you live in Limehouse.

IRIS   All my life, except when we were evacuated during the war. I grew up on the Causeway, and now I run Friendship Noodle with my husband Johnny. On Pennyfields? Just over there.

EILEEN   I think I've walked past it.

IRIS   You should come in. Our lo mein is famous.

EILEEN   That's one of the places they're planning to tear down.

IRIS   They said they'd try to find somewhere else for us.

EILEEN   And you're not going to let that happen.

IRIS   I don't know that we have much choice.

EILEEN   But you're going to make a stand.

IRIS   I don't like to cause trouble.

EILEEN   I'm confused, Mrs Wong. Why would you want to join my hypothetical committee?

IRIS   What you said about preserving the history of the place. I agree with that.

EILEEN   But that comes with preserving the place itself.

IRIS   They say these buildings have to come down. There's a government notice and everything. I don't want to go against that.

EILEEN   Very well. Good evening, Mrs Wong.

IRIS   Is that it?

EILEEN   You don't want to make a fuss. Nothing ever changes unless someone is willing to make a fuss.

IRIS   My mother was Frances Foong.

EILEEN   I'm afraid I don't–

IRIS   You know, the Frances Foong? *(Awkward pause)* I thought you said you grew up in Limehouse.

EILEEN   I was six when we left.

IRIS   She set up the Chung Kuo School. Maybe that was later. She'd come over from Hong Kong, and was scandalized to see so many Chinese children who didn't speak a word of their parents' language.

EILEEN   How fascinating. I'd love to meet her.

IRIS   She passed away during the war. My dad too.

EILEEN   I'm sorry. She sounds like a wonderful woman.

IRIS   That's why I thought – when you said, the history of the area, I thought she should be part of it.

EILEEN   How do you mean?

IRIS   What she did was important. I'd like her to get some acknowledgement.

EILEEN   History has a way of leaving people behind.

IRIS   But you could stop that.

EILEEN   Me?

IRIS   You said, about preserving the past. That's why I was excited to hear your talk. Because you want to save Limehouse, and what she did was part of Limehouse–

EILEEN   I see.

IRIS   I just felt I had to run after you. You seem to know what you're doing.

EILEEN   And the school?

IRIS   The building was bombed.

EILEEN It's hard to remember a place, when it's gone.

IRIS She's a person, not a place. You remembered Limehouse, you said. It wasn't gone, but you were.

EILEEN My daddy talked about this place, and I could remember some things, in a shadowy way. But then I came back, and everything was all different. And now it's going away–

IRIS Nothing ever stays the same.

EILEEN I like cities when they evolve. They accumulate layers, like coral. You should be able to see who was here before you.

SCENE THREE

Moving images projected onto the walls: someone moving through the streets of present-day Limehouse with a handheld camera. We don't see the operator. It's morning, probably. From time to time, whoever is behind the camera holds out a photograph – perhaps one of Eileen's, perhaps one we haven't seen. The camera lingers on a church building, and–

SCENE FOUR

The hallway of Holy Trinity Brompton, after a service. Mary Cheah sits behind a table. Eileen comes up to her.

EILEEN Mary, isn't it? That was a wonderful reading. Your voice has so much warmth in it. And I do adore your accent.

MARY Thank you. Have we–?

EILEEN Oh, not formally. Eileen Cunningham. Charmed. *(Offers her hand)*

MARY Mary Cheah. Can I interest you in one of our groups? Perhaps I'll put you down for cross-stitching the prayer stools? Very fine work. Or there's flowers.

EILEEN I'm not actually planning in joining any groups.

MARY Really? Please reconsider, we'd love to have you.

EILEEN That's darling of you to say, but there was something else I wanted to talk to you about.

MARY Yes?

EILEEN I meant in private. When you're finished here, I could buy you a cup of tea?
MARY I'm afraid I'll need to get back. Gregory will be waiting.
EILEEN Your husband?
MARY Gregory is my cat.
EILEEN It needn't take long.
MARY *(to a woman walking past)* Felicity! Hold up, you'll need one of these. *(Hands her a mimeographed sheet, then turns back to Eileen)* I'm sorry.
EILEEN It's like this, Mrs Cheah–
MARY Miss.
EILEEN I couldn't help noticing that you were, correct me if I'm wrong, Chinese.
MARY Half.
EILEEN Oh, me too, but one drop of blood and all that.
MARY Fook Man on the Barons Court Road.
EILEEN Excuse me?
MARY I knew what you were about to ask. Everyone wants to know the best Chinese food around here, and I always say Fook Man. Try the Shanghai dumplings, though I suggest leaving off the spicy sauce if you value your tongue.
EILEEN That wasn't what I was about to ask.
MARY Oh? I thought, you seem to be new in town–
EILEEN I've actually found some rather splendid places on my own. That's what I wanted to ask you about, in a way. Are you familiar with Limehouse?
MARY In the East End?
EILEEN Is there more than one?
MARY There's probably a Limehouse, Nevada or Limehouse, California.
EILEEN I meant the one here.
MARY I'm from there. Grew up on Pennyfields.
EILEEN You? But you seem so–
MARY Proper? Grammar school.
EILEEN So you left.

MARY   Yes, for the typists' pool at SOAS and a rented bedsit in Earls Court. Every girl's dream.

EILEEN   So you know what's going on there.

MARY   Not very much, I'd imagine. It's not the most eventful locale.

EILEEN   I meant the clearances.

MARY   Oh, yes, it's time someone dealt with those buildings. Eyesores.

EILEEN   Doesn't it matter to you, that your childhood home is being torn up?

MARY   No one expects their childhood home to stick around forever, unless maybe they grew up in Buckingham Palace. What's Limehouse to you, anyway?

EILEEN   I lived there. Cheah – on Pennyfields – did your father run a laundry? Sort of canary-coloured, the name in red?

MARY   'Cheah' in curly writing, looked like the word 'Clean'.

EILEEN   He had a funny little beard, just his chin, not the sides of his face. Your mother had red hair.

MARY   Had is right. Pure white now.

EILEEN   They'd give me candy when I stopped to say hello. I don't remember you.

MARY   Probably not born yet.

EILEEN   We might have been friends, if I'd stayed.

MARY   That was a long time ago.

EILEEN   I was hoping you'd join my committee – for the preservation of Limehouse.

MARY   Seriously?

EILEEN   It's nothing really. It's just me so far, actually.

MARY   I don't think so.

EILEEN   I'll join one of your groups.

MARY   It doesn't work like that. Anyway, no, I couldn't in good conscience. I don't want Limehouse preserved. I want it thoroughly disinfected and steam-cleaned.

EILEEN   Aren't you even a little upset that it's going?

MARY   You've been away too long. You've forgotten how bad it smells in the summer, all those open drains. No hot water, queuing up five deep to brush your teeth. Lots of people were sent away during the war and didn't bother coming back.

EILEEN I'm not saying pickle it in vinegar. But they want to tear up every last scrap. Years from now, people will walk round Limehouse and have no idea there was ever a Chinatown here.

MARY You're too late. You should have got here years ago, back when there was still something to save. They're going to build a modern new council block and give my parents a flat in it. Running water and their own bathroom and a modern kitchen. I'm not going to stand in the way of that, and I wish you wouldn't either. *(To a passing man)* Mr Holness! Don't forget choir practice on Tuesday. You're our last tenor.

SCENE FIVE

Friendship Noodle restaurant, about three in the afternoon – the end of the lunch rush. Stanley cleans up, while Johnny prepares for the dinner crowd – chopping vegetables etc. Three customers, Jenny, Chuang and Mabel, linger over their tea.

STANLEY Feet.

Mabel raises her legs. Stanley sweeps underneath them.

JOHNNY Old man, why don't you clean over there? Let the girls finish their tea in peace.

JENNY We'll be ever so quick.

JOHNNY No rush.

CHUANG 好茶。特别浓！ [Good tea. Very fragrant!]

JOHNNY Eh?

MABEL She likes the tea.

JOHNNY That's a good blend, proper Silver Jasmine. Got it off the Shanghai Clipper – just docked from Amoy.

JENNY Isn't that where you're from, Stanley? Amoy?

STANLEY No. Canton.

JENNY Just imagine, tea coming all the way from over there. I wish I could visit.

CHUANG Not these days. Bad government.

EILEEN *(entering)* Oh, isn't this charming!

JOHNNY We're closed.

EILEEN No! I've come all this way, hoping to sample a genuine East End meal.

JOHNNY All the way from America?

EILEEN You spotted the accent, how clever of you. No, merely the West End, but that seems quite far enough on a hot day like this.

JOHNNY We close the kitchen between lunch and dinner.

EILEEN But there are still customers!

MABEL We're going in a minute.

EILEEN I don't mean to drive anyone away.

JOHNNY You're not. I am.

EILEEN You must be Johnny Wong.

JOHNNY Who's been telling tales?

EILEEN Everyone knows the dashing master chef of Friendship Noodle. Right, girls?

JENNY Yes, and we're all dreadfully envious of Iris.

JOHNNY Get along with you.

MABEL We're going.

CHUANG Bye.

EILEEN Before you go – let me give you my card. You seem like bright young people. I might have a little job or two for you.

JENNY Cheers.

CHUANG *(as they exit)* 那女人好怪！[That woman is so strange!]

JOHNNY We open again at six.

EILEEN I don't think I can stay that long. It's a shame, I'd heard so many wonderful things about this place, my mouth was watering.

JOHNNY Well, look, just this once, I could whip you up something quick. If you don't mind us chopping and cleaning around you.

EILEEN I think that would add to the atmosphere.

JOHNNY Stanley, set a place for the lady.

STANLEY Over here?

EILEEN Gracious, no. I prefer to be near the kitchen. Close to the action.

JOHNNY I'll do you a bowl of our lo mein. It's famous.

EILEEN Delightful.

Through the following, Johnny creates the meal effortlessly on his single hob and wok, never taking his attention off Eileen.

JOHNNY What was that about, having a little job for the girls? Nothing dodgy, I hope.

EILEEN Behave, Mr Wong! It's just a small project of mine. Urban preservation.

JOHNNY What's that when it's at home?

EILEEN Making the city better. Not letting it change too fast. Protecting the character of the neighbourhood against development–

JOHNNY Oh, that. My wife's been going on about that too. Went to some kind of loony meeting at the Town Hall – some people have another think coming.

EILEEN Your wife may have a point, Mr Wong. Take this place, take Limehouse – don't you think it's worth saving?

JOHNNY Ha, good luck with that. No offence.

EILEEN How do you mean?

JOHNNY There's no sense trying to hold on to the past. Look around here – Limehouse Causeway gone, and they're coming for this place next. Slum clearance, they say. I've lived here twenty-nine years, man and boy, and it's news to me I grew up in a slum, but what're you going to do?

EILEEN You could try to stop it.

JOHNNY Little people like us, we just go where we're told. Might be a blessing in disguise, being given the shove. Business has been falling off.

STANLEY The docks – not so many sailors.

JOHNNY Yeah, Stanley here used to run a sailors' hostel. Had to shut down. Not enough customers.

EILEEN And you still live in Limehouse, Mr–?

STANLEY Lim. Yes, here.

JOHNNY He means here in the restaurant.

EILEEN Actually in the restaurant?

JOHNNY It was meant to be a temporary thing, but, well. And there's not any room upstairs.

EILEEN What's going to happen to all of you?

JOHNNY   They said they'd offer us another space around here, but I don't know. It might be better to strike out and find somewhere new.

EILEEN   But there's a community here. You've got your regulars, don't you? I saw how friendly you were with those nice boys. If everyone goes off in different directions, you won't see each other anymore.

JOHNNY   So? We'll make new friends.

EILEEN   It's more than just friends.

JOHNNY   They'll take a bus anywhere we move to, for a taste of my lo mein.

EILEEN   Where will you go?

JOHNNY   Who knows? Cricklewood, Kilburn, somewhere like that. No Chinese takeaway around those parts. It's getting so that every neighbourhood has one. Better get in while we can.

EILEEN   But your responsibilities, Mr Wong. You're abandoning the community that depends on you.

JOHNNY   Careful who you call irresponsible. I'm going to be a family man. Baby on the way. That's who I'm responsible to, not some 'community'.

EILEEN   I just meant–

JOHNNY *(slapping a bowl down in front of her)*   Here's your lo mein. Eat it before I change my mind.

EILEEN   I honestly wasn't trying to–

JOHNNY   Eat.

EILEEN   This is delicious.

JOHNNY   Do you want a fork?

EILEEN   No, I'll cope. My daddy would be shocked to see me eating noodles with a fork, god rest his soul. Mm, is that scallions and – ginger? In the sauce?

JOHNNY   Secret recipe.

EILEEN   Well, I shall have to tell all my friends to call in on you.

JOHNNY   Tell them to do it in the next three months.

EILEEN   That quickly?

JOHNNY   It takes the Council forever to make up their minds about something, but once they do–

EILEEN   I'd have thought a man like you would be leading the protests, Mr Wong.

JOHNNY	What protests?
EILEEN	You're not just going to roll over and let them do this, are you?
JOHNNY	It's done. Everything's been decided.
EILEEN	But this restaurant–
JOHNNY	We took it over from someone else. He moved on, and now we will too. If everyone wanted things to stay the same, where would progress come from?
EILEEN	What kind of progress is this?
JOHNNY	We could get a bigger place. Maybe even open a branch. Chinese food is going to be enormous. Wait and see. I heard they've started serving chow mein at Butlin's.
EILEEN	If everyone just looked out for themselves, then what happens to Chinatown? Who's looking out for the community?
JOHNNY	What is this community you keep talking about? Is community going to pay our bills? The way they keep raising the rates–
EILEEN	How can you be so callous?
JOHNNY	What does that mean?
STANLEY	Callous. Adjective. Unfeeling, lacking in empathy.
EILEEN	Goodness.
STANLEY	I read the dictionary. Spare time. Improve English.
JOHNNY	Who are you calling unfeeling?
EILEEN	Mr Wong, I don't believe you can care so little about the area you and your wife grew up in. All I'm saying is that there's a vital piece of history in these streets. You mustn't let short-term gain drive you into throwing that away. I know change is frightening, but–
JOHNNY	Oh, so now I'm a coward.
EILEEN	That's not what I said.
JOHNNY	I think it's time you left. We don't need some do-gooder to come in telling us how to run our lives.
EILEEN	I didn't mean to offend you.
JOHNNY	Yeah, I'd hate to be around when you were trying to be rude.
IRIS *(entering)* Johnny, it smells like dead fish in there, you'll need to look at the dr– *(Sees Eileen)* Bleeding hell.
EILEEN	Hello, Mrs Wong.

IRIS   I didn't think you'd actually– This is my husband Johnny.

EILEEN   We were just having a lovely chat. *(To Johnny)* Eileen Cunningham. Charmed.

JOHNNY   Iris? You know her?

IRIS   This is Mrs Cunningham. The lady from the talk? The Town Hall?

JOHNNY   The one who's going to save all of us? Like Jesus.

EILEEN   I said I'd drop by to see your wife, Mr Wong.

JOHNNY   What was all that about wanting a meal?

EILEEN   I did want a meal. I was starving. All morning I've been tramping up and down this street, documenting what buildings are worth preserving, talking to families.

JOHNNY   I don't know what you've done to Iris, but ever since she came back from that Town Hall meeting, it's been Mrs Cunningham this, Mrs Cunningham that. Teacher's pet. You've got her all worked up. They're going to tear this place apart, and you won't be able to stop them. Why not make the best of it?

EILEEN   Your wife might have her own views, Mr Wong.

JOHNNY   Iris? What do you have to say to that?

IRIS   You know what I think.

JOHNNY   Don't want the kid growing up in a slum, do we?

EILEEN   This is a wonderful place you have, Mrs Wong. I was just telling your husband. So authentic. Just like the places I remember.

IRIS *(to Johnny)*   Mrs Cunningham grew up around here.

EILEEN   Till I was six. Then America called, and–

JOHNNY   I think I hear it calling again. Why don't you get back there?

IRIS   Johnny! Why are you being so rude?

JOHNNY   Mrs Cunningham, my wife doesn't have time for this nonsense. Look at her. She's got the whole restaurant to run, and there's a baby on its way any day now.

IRIS   Johnny.

JOHNNY   We've talked about this. Isn't that what you want too?

EILEEN   You could stay, if you wanted. They could make Limehouse better, without driving everyone out. You don't have to leave.

JOHNNY   What's left here for us? Iris's parents came all the way from Hong Kong, didn't they? And my dad. Where'd we be, if they'd decided they'd rather stay put where they were?

IRIS   How do you know we'd be worse off?

JOHNNY   Ask Stanley. Stanley, do you ever wish you'd stayed in China?

IRIS   That's not fair.

JOHNNY   Go on, Stanley. You ever think of going home?

IRIS   You're being unkind now. It's alright Stanley.

STANLEY   Okay. *(He exits)*

JOHNNY   I was just teasing. He doesn't mind.

EILEEN   This is where you belong! You can't give up on it that easily.

JOHNNY   Look around you. This place is a disgrace. When a place gets this run down, best thing is to just tear it down and start over. You don't know the first thing about our lives. Who are you, barging in–

IRIS   Johnny, don't get like that.

JOHNNY   Nah, people will be coming in soon, wanting their tea, and she's still sitting there over lunch. You need to go, Mrs Cunningham. Never mind paying for your lo mein, have it on the house. Call it a farewell present, because I don't want to see you here again.

SCENE SIX

Iris emerges with a basketful of laundry, which she proceeds to hang on the line. After a moment, Johnny appears with a cigarette in his hand.

IRIS   You didn't need to be so rude to her.

JOHNNY   Yeah. Sorry. She put my back up.

IRIS   That's the Americans. They're direct, see. It's not her fault.

JOHNNY   I don't mind direct. I'm direct. But thinking she knows better than us–

IRIS   She's done it before, she said. She knows how these things work.

JOHNNY   We don't need her. Listen, this is an opportunity. The Council will give us something towards relocating. We'll go somewhere better. North London. This is the best shot we'll get. Miss it and we're stuck here.

IRIS I didn't think you minded here.

JOHNNY It's all right. But that doesn't mean there isn't something better.

IRIS I don't want to lose this.

JOHNNY You won't.

IRIS But if it's gone—

JOHNNY Unless you get a knock on your head and lose your memory, it'll be in there.

IRIS Places matter. She said...

JOHNNY Never mind her. Why don't you ask her to come live with us for a week and see if she still feels the same way? She can kip down next to Stanley.

IRIS She's trying to help. There's no need to be like that.

JOHNNY Let her find someone who needs her help, then. We're fine.

IRIS I just wanted—

JOHNNY What?

IRIS You'll laugh.

JOHNNY I won't.

IRIS My mother.

JOHNNY I know. She won't be forgotten.

IRIS How do you know? You've forgotten everything she taught you.

JOHNNY How does living here help?

IRIS I didn't say I wanted to live here.

JOHNNY Your Mrs Cunningham thinks you should.

IRIS She doesn't realize.

JOHNNY Must be nice, not needing to realize. Having a husband rich enough to buy you a big house in Knightsbridge. Bet you wish you'd snagged one of those.

IRIS What am I supposed to say to that? You'll do.

JOHNNY Will I? That's big of you.

IRIS Ma loved you. She always said, 'He's not shifty, that one. He'll always be straight with you. That'll be valuable. You'll see.'

JOHNNY We can call the new place The Frances Foong.

IRIS What kind of name is that for a restaurant?

JOHNNY Name a dish after her, then. Dumplings a la Foong. Spicy.

IRIS Or a cocktail. 'Bartender! I'll have a Frances Foong.'

JOHNNY That'd just be a big glass of gin.

IRIS You do make me laugh.

JOHNNY Part of my charm.

IRIS Johnny, what's going to happen to Stanley?

JOHNNY He can't come with us, so don't ask.

IRIS I wasn't going to.

JOHNNY He's like a big kid. We'll have our own child to take care of.

IRIS You make him sound like a stray cat.

JOHNNY Tell you what, send him to live with Mrs Cunningham. I'm sure she's got a spare room in that mansion of hers.

IRIS It's not a mansion.

JOHNNY Have you seen it?

IRIS She said it's modest. Her husband's not that high up in his bank.

JOHNNY High up enough that they brought him over here.

IRIS I'm not going to argue with you. I'm tired.

JOHNNY Are you feeling blue?

IRIS Stop it.

JOHNNY Maybe Limehouse Chinese Laundry Blue?

IRIS I'm not in the mood.

JOHNNY *(singing)* Oh Mr Wu, what shall I do?

IRIS *(overlapping)* You know I hate that song.

JOHNNY *(singing)* I'm feeling kind of Limehouse Chinese Laundry Blues...

SCENE SEVEN

Mary Cheah's bedsit in Earls Court. Mary and Eileen sit on the sofa.

MARY You still haven't explained how you got my address.

EILEEN Church office. It's remarkable how many people will give you information they really shouldn't, if you just exercise a bit of charm.

MARY They told you where I live?

EILEEN I said you had a cold and I wanted to surprise you with some flowers.

MARY *(doesn't have a cold)* So where are they? *(Eileen reaches into her handbag and pulls out a little potted African violet. She places it on the table in front of them)*

MARY The cat's going to eat that.

EILEEN Put it on a shelf.

MARY This isn't very convenient. I'm expecting a telephone call.

EILEEN I won't keep you too long.

MARY Well, as you're here.

EILEEN Aren't you going to offer me tea?

MARY Do you want tea?

EILEEN No, it just seemed so English, to be asked.

MARY I do wish you'd come to the point.

EILEEN I don't want to say the wrong thing. You seem so prickly. I shouldn't have said that. It's just so clear to me why Limehouse should be preserved, I don't know how to convince you.

MARY Maybe in an ideal world–

EILEEN You're a bit younger than me. One day you'll realize the road doesn't stretch ahead forever. That's when you'll want to look back.

MARY You're not old yourself. How would you know?

EILEEN I've seen it in others. My father.

MARY My parents seem quite happy to be moving somewhere clean and modern.

EILEEN That's what they say, because they want you to stop worrying about them. But they also wish at least some of the buildings would be kept the way they are.

MARY   How would you know?

EILEEN   He told me, your dad. His shop might not be there anymore, but he said he'd miss walking past and seeing where it used to be. Even if it is a bookie's joint.

MARY   When did you see him?

EILEEN   It was the funniest thing. I was walking down Ming Street and saw this couple I thought I recognized. So I asked if they were the Cheahs, and sure enough... I told them I used to come into the laundry sometimes, and they'd give me candy. And they remembered eating at my dad's restaurant, his special Yee Leng Sweet and Sour Pork. They invited me up to their place for tea.

MARY   I can put the kettle on.

EILEEN   It is somewhat characterful.

MARY   That's a polite way of saying dingy and full of mould.

EILEEN   I can see why you'd want them to move.

MARY   And the stairs are a trial to them.

EILEEN   I noticed.

MARY   There might even be a lift in the new place! Sorry, an 'elevator'.

EILEEN   It's not that I want to take any of that away from them. Why shouldn't they have a modern flat? It's 1958. No reason to live like it's 1928.

MARY   Here's a puzzle for you. How do we hang on to this 'history' you keep banging on about, when we all want to live in the present?

EILEEN   There must be some way to compromise.

MARY   Compromise doesn't seem to be your way.

EILEEN   I know I come on strong, but I'm perfectly willing to listen to the other side.

MARY   So what do you propose?

EILEEN   I'm not clever enough to come up with all the answers myself. That's why I wanted a committee.

MARY   Well, I wish you luck but I really must – I don't mean to be rude, my mother usually telephones around this time–

EILEEN   Yes, I know.

MARY   You know?

EILEEN She mentioned it, your little Wednesday night ritual, how they're not on the phone so she has to use the one in Friendship Noodle. She said she'd be sure to mention my visit.

MARY Well, you've told me now, so–

EILEEN My next visit. This weekend.

MARY What?

EILEEN They've invited me to Sunday lunch. I think they'd like the company. They were saying they don't see you nearly often enough.

MARY I have a lot to do. They're right across London.

EILEEN I might have implied we were close friends, from church. You don't mind? It would have been odd otherwise.

MARY You lied to my parents?

EILEEN I gave them a certain impression. It wasn't a lie, I'm sure we'll be great friends. I sense a kindred spirit in you. Oh, and no reason you would, but if you ever meet Alfred and he asks about this Sunday, be sure to say we had lunch together, but no need to mention Limehouse. I told him there was a church ladies' luncheon.

MARY This is getting too complicated.

EILEEN Not at all. We'll have a nice lunch, that's all. We can leave together from church.

The telephone rings.

MARY But–

EILEEN That'll be her. Go on, don't keep your mom waiting. I'll see myself out.

SCENE EIGHT

Friendship Noodle, night. Stanley sorting through his suitcases. He pulls out a stack of records, and goes through them. Furtively, he puts one on the record player. We hear Zhou Xuan singing 'Waiting For Your Return' (何日君再来), softly at first and then louder, Stanley looking towards the staircase for any sign that he is disturbing Iris and Johnny. Nothing. He settles down to listen.

A man appears – younger, dressed as a sailor from the 1930s. A figment of memory – someone he used to know. The sailor approaches Stanley and pulls him to his feet. They dance till the song ends.

SCENE NINE

Cathay Restaurant, Glasshouse Street. Iris and Eileen having lunch.

IRIS I shouldn't be here, really.

EILEEN It's important to make time for yourself. How long's it been since you had lunch with a girlfriend?

IRIS I feel bad, leaving Johnny to mind the restaurant.

EILEEN It was nice of him to let you out.

IRIS He doesn't know I'm here. He'd wring my neck. He doesn't approve of flashy establishments. Or the West End. Or you. I told him I was going to the doctor. You can use that one often as you like, when you're pregnant.

EILEEN Clever girl.

IRIS Why did you want to see me, Mrs Cunningham?

EILEEN Let's order first. Get anything you want. You're my guest.

IRIS That's very kind.

EILEEN Nonsense, I'm glad you were able to come. To tell you the truth, I wasn't expecting you to show up. Our last encounter ended on such a bad note.

IRIS It's Johnny's temper. He doesn't mean it, not really, but he can't bear to be crossed. You weren't to know that. It's best to let him think he's getting his way.

EILEEN And then go behind his back?

IRIS Do you tell your husband everything?

EILEEN Alfred? Of course. It's not like he ever listens to a word.

IRIS What are you having?

EILEEN It all looks so unfamiliar. Sounds silly, but I've never seen a menu like this. Everywhere back home is choose one from Column A, two from Column B. They don't even have chop suey here.

IRIS What's that?

EILEEN To tell the truth, we hardly ever go to a Chinese place. Alfred can't stand the smell.

IRIS 服务员！ [Waiter!]

Waiter enters, a little harried but still uniformed and neat – a world away from the chaotic service of Friendship Noodle.

IRIS 点菜。来一锅咸菜汤、一个鸭舌头、一个佛跳墙，嗯，还有两碗米饭。[I'd like to order. Bring us some pickled vegetable soup and a plate of duck tongues, a Buddha-jumps-over-the-wall, mm, and two bowls of rice.]

WAITER 茶要吗？[Do you want tea?]

IRIS Tea? *(Eileen nods)* 嗯，铁观音。[Yes, the Iron Goddess of Mercy.] *(Waiter exits)* I hope you like it. We can share, Chinese-style.

EILEEN Was that—?

IRIS Cantonese.

EILEEN And you were born in London.

IRIS My mother's doing. She used to say, how could I advertise the school if my own daughter doesn't speak the language of her ancestors?

EILEEN It sounds so musical. The two of you, twittering away like birds. I wish I could join in.

IRIS Didn't your father—?

EILEEN He tried, but I knew I wasn't going to be stuck on Mulberry Street forever. What would I need the language for after I'd escaped?

IRIS Is that where your father's restaurant was, Mulberry Street?

EILEEN Yes. Poky little place, kind of like yours. No offence.

IRIS One from Column A, two from Column B.

EILEEN Customers get used to certain things.

IRIS I've heard some places over here have added chips to the menu.

EILEEN Chow mein and chips! Whatever next.

IRIS Mrs Cunningham, if there's something we need to talk about, I think we should come to the point. I'm enjoying this place and all—

EILEEN But that's just it, Mrs Wong. This place.

IRIS This place?

EILEEN Just look at it.

IRIS It's nice. Very grand.

EILEEN   I wanted you to see what a Chinese restaurant could look like. Have you ever been anywhere like this?

IRIS   We don't get out very much. And when we do have a night off, the last thing we want is more Chinese food.

EILEEN   If we were to jazz up your place a little – a nice coat of paint, get rid of that dreadful linoleum–

IRIS   Our place? Friendship Noodle?

EILEEN   And those dreadful tables. Where are they even from?

IRIS   Job lot from Old Chang, when his place closed down. But–

EILEEN   Get something modern. Formica.

IRIS   What?

EILEEN   I'm trying to tell you – don't give up your shop. Keep it open, become the owner of a fine dining establishment. Your husband's cooking is certainly good enough. Limehouse could become synonymous with Chinese food again, like it was in my daddy's day. The Far East rising in the East End! This place is all very well, but when have the Chinese lived in Glasshouse Street?

IRIS   I don't know what to say.

EILEEN   Say you'll think about it.

IRIS   Mrs Cunningham, did you ask me here to insult our restaurant?

EILEEN   Merely making suggestions.

IRIS   You said 'dreadful' twice.

EILEEN   Oh what do you care, you're getting rid of it anyway.

IRIS   We have no choice.

EILEEN   But you do. You could fight this.

IRIS   Why would we?

EILEEN   It's where you belong. Didn't you say you wanted to keep your mother's memory alive?

IRIS   I was just thinking a plaque somewhere. Maybe a mention in the history books.

EILEEN   You people with your small dreams.

IRIS   Look at you, Mrs Cunningham. This is where you should be, in Soho. I've never seen anyone more uncomfortable in our restaurant. Why do you care if the East End goes away?

The Waiter reappears with their food.

EILEEN   I was born there.

IRIS   And you left.

Waiter   咸菜汤、鸭舌头、佛跳墙、米饭、茶。到齐了，请慢用。 [Pickled vegetable soup, duck tongues, tea. That's everything, enjoy your meal.]

IRIS   有没有辣椒油？ [Do you have chili oil?]

WAITER   嗯，请稍等。 [Yes, just a moment.] *(Waiter exits)*

IRIS   We should eat. I don't have much time.

EILEEN   What are these?

IRIS   Duck tongues in sesame sauce.

EILEEN   You're joking.

IRIS   What?

EILEEN   I'm hoping that's some kind of colourful metaphor? No. Actual tongues, ripped out of actual duck mouths–

IRIS   I thought you grew up in a Chinese restaurant. Yes, I know. Column A, Column B.

EILEEN   You don't have to remind me, Mrs Wong. I know I don't fit in. Not Chinese enough for you. A little too exotic when I visit Alfred's club.

IRIS   I didn't mean that. Plenty of people are mixed. Johnny is. There's no harm in it.

EILEEN   I don't belong anywhere. Not that I wish I'd stayed at Mulberry Street, but–

IRIS   You want it to stay the same, even though you've changed.

EILEEN   Something like that.

IRIS   Limehouse isn't a photo album for your childhood memories. We're allowed to change too. You've found something better for yourself, why can't we?

EILEEN   Is this better?

IRIS   I promise you, it is.

Waiter enters.

WAITER   辣椒油。 [Chili oil.]

IRIS   谢谢。 [Thank you.]

Waiter exits.

EILEEN   I seem to be saying all the wrong things today.

IRIS   Don't mind me. Having a human being strapped to your front does wonders for the temper.

EILEEN   Mrs Wong, I want to save Limehouse. At least a little corner of it. When they're done there'll be no evidence there were Chinese in Limehouse.

IRIS   We'll know.

EILEEN   And your child? Don't you want it to know where its parents came from?

IRIS   We're just trying to keep our heads above water.

EILEEN   I could help.

IRIS   Are you offering me money?

EILEEN   Call it a loan.

IRIS   I think you've got the wrong idea, Mrs Cunningham.

EILEEN   I didn't mean to insult you. Please, sit down.

IRIS   I should get back to Johnny.

SCENE TEN

Friendship Noodle, night. Stanley is asleep on his makeshift bed – perhaps a bench and a couple of chairs shoved together. A German soldier enters.

SOLDIER   Achtung. Ich bin Luftwaffe. Du bist das deadmeat, ja?

STANLEY   别过来。你来错了地方。 [Don't come any closer. You've come to the wrong place.]

SOLDIER   Nein, ich suche dich. Hast du vergessen?

STANLEY   战争已过去了，你怎么还在？ [The war is over. Why are you still here?]

SOLDIER   Ach, Stanley, der Krieg ist immer hier. In dein Kopf. Dummkopf!

STANLEY   放过我，求求你，我是无辜的。 [Let me go, I'm begging you. I'm innocent.]

IRIS   Stanley?

Iris enters, turning on the lights. The German soldier vanishes.

STANLEY 他又来了，那德国人。他一直缠着我。 [He came again, the German. He won't leave me alone. He won't leave me alone.] Nothing, bad dream.

IRIS Was it the war again?

STANLEY So many times, I tell myself it is over. But still they come.

IRIS Let me get you some water.

STANLEY Don't go.

IRIS It's all right, I'm not leaving. Just over here, to the urn. It's still warm, good. Drink this, you'll feel better. Nice warm water.

STANLEY Thank you.

IRIS You are safe here.

STANLEY You are kind woman.

IRIS Don't worry about it.

STANLEY Why you so kind to me?

IRIS Has it gotten worse lately, Stanley? It seems to be happening more often.

STANLEY I don't know.

IRIS That's twice now, this week.

STANLEY Are you angry?

IRIS Of course not. Just worried about you.

STANLEY So many bad dreams. Don't know why.

IRIS Is something bothering you?

STANLEY No.

IRIS Is it because we might be moving soon?

STANLEY Don't want.

IRIS I don't think we have a choice.

STANLEY Like being here.

IRIS Me too.

STANLEY I want my time back. When I had the rooms, and I sat with Ah Lok and Shuang and the Swedish man, we played cards and they knew so many songs. *(Sings)* Oh Danny Boy, the pipes, the pipes are calling...

IRIS That was years ago. Do you know what year it is, Stanley?

STANLEY   I'm not stupid.
IRIS   I didn't say you were.
STANLEY   I remember everything. All the good and bad. My head has too many things.
IRIS   We'll find somewhere for you to go, when this is gone. Try not to think about it.
STANLEY   I never try to think. It happens.
IRIS   Go back to sleep, Stanley. I'll see you in the morning.

SCENE ELEVEN

More projections – the handheld camera going down Pennyfields, now in the early afternoon, again with the unseen camera operator holding up pictures of the buildings from the 1920s. We stay on one of these, which expands as we pan along it. For a moment it lingers, as lights come up on Mary and Eileen, the backdrop to their stroll through Limehouse.

EILEEN   Over there – near as I can make it – that's where my father's restaurant used to be. Even the way the street lies is all different now.
MARY   Lots of these ones were bombed in the war.
EILEEN   No, it went before that. The slum clearances, in the 1930s.
MARY   I'm sorry.
EILEEN   I remember – or was it a dream? Running down the road for my father. Holding a piece of paper, with Chinese writing–
MARY   Oh, puck-a-poo, yes, we all did that.
EILEEN   That's what it was called?
MARY   You crossed out Chinese characters on a form. They picked ten cards out of a hat, and if those were the same characters you'd crossed out, you won enough money to buy a house. My dad never got more than two right. Two meant fish and chips for supper.
EILEEN   I can't imagine London not having a Chinatown. This isn't nearly as big as the New York one, but it was comforting to imagine this still here.
MARY   There are a few restaurants and supermarkets up in the West End. Lisle Street, Rupert Street that kind of area.

EILEEN   Are they calling that the new Chinatown? Who actually lives there?

MARY   We live everywhere. Who says we have to all be in the same place? It's not a holiday camp.

SCENE TWELVE

Eileen's living room. Bao, Chuang and Jenny are on the floor, painting a large banner. Perhaps it says 'Let Limehouse Live' or the Chinese characters 保留唐人街.

CHUANG   这有什么作用？[What's the use of this?]

BAO   有钱拿，你管得着？[What do you care, as long as there's money to be earned?]

CHUANG   浪费时间。[Waste of time.]

Eileen enters with a tray full of tea things.

EILEEN   Careful not to spill tea on it, after all your hard work. *(Pours tea)* I hope this is all right. Sugar's on the side.

JENNY   Thank you.

CHUANG   说自己是华人，连中国茶都没有。[She calls herself Chinese, then doesn't even serve us Chinese tea.]

BAO   好了！[Be quiet!]

EILEEN   How clever you are. I'm not good at working with my hands. My great skill is delegation.

JENNY   Do you really think this will do any good?

EILEEN   Who can say? You've got to get people's attention, somehow. It's like scattering wildflower seeds. Most of them won't take, but keep at it long enough and some will.

BAO   But you – angry people?

EILEEN   You're not going to get very far, if you're afraid to annoy people now and then.

BAO   典型的美国鬼。[Spoken like a true American devil.]

CHUANG   Don't need get far. I am happy here.

EILEEN   Where you are isn't going to be there much longer.

JENNY   They said they'd find us alternative housing nearby.

EILEEN   It won't be the same, though?

JENNY Just want a quiet life.

EILEEN Well, it's good of you to help me, even if you aren't quite on the side of the cause.

BAO Five shillings.

EILEEN Right, yes. *(Finds her handbag, rummages in it)* I'm still not used to your money. Is this right?

JENNY Yes, ta.

CHUANG Ta.

EILEEN And don't forget, two o'clock next Thursday Town Hall. We'll give them something to think about. And Jenny – work on your speech.

SCENE THIRTEEN

Town Hall. A meeting has been assembled for the Council to hear objections to the Chinatown redevelopment scheme. Councillor Eric Brinkman presides. At present, Jenny Szeto is reading out her complaint. Everyone looks a bit tired – it's been a long session.

JENNY And furthermore, many families have told me they will be unable to find ingredients of this quality in any convenient location. It is not reasonable to expect Limehouse residents to travel to the West End merely to do their grocery shopping. I urge the Council to bear this in mind in their plans. Thank you.

Applause. Cries of 'Well said, Jenny!'

BRINKMAN Thank you, Miss Szeto. Now, I believe we have one more petition to hear?

Johnny steps up to the makeshift podium.

JOHNNY Jonathan Wong from the Friendship Noodle restaurant. Councillor Brinkman. Thank you for this opportunity. My wife and I have run Friendship Noodle Restaurant for six years, taking over the premises from Oswin Chang. This area has always been known for its Chinese food. We have built up a loyal clientele, who come from near and far for our famous lo mein – including yourself, Councillor Brinkman. We also serve dock workers, many sailors have told us ours is the first place they come to when their ships are in harbour. If the Councillor cannot provide a reassurance that a suitable accommodation can be found, we will have no choice but to leave the area that has been our home for almost thirty years, and set up shop elsewhere.

Applause. 'Hear, hear!' etc.

JOHNNY   Thank you. *(He sits)*

BRINKMAN   Thank you, Mr Wong. This brings us to the close of the inquiry. I assure you all of your objections will be considered in our deliberations.

For my own part, I wish to commend all of you for the candour and civility with which you have shared your views. We on the London County Council understand only too well the disruption that can occur with these development works, and it's only severe need that has made us recommend such drastic renovation work. The Abercrombie Plan of 1943 refers to the 'drabness and dreariness' of 'the depressed housing areas and obsolescence of the East End', and regretfully little has changed since then. Many of the pre-fabricated structures intended as emergency housing after the war are still here, fifteen years on. Meanwhile, more and more young families are desperate for accommodation. The situation is untenable.

There will have to be a certain amount of inconvenience, yes, but the results will be worth every bit of trouble. Limehouse, like the rest of London, must be brought into the modern world. Wiser heads than mine have put together the Administrative County of London Development Plan calling for slum clearance, and even the Tories recognize the need for more housing, with Harold Macmillan calling–

EILEEN *(off)* Let Limehouse live! Let Limehouse live!

BRINKMAN   Uh, Harold Macmillan calling housing 'the most urgent of all social services.' Standards will be raised.

EILEEN   Let Limehouse live. Let Limehouse live. Let Limehouse live.

A group of protesters arrive from the back of the hall, waving the banner and placards. They include Jenny Szeto, Mabel and Chuang.

IRIS   Mrs Cunningham?

RESIDENT ONE   This is an official inquiry.

EILEEN   And we're here to make our objections. Isn't that why we're here?

BRINKMAN   All objections must be filed with the Council Clerk no later than three days before the–

EILEEN Yes, all right, all right.

JOHNNY She couldn't make an objection anyway. She's not from round here.

EILEEN You're all missing the point. Someone has to say it. Don't you see? You're missing the wood for the trees.

RESIDENT TWO It's a disgrace! People barging in like this.

EILEEN Ingrates. I'm only trying to help. *(Outrage. Perhaps someone boos)* No, listen! I so hoped someone else would say it, but all the objections were so short-sighted. I need this, we stand to lose that – we have to think about more than that. More than what we personally have to gain from this. Chinatown isn't just a place. It's a home for all of us. Even if we don't live here. The Chinese need somewhere in London we can call our own. And if this is taken away, where will we belong?

BRINKMAN Madam, look around you. The Council Health Officer has certified a number of buildings unfit for habitation, and I must say I cannot argue with his view. The sanitation here is – well. We seek to provide all residents with clean, modern apartments. Indoor bathrooms and community amenities. Who could be against that?

EILEEN Your plans don't take into account the character of the place. The Chinese have always lived here–

JOHNNY Less than a hundred years.

EILEEN Whose side are you on?

JOHNNY Not yours.

BRINKMAN Alternative accommodation will be found–

EILEEN You can't just tear up a neighbourhood and expect people to hang around. They'll go elsewhere. There are few enough as it is–

BRINKMAN Precisely. There can't be more than fifty Chinese families left in the area. The spirit of the place is not something I can quantify. There are real, concrete needs that have to be met, and it's my responsibility as an elected representative to see that this happens. There is simply no economic reason for keeping Limehouse in its present form.

Now, if you'll excuse me I have another meeting–

EILEEN Turning tail. Coward.

BRINKMAN Good day to you all. *(Exits)*

RESIDENT ONE Now look what you did, you stupid woman. You frightened the Councillor away.

EILEEN *(calling after him)* You're supposed to be serving these people!

JOHNNY Who are you calling 'these people'?

EILEEN If he was meeting the people's needs, then why are there so many objections?

RESIDENT TWO We had questions. That's all. We wanted our views to be heard. Why are we wasting our time talking to her?

JOHNNY No one asked you here. Just go.

IRIS Mrs Cunningham, it might be better if you left. We can–

EILEEN Oh, sure, like you tried to keep me away in the first place? You might have mentioned this was happening.

IRIS I was afraid you'd make trouble.

EILEEN It's all very well to sit here and make polite conversation, but the truth is the Council will put through compulsory purchase orders whatever you say. Just come in and buy up the land from under you.

IRIS Yes, but–

EILEEN So what, Mrs Wong, is gained by all this talk? What would your mother do? If you want to stop this from happening–

RESIDENT ONE Who says we want to stop this?

EILEEN More fool you if you don't. This place is the one thing you truly own, and you'd throw it away for what, central heating?

RESIDENT TWO That's easy to say. You look like you've never been cold.

EILEEN I was born here. When I tried to find my father's restaurant – I knew it was gone, of course, but not even being able to tell where it had been, not the slightest trace he was ever there – I can't tell you how it broke my heart.

JOHNNY Boo hoo.

EILEEN Let Limehouse live! Let Limehouse live!

The protestors join in. Stanley, who has spent the last few minutes with his hands over his ears, suddenly stands and runs outside, howling.

EILEEN What's the matter with him?

IRIS He doesn't like loud noises.

SCENE FOURTEEN

Another meeting room in the Town Hall. Stanley cowers in a corner. Eileen enters, out of breath.

EILEEN Oh thank heavens. Everyone's out looking for you. *(Silence)* Mr Wong went back to the restaurant in case you were there. I was sure you hadn't left the building, though. It's always safer to be indoors. *(Silence)* Are you going to talk to me?

STANLEY No.

EILEEN I'm sorry I got everyone angry. Well, I'm not, but I'm sorry that upset you.

STANLEY Okay.

EILEEN Will you come with me? Mrs Wong was very worried about you.

STANLEY No.

EILEEN I promise I won't do any more shouting.

STANLEY Don't believe you.

EILEEN Well, stay here and I'll go get Mrs Wong. Is that all right? *(Silence)* What happened to you, Stanley?

STANLEY When?

EILEEN You weren't always like this, were you? Mrs Wong said something about the war.

STANLEY Don't like to talk.

EILEEN I was in the war too.

STANLEY You are lady.

EILEEN I was on a ship. As a nurse.

STANLEY I was on ship.

EILEEN You too?

STANLEY Not fighting. Merchant ship. We transport, all over world.

EILEEN Military supplies and whatnot.

STANLEY Materiel. Yes. Sometimes people. Whatever needs to move. I was just ordinary sailor, ship's cook sometimes, but then the war, and we must all help, there is no other work. Not like before, there is a navy ship beside us, following.

EILEEN An escort. Yes, I've seen those.

STANLEY   So we should be safe.
EILEEN   That's never a guarantee, but it helps. I saw a fair bit of action, even in my humble role, but someone must have been looking out for me.
STANLEY   No one look out for me. A German airplane bomb hit my ship. We sank so fast I could not believe, maybe twenty minutes. No time for lifeboat or anything. I hold piece of wood.
EILEEN   You survived.
STANLEY   I don't know how many hundred people on that ship. The water is cold. There are dead bodies near me, then they sink. I float for how long, maybe hours.
EILEEN   Stanley.
STANLEY   And that day and night, there are more airplanes above, I do not know if they are German looking for us, or others for rescue. I shout but there is no one, you will not believe the ocean is so flat but you cannot see who else is there, everything is gone and then I am alone in the middle, flat blue water in all direction, sky, nothing else, and I think how big the sea underneath me, how small I am in all that water so many miles down and all around.
EILEEN   We never thought what would happen if we were hit. You couldn't.
STANLEY   Then maybe I faint, and when I wake up I am on a ship and they say okay, we are British, we will take you to safety. When we arrive in port, I say thank you, and now I will never get on ship again. So Limehouse is now home.
EILEEN   Don't you want to go home home?
STANLEY   Limehouse is home. What is left in China? The Communists took charge and now only bad things happen, no food and even worse.
EILEEN   Your family–
STANLEY *(shakes his head)* My China is gone.
EILEEN   And now this place too.
STANLEY   Iris says she will help me find somewhere.
EILEEN   Wouldn't you like to keep living with them?
STANLEY   I am fine. Life is not supposed to be easy.

Iris enters. They do not notice her.

EILEEN	If they'd just listen to me, maybe some of Chinatown could stay the way it is and you wouldn't have to move.
IRIS	Don't make promises you can't keep.
EILEEN	Mrs Wong–
IRIS	It's not fair.
EILEEN	Why do you all give up so easily?
IRIS	We can't afford to make a mistake.
EILEEN	Giving up might be the biggest mistake.
IRIS	I have to think what's best for the baby. I'm not taking risks with her future. You asked what my mother would have done. She'd have made sure first of all she wasn't hurting anyone else. Come on, Stanley. We're going home.

SCENE FIFTEEN

More video projections. It's becoming clear that the person with the handheld camera is heading towards Limehouse Town Hall. Perhaps we hear snatches of her voice – "She said cobblestones here. Suppose they've all been dug up." It is late afternoon, almost evening. More pictures of the old days, though these might be more 1930s or even 40s.

SCENE SIXTEEN

Johnny is sitting at a table in the restaurant, dozing. Perhaps a bottle of beer next to him. Frances Foong (aged 27) appears, dressed in a rather smart 1920s outfit.

FRANCES	Little Johnny.
JOHNNY	Miss Foong?
FRANCES	I hope you've been studying. 香港。
JOHNNY	Hong Kong.
FRANCES	That was an easy one. 女人。
JOHNNY	Something person.
FRANCES	Woman. 愛你。 [Love you.]
JOHNNY	I don't know.
FRANCES	Johnny, I'd like you to meet my little daughter. Iris.

JOHNNY   Iris?
FRANCES   Don't be shy, say hello to my little Iris.
JOHNNY   Iris!
IRIS *(entering)* What? What's wrong? *(Frances vanishes)*
JOHNNY   You're here.
IRIS   ...Yes?
JOHNNY   I dreamt we were kids again. Your mum was there. Sometimes I forget how long ago that was. I've known you for twenty-three years.
IRIS   To be fair, you spent the first five pulling my hair.
JOHNNY   Everything else has gone. Your mum's lessons.
IRIS   I guess I'll be the one teaching our kid Chinese, then.
JOHNNY   Chip off the old block.

They kiss. Mary enters.

IRIS   We're not open yet.
MARY   Are you Mrs Wong?
IRIS   Yes?
MARY   My name is Mary Cheah. I'd like to talk to you about Eileen – Mrs Cunningham.
JOHNNY   Not Uncle Fatt Heung's daughter?
MARY   Yes.
JOHNNY   Haven't seen you around here.
MARY   I live in Earls Court.
IRIS   What were you saying about Mrs Cunningham?
MARY   I heard about the council meeting.
IRIS   There was – an incident.
JOHNNY   She's got too much time on her hands.
MARY   Eileen means well, I'm sure she does. And my parents adore her. She can be very charming when she wants to be.
JOHNNY   I'll believe it when I see it.
MARY   She just wants to keep Chinatown the way it is now. I don't know how you feel about the clearances?
IRIS   I'll miss all of this, I won't lie.
JOHNNY   It's no place to bring up a child.

IRIS	They say it'll be better–
JOHNNY	Eventually.
MARY	So you're leaving?
IRIS	Probably.
JOHNNY	Definitely.
MARY	That's what she was afraid of, I think. Not just the buildings going. The people too. And then what's left?
JOHNNY	You left.
MARY	That's what happens. You can't stop people going where they want to. It's like water, it has to slosh around, find its own level. Earls Court is where I ended up. Hardly as far as any of our parents travelled.
JOHNNY	My mum's from Canning Town.
MARY	Eileen's barking up the wrong tree, but she really does have good intentions. And we're friends, I think.
JOHNNY	Did you come all the way here to tell us you're friends?
MARY	I got the strangest phone call last night. I think she'd been drinking.
IRIS	Mrs Cunningham?
MARY	She said there'd be a sight to behold in Limehouse this afternoon. Something to shake everyone up a bit. And then she cackled. I didn't think anyone actually did that.
JOHNNY	Maybe she's got a bomb.
MARY	I thought she might have said something to you. She's mentioned her plans for your restaurant.
JOHNNY	Her what?
IRIS	She had a few suggestions. For making the place better.
JOHNNY	I've got a few suggestions for her.
MARY	It may be nothing, but–

Stanley enters from outside, dressed in some approximation of a 1920s sailor outfit.

STANLEY	Pardon me.

He goes to his suitcases (stowed behind the counter during the day), rummages through them, finds a little nautical telescope, and exits. A pause. The others exchange glances and run after him.

SCENE SEVENTEEN

Pennyfields. A couple of men run in dressed as thugs for a staged 1920s gang-fight scene. Choreographed fight scene ensues. Someone appears to have set up an opium den in the street. A man reclines on a chaise-longue, while a servant offers him a pipe.

MAN Ah, such a sensuous aroma.
SERVANT The dragon is strong tonight.
MAN Truly, life holds no greater pressure.
EILEEN Pleasure! *(She appears, holding a sheaf of papers – her script)* I mean, think about it. 'No greater pressure' doesn't make much sense, does it?
MAN Sorry.
EILEEN Let's go back to 'So this is the Blue Lotus' and let's try to stick to the actual words.

Iris, Johnny and Mary come into view, looking fairly shell-shocked.

MAN So this is the Blue–
IRIS Mrs Cunningham – what is this?
EILEEN Oh hello, everyone. Come to join in the fun?
JOHNNY What the hell do you think you're doing?
IRIS Johnny! Language.
EILEEN Just a little demonstration. Something I've thrown together to show Limehouse off.
MARY Show it off to whom, Eileen?
EILEEN Anyone who cares to look! You were all saying that Chinatown's had its day, that I'm too late. Well then, let's turn the clock back. When was this neighbourhood important? Let's remind people of the glory days.
MARY But what for?
EILEEN I've tried reasonable argument, and that didn't get anywhere, so to hell with logic! I just want attention now. You've got to make trouble, before people will listen to what you say.
IRIS Mrs Cunningham–
EILEEN You were right about one thing, though. This area is dead. Every single person I asked was happy to put aside whatever they

were doing and join in our little pageant. I'm not even paying that much. Charleston, everyone!

A group rushes in, dancing the Charleston frenetically. Eileen calls out directions.

EILEEN Nice straight arms! Bend at the knees – now! And up. Good, good, keep to the beat. Jenny, hands!

JENNY Sorry!

EILEEN Keep going, don't stop. And turn-kick-back-kick.

IRIS Mrs Cunningham, I don't understand–

EILEEN Join in! You probably couldn't do the dancing, but we're shorthanded at the puck-a-poo stand.

JOHNNY My wife isn't doing anything of that sort. We've left all that behind. There's none of that opium gambling den nonsense around here.

EILEEN Did you know there used to be authorized tours from the West End to Limehouse? People would get on a charabanc and head out here. They wanted to see the bad old Chinatown, opium dens and all.

IRIS Yes. I saw them sometimes, gawping at us.

EILEEN And some days, if there wasn't enough going on, they hired people to run around shouting with pigtails or whatever.

JOHNNY What's your point?

EILEEN You heard the Councillor. No economic reason to preserve Limehouse. I'll give them an economic reason.

Stanley walks past, waving his telescope.

STANLEY Shiver my hearty timbers.

EILEEN No, no, Mr Lim. It's 'Shiver my timbers, me hearties.'

IRIS Is he meant to be a sailor or a pirate?

EILEEN Who knows the difference?

MARY But what are you trying to do?

EILEEN Shut down the street! All the streets if need be. We'll have a carnival, I'll make sure the press witnesses everything, we'll see if we can't embarrass them into keeping Chinatown open. How dare they. All this history, all gone. Not if I have anything to do with it. They won't be able to ignore what this place stands for. We'll rub their noses in it.

JOHNNY This is enough. I've had enough of this.

EILEEN Yet look how many people have joined in.

JOHNNY Of course they have, you're paying them! They're all still going to move, when the Council tells them to. The changes are going to happen, whether you want them to or not.

EILEEN This is so horrifically short-sighted. You'll see one day, when it's all gone. You'll wish you'd done something, and it'll be too late.

JOHNNY And we'll be weeping into our tea. "If only we'd listened to that wise Mrs Cunningham, she was so clever." Do you really think you're the only one who sees this? We all understand what we're giving up here. Iris and me, we grew up on the Causeway. Everyone here is from here, it's our home, but we also know we deserve better. We've seen how the rest of the country lives.

EILEEN You don't have to throw out the baby with the bath water. Yes, get your central heating if you must, but don't let your whole history get wiped out.

JOHNNY We're past that. Look around you. If this had been kept up maybe if these buildings had been well-constructed in the first place... It served its purpose. Limehouse was fine when it was all sailors and Chinese laundrymen just off the boat. Why do you want to trap us here? You got out.

EILEEN And I feel lost! I don't know where I belong. That's the truth. I don't feel like I belong here, but I want it to stay. I'd feel better, knowing it was here.

IRIS Just pretend it's still here.

EILEEN Your mother – she saw something that needed doing, and she came in and did it. There'd have been no Chinese school if not for her. Are you saying she shouldn't have?

JOHNNY She did something useful, something that people wanted. No one wants you here.

EILEEN That's not true. Your wife ran after me, that first day, when I was about to leave. Did she tell you? She said I was needed here.

IRIS That's not what I said. Johnny, it wasn't like that.

JOHNNY I don't care. I know better than to believe a word that comes out of her mouth.

EILEEN You can hate me, if you want. I don't expect thanks. This is my last shot at saving Limehouse, and then you're on your own.

JOHNNY Why don't you just leave now?

He tries to push her away. She hits back. Iris tries to hold Johnny back. Maybe Stanley and the others join in the scrum. A couple of men run in dressed as thugs, ready for their staged 1920s gang-fight scene – assuming this is part of it, they pile on. It quickly becomes a proper street brawl, and Eileen's tenuous leadership of the mob completely evaporates. In the confusion, Iris lets out a bellow and lowers herself to the ground.

JOHNNY	Iris?
IRIS	I'm just going to rest here for a bit.
JOHNNY	Get help, someone, don't just stand there.
EILEEN	Here, elevate her feet.
JOHNNY	Get away from her.
EILEEN	It's quite all right, I'm a qualified nurse.
STANLEY	She is, it's true.
JOHNNY	Has everyone gone completely mad?

EILEEN Stay out of this, it's women's business. Jenny, go boil some water. As much of it as you can. Mabel, run and fetch some towels. Clean ones.

JOHNNY Listen–

EILEEN Don't fight with me, Mr Wong. We can do that later. Better?

IRIS Yes, thanks.

EILEEN Never mind thanks. It's time to call the doctor.

JOHNNY What?

EILEEN Don't worry.

JOHNNY Iris, hold on, you'll be all right.

EILEEN More than all right. There's absolutely nothing to worry about. Go home, everyone. We're done here. And breathe.

SCENE EIGHTEEN

Friendship Noodle. Stanley at the stove. Mary seated.

MARY She's going to be all right. There's no need to fret.

STANLEY I am not fretting.

MARY I thought Mr Wong did all the cooking.

STANLEY Usually. Sometimes he lets me. I was ship's cook, you know. Here. *(He places a small plate of dumplings in front of her)*

MARY Oh, I don't–

STANLEY	You should eat. On the house. I am in charge now.
MARY	These do look good.
STANLEY	Dip in the sesame, then in the ginger.
MARY	Delicious.
STANLEY	You should not be afraid.
MARY	I'm sorry?
STANLEY	You are not happy, I think? You worry about other people a lot, and you do not do things for yourself. Your life will not change if you do not change it yourself.
MARY	I like my life the way it is.
STANLEY	Really?
MARY	I just met you. What do you know about me?
STANLEY	I know you like dumplings.
MARY	Everyone likes dumplings.
STANLEY	I am not saying you must do anything, just consider.
MARY	Consider?
STANLEY	Consider. Verb. To entertain possibilities.
MARY	I know what it means.
STANLEY	So consider.
MARY	It's sad this place is going.
STANLEY	Why? You hardly came here before.
MARY	My parents like it.
STANLEY	Everything will end.
MARY	Are you always this philosophical?
STANLEY	Usually I am quiet. But now there is no one else talking, so.
MARY	What do you think about all this?
STANLEY	It does not matter what I think. So I do not.
MARY	You must have an opinion.
STANLEY	I think Mrs Cunningham is right.
MARY	She is?
STANLEY	Oh yes. She can see what Chinatown will become.
MARY	Well. I'm still happy that my parents are getting a new flat.

STANLEY   Of course.

MARY   And there's not much left, is there? Let's face it. Chinatown might have been worth saving thirty years ago, but look at it now. Bombed out, everyone old and dying – no offence – and full of unbelievably nasty smells. Preserving the bricks and mortar – why? It's a relic.

STANLEY   Like coral. Leaving behind, even after animal is gone. On the ship, sometimes we dive down in shallow ocean, break off piece of coral to sell.

MARY   You probably shouldn't have done that.

STANLEY   Coral does not care. It is dead.

SCENE NINETEEN

Eileen's living room, full of packing crates. The furniture is piled up. Iris and Eileen sit on a crate, using another as a table for their tea cups. Iris is no longer pregnant.

IRIS   Oh this is so nice. Listen to that. The silence. It's been such a long, long time since I heard silence.

EILEEN   She can't be crying all the time.

IRIS   She stops when she's asleep. But when that happens, I sleep too. It's my only chance. I can't remember the last time I had my eyes shut more than an hour.

EILEEN   You've only had her three weeks.

IRIS   Is that all? My mother would be scandalized. You're supposed to sit out the month and eat special nourishing foods. Not leave your baby with your husband and go off gallivanting.

EILEEN   Where did you tell him you were?

IRIS   He's not a monster. Of course he said I could come say goodbye.

EILEEN   We got off on the wrong foot somehow. Well. Too late now.

IRIS   I wish you weren't going.

EILEEN   Never mind me. I want to hear more about the baby. What's her name?

IRIS   We're calling her Frances. I'd still like to see my mum get into the history books, mind. But for now–

EILEEN   It's perfect.

IRIS   What will you do next?

EILEEN   The usual. Luncheons. Whist drives. Someone will ask me to be on their committee, and I'll accept. It usually goes on from there.

IRIS   Moving on to the next cause.

EILEEN   It's not like that. Limehouse really does mean something special to me.

IRIS   Maybe it's good you're going, then. You won't be around to see it get torn down.

EILEEN   Alfred's bank decided he'd be more useful to them back in Boston. They called it a promotion. I don't know.

IRIS   I'm sorry it turned out this way.

EILEEN   It was foolish of me to think I could change things. But I had to try.

IRIS   Yes.

EILEEN   I've always been a fighter. If I'd been born earlier I daresay I'd have been a suffragette.

There's always something worth changing. Just before we came over, I heard Jane Jacobs at a rally – she was speaking about not letting them tear apart Greenwich Village for the sake of some expressway, and I thought that was right. You can't just rip things to pieces and call it progress.

IRIS   It's working out well for us. They're giving us a bit of money to help us move. We might even go outside London. There are still plenty of towns where they don't have Chinese takeaways yet. Johnny's convinced we have to get in there now.

EILEEN   I never did get to finish my lo mein.

IRIS   You'll just have to visit again.

EILEEN   I don't think I'll be back. What for?

SCENE TWENTY

Video: Limehouse changing, the final Chinatown buildings coming down, council flats going up, new roads being paved. A counter shows the years ticking ahead, 1959, 1960, 1961, 1962, 1963, 1964. Then we are at a party. Some fashionable young people are dancing the twist.

Mary talks to Colin, who is maybe 30.

COLIN   No way.

MARY   Don't make me say it again.

COLIN   You can't be.

MARY   Fine, forget I said anything.

COLIN   No, it's good, you definitely don't look–

MARY   Don't you say it either. It's ridiculous, at my age, going back to school. But there I was, typing up academics' notes all day, thinking 'I bet I could do this.'

COLIN   And here you are.

MARY   I feel ancient. Especially with a lecturer who looks about twelve.

COLIN   I wish I didn't! People might take me seriously.

MARY   God. This music.

COLIN   We could go somewhere else.

MARY   No, I should try to get used to it. I do want to experience all of undergraduate life, not just the studying. I feel I missed out.

COLIN   What made you take the plunge?

MARY   I met a lady – I guess you could call her a force of nature. American, of course. When she wanted something, she just went out and made it happen.

COLIN   That must be nice, always getting your own way.

MARY   Oh no, it blew up in her face. I mean, she was really, really wrong-headed in a lot of ways. But the important thing is she tried.

COLIN   I don't think that's true. I think succeeding is the important thing.

MARY   You're young. You haven't spent years not doing anything because you were afraid of not succeeding.

COLIN   I think you'll succeed.

MARY   What in?

COLIN   Whatever it is you decide to do. I have a feeling.

SCENE TWENTY-ONE

Video – more time passing. The first skyscrapers appearing. The Limehouse docks closing for good. More years tick by, leaving us in 1976, in an East End nursing home. Johnny and Frances Wong are visiting Stanley. A nurse gives him the last of his medication.

JOHNNY	All right, old man?
NURSE	He might not answer you. We're having a slow day, aren't we, Mr Lim?
JOHNNY	Does he take all that every day?
NURSE	More or less. I don't think he minds. It's just part of the routine.
FRANCES	Dad, can I wait in the car?
JOHNNY	Say hello to your Uncle Stanley.
FRANCES	He doesn't know I'm here.
NURSE	I'll leave you to your visit. *(Exits)*
JOHNNY	Of course he knows. He's very glad you came.
FRANCES	How do you know?
JOHNNY	He's smiling.
FRANCES	That's not a smile.
STANLEY	Iris?
FRANCES	What?
STANLEY	Iris, hello.
FRANCES	Uncle Stanley, it's me. Frances. Iris is dead.
JOHNNY	Fran!
FRANCES	What? He was at the funeral!
JOHNNY	He doesn't remember! Be gentle.
FRANCES	This is really creepy.
JOHNNY	You look a lot like your mother, that's why.
STANLEY	Iris?
JOHNNY	No, old man. It's not her.
FRANCES	This is – I can't. I'm waiting outside. *(Exits)*
STANLEY	I want Iris. She was nice to me. Not like these people.
JOHNNY	She's gone, old man. I miss her too.

STANLEY   Iris?

SCENE TWENTY-TWO

More projections, more pictures. The DLR makes its first appearance, Canary Wharf blossoms. Years tick by. Hatchards, 1988. Mary, behind a table piled high with her books, talks to her audience after a reading.

MARY   I didn't expect this much attention. This started out as an academic book, then I began writing what I remembered. When I talked to the older residents, my parents' friends, they had so many stories for me. And they said, we want to tell these before we go, and there's no one left to remember. At first I thought, I'm not a historian, let someone else do it. But no one else stepped up.

What is it about Limehouse? This wasn't the first Chinatown in the world, and it won't be the first to disappear, but it still matters. A lost civilization, in its own way. There was more to this than a place we lived, somewhere to visit for cheap noodles. It stood for belonging.

And now – well, it's doubly lost. As you leave here, just go for a little wander. Try to find signs that there was ever a Chinatown here. It was important enough once that everyone in London was terrified of opium dens and white slavers. You'd think there'd be something left behind. Some residue.

I was here in '58, you know. I wish I could say I tried to stop it happening, but like everyone else I just wanted the area to stop being so run-down. They promised us the new buildings would be clean and modern, which they were. Modernist, anyway. But what character do they have? No offence, but Limehouse is dead, its soul sucked right out of it.

Jane Jacobs wrote this in 1958: "The point, to repeat, is to work with the city. Bedraggled and abused as they are, our downtowns do work. They need help, not wholesale razing. Designing a dream city is easy; rebuilding a living one takes imagination."

SCENE TWENTY-THREE

More time passes. Frances Wong's wedding, 1994.

JOHNNY   I asked Fran what she wanted me to talk about, and she said, 'Whatever, dad, just keep it short.' Fair enough, no one wants to hear an old man rambling on. I'll skip the usual stuff about my little princess being the most beautiful angel in the world.

I'd hoped my little girl would take over the restaurant, but of course those two are making far too much money where they are. I don't mind, banking's a good solid job. And the H in HSBC stands for Hong Kong, so it's not like she's forgotten where she comes from.

Her office must be half a mile up in the sky. From that tower in Canary Wharf, she can look down at where her old man's restaurant used to be. It's all gone now, of course. All in the past. I'll take my beef lo mein recipe to the grave.

Oh Frances, my pet, I wish you happiness. I just wish your mother – I wish Iris had lived to see – I'm drunk, sorry Fran. I'll sit down now.

SCENE TWENTY-FOUR

More video footage of present day Limehouse. Then someone turns off the projector and puts the lights on. It is Chloe Mann, in her 20s, Iris and Johnny's granddaughter.

EILEEN   Is that the whole thing?

Eileen Cunningham steps into the light, She's looking quite good, considering she's 93 and has just got off a plane.

CHLOE   There are a few other bits, but that's the main idea.

EILEEN   I see.

CHLOE   You hate it.

EILEEN   Not at all. It's just – seeing all this, after such a long time.

CHLOE   Should have taken you to the hotel first.

EILEEN   I don't need rest. I'm just – overwhelmed.

CHLOE   It's good of you to come all this way.

EILEEN   It's good of you to pay for my flight.

CHLOE   It wasn't my money exactly, I had an Indiegogo. That's a thing where you say what project you're doing, and–

EILEEN   I know how the internet functions, thank you. In fact, I looked at your work on the YouTube.

CHLOE   Oh?

EILEEN   Don't be alarmed.

CHLOE   I'm still at art school.
EILEEN   I know.
CHLOE   This is my final project.
EILEEN   I'm sure you're trying very hard.
CHLOE   Why'd you agree to take part, if you don't like my work?
EILEEN   Honestly? It got me back over here.
CHLOE   You could just have come anytime. It's not like you needed your flight paid for.
EILEEN   I know. But I said once I wouldn't come back, and then it felt dishonourable, without a reason. An invitation.
CHLOE   But you wanted to?
EILEEN   I was born here. And there's something that happens, approaching the end of life, that gives you a mighty hankering to take it full circle, to see where you came from.
CHLOE   My granddad would have liked to have seen you. He'd never admit it – he called you "that damned woman" right up to his death, but he did mention you a lot. You got under his skin.
EILEEN   You can miss enemies as much as friends.
CHLOE   You weren't enemies, were you? I mean you were on the same side, kind of.
EILEEN   The sides weren't that clear. What we were a part of, it was complicated.
CHLOE   But you did take on the council. Like Occupy Wall Street.
EILEEN   It was nothing like Occupy Wall Street. Unwashed bums.
CHLOE   Are you angry? I hope I haven't upset you.
EILEEN   You haven't upset me. I'm always angry.
CHLOE   Why?
EILEEN   It's what keeps me alive.
CHLOE   I've walked around Limehouse, trying to see the Chinatown. There's a couple of street signs – Amoy Lane and so on – and a weird dragon statue thing, but not much else. They really did get rid of it.
EILEEN   I said they would.
CHLOE   That made me furious. It's where my grandparents had their restaurant. I would have liked to see it.

EILEEN	And that's why you made your piece.
CHLOE	I know it sounds simplistic – but I thought that could be moving, a video tour showing Limehouse now and then.
EILEEN	Things can be both simplistic and moving.
CHLOE	And with you telling your story–
EILEEN	You said 'appear'. I have to speak too?
CHLOE	Well, that's the whole point. I need your voice. I could have asked Mary Cheah, if she were still alive, but there's just you now.
EILEEN	Yes, I've outlived them all. Can't you just use Mary's book?
CHLOE	It's not the same. Maybe you could read a bit from it – but we'd also like to hear from you. What happened back then.
EILEEN	I can say what I remember, but it's all blurry. There's too much now to keep it all separate. One day just bleeds in to the next. Some days I think I have a dental appointment, then remember my dentist died in 2007.
CHLOE	You should get a new dentist.
EILEEN	My teeth have lasted this long. I doubt they'll give out in the home stretch.
CHLOE	You look well.
EILEEN	I look like crap. That's what happens when you're ancient.
CHLOE	It's good to meet you.
EILEEN	Yes, you've said that.
CHLOE	I'm glad you came. It doesn't matter if you don't like my work. I'll make it better.
EILEEN	Do what you want to do. My opinion doesn't matter much.
CHLOE	But I so wanted to get this right. My grandparents were driven out of Limehouse by the clearances, and you tried to stop that happening. Even if you didn't succeed, you're still a heroine.
EILEEN	I promise you, it wasn't like that.
CHLOE	What was it like?
EILEEN	Are you taping this?
CHLOE	Do you want me to?

EILEEN　　　　It was the least organized movement ever. It wasn't even a movement, if I'm honest, it was me. Mary talks it up in her book, I suppose she had to create drama somehow. The remarkable thing was how quietly it all went. Moving families one by one till the buildings were empty, then one day the bulldozers came in, and a couple of years after that – well, you've seen.

CHLOE　　　　I didn't really understand what Limehouse was, until I started doing my research. I'd always thought the Chinatown in Soho was the one that had always been there.

EILEEN　　　　Most people do. Why wouldn't they? There's no evidence to the contrary.

CHLOE　　　　So this is a first step. Just to say there was something here. I don't know what else to do.

EILEEN　　　　It's hard, once something's gone, to hold on to it. Memory is slippery. Do you know who Frances Foong was?

CHLOE　　　　My great-grandmother. My mother was named after her, you know.

EILEEN　　　　I did know that. Well, that's something salvaged, at least. Something from the wreckage.

CHLOE　　　　I wish you'd managed to do it. I wish you'd succeeded.

EILEEN　　　　Who's to say this place wouldn't have been destroyed anyway? We all wanted different outcomes, and I don't know that my version of things would have turned out any better.

But it felt important to do something. We tried. Or I did. I really did try. I wasn't under any illusions that this would become my home again, but for a few weeks, a short span of time, I felt like I belonged somewhere.

The end.

JAMAICA BOY

For *Jamaica Boy* I wanted to see things on stage you weren't expecting. I wanted to show things you didn't know about. Challenge your preconceptions about people places and things. *Jamaica Boy* is set in present day London and 1960's Jamaica. It explores being British Chinese, Jamaican Chinese, Black British, diasporic, outside, under represented, hapa, hooded and homo. *Jamaica Boy* was developed with Rikki Beadle-Blair and the Theatre Royal Stratford East and later with Yellow Earth and Soho Theatre.

My interest for *Jamaica Boy* starts firstly with my father. Learning about how he moved to the UK from Malaysia and how his Chinese ancestors moved to Malaysia from China. I was fascinated by where Chinese communities had ended up. Alongside this, lies my interest in sexuality and identity. How young gay boys negotiate their environment and struggle to uphold ideas of masculinity.

Stephen Hoo studied Theatre at The Brit School before completing his BA in Modern & Classical Chinese at SOAS. He then went on to do his MA in Theatre Lab at RADA. Stephen was a member of The Royal Court's Critical Mass writing programme and the BBC Writers room.

www.stephenhoo.com

JAMAICA BOY

STEPHEN HOO

Characters

Present-day London

OPHELIA	Black, Jamaican, round, 60s.
CHRISTIAN	20s, half Chinese/white.
PYRO	Black, geek, bespectacled.
MISHECK	Black, sporty, wiry.

1960s Jamaica

OPHELIA	Beautiful dark skinned 19 year old girl.
CHONG	Handsome Jamaican Chinese, early 20's, strong.
CLINTON	Tall, black, intense, 22 year old. Ophelia's brother.
SNITCH	Wiry, mixed, scruffy, 23.
LIM	Chong's father, a shopkeeper, 50's, rotund, proud and grumpy.

SCENE ONE

PRESENT DAY LONDON / CROYDON – The back of a brick house. A back garden / allotment. A ton of mess. A shed. Ophelia is facing Christian, who has his hood up, almost totally covering his face. Ophelia is holding a file.

OPHELIA	Late!
CHRIS	It's ten!
OPHELIA	Five past.
CHRIS *(kisses teeth)*	Shut up.
OPHELIA	Watch your mouth.
CHRIS	You gonna report me for being five minutes late? Waste gash!
OPHELIA	Yes. And it need clearing.

CHRIS You what?

OPHELIA The waste. I want you to clear the waste. You see it there?

CHRIS …

OPHELIA Move all of that to over there then I want you to take up di slabs, put them in the wheelbarrow, I'll let you know what next. *(Handing him some gardening gloves)* No smoking, no friends, and no entry. *(Indicates her house)* Ya hear me?

CHRIS What if I need a slash?

OPHELIA Knock pon di door. I'll accompany you.

CHRIS Fink you can treat me like dog like?

OPHELIA *(mocking)* A dog would do it outside. Like a dog like.

CHRIS You don't know me, man.

OPHELIA I know that you are a late comer, I know I am not a man. And I know what you are here fi do.

CHRIS Look–

OPHELIA And I know what my function is.

CHRIS And I know that I'm not a dog. I know my rights and I know that now it's ten past so now you're making me more late innit. Crusty old– *(Ophelia gets an instant Kodak camera out and takes a picture of Christian)* Fuck d'you fink you're doing?

OPHELIA Proof of arrival.

She waits for it to process, waves it to dry it.

CHRIS What? Look woman I don't give a–

OPHELIA Miss Randles.

Beat.

CHRIS You didn't arks my name.

OPHELIA You didn't introduce yourself. You bowl in like this. No manners, no courtesy. Just insolence probably born from a life of indolence, indifference and bone idle inertia.

CHRIS What?

OPHELIA What this, what that. Wotless! Char! *(Ophelia opens a file she is holding)* Chiang Weng O'Riordan.

CHRIS It's Christian! *(Ophelia gives him a look)* My name's Christian.

OPHELIA *(giving side eye, still drying the photo)* Um hem. Is required to fulfil the terms of community service for a period of exactly twelve weeks.

CHRIS ...

OPHELIA Said offender will work for a period of twenty hours a week. *(Chris kisses his teeth)* Unpaid. Said offender will arrive on time.

CHRIS Was.

OPHELIA Will be subject to daily progress reports. Punctuality report.

CHRIS Fuck sake!

OPHELIA Civility Report.

CHRIS I know this.

OPHELIA Other conditions include. No back chat. Improved manners and have a shower in the morning. *(Wafting the report)* Oh lordy! You g'warn tink up di place bwoy.

CHRIS *(trying to grab the report unsuccessfully)* You're making it up.

OPHELIA He will not steal–

CHRIS I ain't not no teef!

OPHELIA Triple negative! Improve his grammar–

CHRIS Where do I start?

OPHELIA *(pointing to shed)* He will fetch the rake.

CHRIS Where?

OPHELIA *(still in report mode)* Where you think? *(Christian makes for the shed)* He will pull up him trousers and he will cover his mouth when him cough.

CHRIS *(off stage)* When he coughs. *(Off-stage clattering)* Why d'you let this place get so mashup for?

OPHELIA My knees aren't what they used to be. And it serves the community, cos now miscreant pickney like yourself have something fi do.

Ophelia studies the Polaroid. Chris comes back from the shed. He's an image of the past.

CHRIS Does it say what I done? *(Beat)* Yo! Eh yo? Miss Randles?

Chris pulls off his hood. Ophelia looks at him.

OPHELIA *(going inside)* Clear up the mess.

Christian looks on bemused as Ophelia shuffles into her back door.

SCENE TWO

1960's JAMAICA – Rocksteady music cross fades with radio broadcast interference.

RADIO BROADCASTER   Good morning Kingston! This is Radio Jamaica and it is 6.30am! Tings hotting up for the island's Independence Day celebrations on di sixth of August. Prime Minister Bustamante announces the biggest parade ever! In other news, unemployment continues to soar as economic reforms fail to provide much-needed... *(Fade out)*

A cock crows.

A Chinese dry goods store. A shop sign – LIM's DRY GOODS. A front entrance with some steps downwards. There is a small improvised makeshift area at the front, which is currently covered by blue tarpaulin. This forms a badly attached annex. There are gas canisters, frying pans, baskets.

Ophelia (aged 19) bursts out of the front of the store doors chased by Chong, who is shirtless. They kiss passionately but are covert. They embrace, Ophelia breaks free. Chong waits at the store's steps. Lights a cigarette.

OPHELIA *(pointing)* This is as far as you go Chong. *(Entranced by her beauty. He moves a bit. Smokes. Cocky)* Eh! Mi nah joke! Behave now! Help me set up di stall. Clinton him soon come.

CHONG   My love for you is foolish you know. Mi lose all sense of caution. Let Clinton come, mi nah care!

OPHELIA   I care! Ya dyam idiot. I know my brother. You wanna ruin everything?

Ophelia starts to set up the annex. Chong smiles.

CHONG   I know how Clinton him stay. Everything gonna be good. Big tings a g'warn! Me a businessman now you know! I know Clinton.

OPHELIA   Hush ya self. If you say that then I think it's time I tell your father, ahem I mean your boss when him comes back from his trip.

CHONG   Ah ah. Now you see that's different, that's–

OPHELIA   Exactly. Hypocritical.

CHONG   Your brother knows that I'm a good man.

OPHELIA   And your papa doesn't know that you are a good lickle bwoy no?

CHONG   Good is good and all but him first need for see me as real businessman. Innovative. Dynamic. Not some pickney that tend di till.

OPHELIA   "Good man". You and Clinton used to go round all the place playing kiss chase with all the girls. Don't think I don't know what you two used to get up to. "Good man".

CHONG   Then your brother him know me well no?

OPHELIA   Yes, him know that you are a dog. And your father still treating you like some pickney bwoy. So you just a lickle puppy dog! *(Chong howls from where he stands. A dog barks in the distance in response)* Hush ya self Chong! Him soon come!

CHONG   First you have to tame me before you can tell me to do dis an do dat! You haffi tame me before you can treat me like some dog!

Ophelia pulls off the blue tarpaulin covering the annex. We now see a simple cooking area and some chairs.

OPHELIA *(preparing the annex)* Help me set up. You know this is a big day for him.

CHONG   For you too Ophelia. For us. There's still time. Let's go back in.

OPHELIA   Absolutely not. The light is coming up.

CHONG   Then mi cyan see every inch of you woman.

OPHELIA   Eh eh?

CHONG *(annoyed)* Ophelia when do I ever get the whole place to myself?

OPHELIA   Opportunist dog. Rampant, rabid, narsty–

They canoodle and kiss, it gets intense.

CHONG   Too long mi a wait for dis. Driving me crazy. Looking but mi cyant touch. One night my Papa leaves. Finally. One night given to me by the lord himself. So mi could love you. Kiss and caress you. Smell you. Do you! *(Picks her up)* Come now, Let me do it one more time. Let's juk. *(Humps her)*

OPHELIA   Oh no, no, no. You cyan't talk to me so?

CHONG *(damage control)* You di most beautiful ting inna dis land. I love you Ophelia. Me talking animalistic-ally, mentally, emotionally–

OPHELIA Stupidly. You talking the talk that is for sure. Good wid di words and all—

CHONG Me good with the good good!

OPHELIA *(disapproving)* My goodness.

CHONG *(grabbing crotch)* Yes! I have di goodness. *(Beat. Ophelia shocked)* You di speechless!

OPHELIA Lord ah mercy! Me cyan't bear so much lasciviousness from you. *(Chong sits down at entrance, kisses his teeth)* What?

CHONG All proper proper proper.

OPHELIA I'm a lady.

CHONG All uptown and ting.

OPHELIA Is what you want? Some harlot? Some nice oriental gyal for cook you di fried rice?

CHONG You're neither of dem tings. You an original, you a classic, exclusive. Tho a bit stushass at times.

Ophelia laughs. Beat. They're in love.

OPHELIA Say them words again.

CHONG *(in Chinese)* 你是，世界上最美丽 的女孩。

OPHELIA If only I could be your China gyal. Then your father won't mind. We both know I'm the real problem here.

CHONG Me nah care for no stodgy China gyal. Me want you!

Chong rushes Ophelia. She squawks. It gets raunchy. We hear a noise. Ophelia and Chong panic. Chong runs inside the store. Ophelia continues setting up. Clinton enters with Snitch. Snitch is rhyming. The two of them are carrying boxes of bananas, canisters of oil, and a huge sign.

SNITCH Call the coffin maker cos di people dem brain dead. Call a voodoo master for him cyan look ahead. This country is rotten. Rotten down to di core. Up there you have the rich rich and down here you have di poor.

CLINTON Snitch. Hush yourself with your politicking.

Snitch drops the bananas down.

SNITCH I'm telling you that this here be some failure waiting to happen.

CLINTON Today. A joyous day. A new start. *(To Ophelia)* I had to listen to Snitch's rubbish all morning. He thinks he's a poet. Chong! Chong! We reach! Snitch. Make yourself useful. *(They both put up a huge* *sign that says "The Original Chinese Jamaican Fritters". It's over-the-top and tacky)* Yah man!

SNITCH Call the coffin maker cos the injustice reach its peak. Call the coffin maker cos dis country's future's bleak. Me know that you cyan't see it, ya blinded by the yellow sun. But trust me my brother you'll regret it when it's done.

OPHELIA I'm not indulging you Snitch. Clinton, why you bring him along?

CLINTON Ophelia. You bowl off at the crack of dawn. Me can't carry all this stuff alone. Chong mekking up excuses. You're both nearly vex me you know.

OPHELIA I was too excited. I wanted to get set up. Couldn't sleep.

CLINTON Too excited to take some stuff with you? Make a few trips?

OPHELIA I was about to come back–

SNITCH Self sufficiency is the way that we can rise. Dependency pon the others is totally unwise. You go sell your banana fritters and you think it's all okay. But the truth is you're a supplicant to the Ching Chong Chiney way.

OPHELIA *(laughing)* Oh Jesus...

SNITCH You can smile and laugh and ting and ting but what me say is the truth. Black man need fi stand alone then you'll have your proof. Facts is facts, tings is tings warnings what I decry. Me talk di truth from pon di roof–

OPHELIA Hush yourself, Snitch! You and your barber shop politics. Me cyan't take it no more. Clinton tell him for g'warn now.

CLINTON You sing and sing and sing sing sing about the destitute. You sing you sing sing sing sing sing. It's all a substitute! Let me get on with my life, and you get on with yours. Instead of waffling on bout the social flaws. *(Ophelia and Clinton laugh)* Chong!? Where him is?

OPHELIA Me nah know. In his father's absence him lie in. Comatose probably. Grateful for some time off. Him soon come.

CLINTON Action speak louder than words, and his INaction speaking louder than my words! Chong!

SNITCH Don't be fooled by the Chiney man Clinton.

CLINTON Not here. Not now.

OPHELIA That Chiney man you talk so bad about. Him help us when our business failing. When we some silly fritter stall inna di side of di road there.

SNITCH You were better on the other side of the road there. Independent!

OPHELIA We were a failing business on the other side of the road there. Now g'warn take yourself somewhere else with your irritation.

Chong enters from the side dangling store keys and greets Clinton and helps set up. Chong kisses his teeth at Snitch.

SNITCH Look at you all. Hush as soon as him come. Treating him like a boss.

CHONG You used to be alright Snitch? What 'appen to yuh? Your head brok.

Chong goes back into the store.

SNITCH When you cyan hear, when you cyan see, then everything is transparency. The Chiney man only care about fokin over the others.

Clinton roughly takes Snitch aside.

CLINTON Why you talk shit for? How many years you known Chong?. G'warn with your stupidness. You're ruining my day.

SNITCH You don't know what I know Clinton. Come with me tonight to the pool club. Meet wit my group man.

CLINTON Crazy.

SNITCH Meet these people Clinton. They'll tell you about business. "Black" business.

CLINTON I have a new business adventure here. No time for di social tings dem.

SNITCH Gonna pay me for helping bring the stuff over?

CLINTON When I make some money from this here business. Jesus!

Snitch leaves.

OPHELIA Why you keep him around?

CLINTON Ophelia. He's a friend.

OPHELIA Him getting crazier by the day. Ever since they let him go from The Fort Clarence.

Chong enters.

CHONG Wouldn't you go crazy working down there? All dem tourists?

OPHELIA We could make more money if we could work down there.

CHONG Already looking further afield Ophelia. Yuh need a permit. What we got here is good. Local reputation. And now you benefiting from di passing trade. *(He looks at the fritter stall. Noticing ingredients)* What's all this?

CLINTON We need it.

CHONG The oil and sugar and flour and all them tings you cyan get from inna the store.

OPHELIA Tivoli Cash 'n' Carry is cheaper than your store Chong.

Clinton and Ophelia laugh.

CHONG *(smiling)* Ah what dat? Then I'll make mine cheaper than theirs!

They all smile at this great idea. Chong turns the radio on.

CLINTON Heat up the oil!

CHONG The Original Chinese! Jamaican! Banana! Fritters! Reach! Come now! Try it out. Free sample! Yea ya know you want fi try it!

Rocksteady music gets louder, everyone is happy. This transitions into a dirty London grime track that then transitions to grime and back again.

SCENE THREE

PRESENT DAY LONDON – Ophelia's allotment. Misheck and Chris are chatting. Chris is making a brick enclosure.

MISHECK These people fam. Dat call themselves diversity role models yea. Go into the schools and talk about gays. Like it's a good fing like. I mean literally coming into the school and doing show n tell n shit.

CHRIS …

MISHECK Like what are they gonna show and tell? How to be a battyman? How to fuck another man in they arse? It's narsty. Pure narsty. What is the world coming to? Homo-geddon. *(Beat)* Why can't people see that hetro-normative binary systems exist for a reason bruv? A good reason. It's nature. The order of things. *(Chris isn't listening, as usual)*

So fam, you a gardener now is it? Is this your lot? It's fucking dumb. What happened to inspiring youngers in this situation? Gardening isn't inspiring? It's meditative. NOT inspiring.

CHRIS It's supposed to be a punishment fool. A service to the community? *(Upward questioning intonation)*

Beat.

MISHECK *(referring to inside the house)* What's she like then?

CHRIS She's a fucking xenomorph blud.

They laugh. Chris does an impression of the Alien from the film Aliens.

MISHECK *(sotto referring to inside)* Anything good?

CHRIS Not allowed inside. Locked and bolted innit. She got a clip board, monitoring me and shit. Twitching curtains. She got this community ting down to a T ya get me.

MISHECK *(loudly)* You ain't no house Chigga then! You white Bitch!

CHRIS Shut up man, she'll come. She's black. She's a granny.

MISHECK COCONUT!

CHRIS Shut. Up!

MISHECK Some proper out in the plantation Chigga innit cuz. She gotta have something worth something. Grannies keep wads of cash in tea pots innit. My granny did anyways. Before she put it all into a high interest rate ISA with Nationwide 1.02% ya know!

CHRIS Patience is a virtue blud. I told you she's hardcore. I wouldn't be surprised she got laser beams n shit in there. *(They laugh)* Wanna sweeten her up but she's proper stamping on my balls over everything I do. Give it time. We'll see what's what. Antiques innit.

MISHECK You ain't never been able to sweeten up gyal blud. And you ain't never had balls.

CHRIS Ain't never had balls?.

MISHECK What?

CHRIS Not NEVER had balls means I had balls all along fool. NOT NEVER HAD BALLS?

MISHECK Shut up talking balls man. It's gay.

CHRIS ...

MISHECK Look yea. If you can sweeten up an old biddy you're on the right path to actually getting lucky wiv gyal ya get me? You gotta start somewhere innit. Yo bruv, I'm gagging to bash some fanny. Even granny fanny ya get meh?. Even acid for blood type xenomorpth type granny!

CHRIS Argh! What has the world come to? Sickness runs deep with you. *(Chris goes to move some clutter out the way. Starts working on a new patch)* Truth yea, why you ain't doing your ting like? Won't you get penalised?

MISHECK You serious? They got me washing a wall. Like a wall. Just a big, white, don't even know what's behind it ... wall. Community officer kicked a bucket and mops and arksed me to clean it. I dusted bruv, nah mate. Fuck that shit. Then I bounce here and look at you. A vision of broken Britain. Pussy whipped. Out in the garden like slave from back in the day.

CHRIS The bitch said if I break rules I get into more trouble–

MISHECK Rules! Listen Chigga. We got in trouble fool. This is trouble. It's done. I'm trouble! I say it with pride bruv. What more can we get into?

CHRIS We're losers Mish! Broken Britain *(sarcastic)*. You say it wiv pride?

Beat.

MISHECK Yea! I say it wiv pride. I've made peace with it. No more cognitive dissonance ya get me?

CHRIS ...

MISHECK You looking lost again. Come n go yea. Little bird tells me sensors broken in Boots. Liftin's piece of piss. Wanna get my hands on that NO7 serum dem gyals go nuts for. Ebay that shit!

CHRIS Pause! Real talk yea. I wanna do this fuckries and move up. Don't wanna teef shit. Don't wanna beef with people.

MISHECK We are products of the construct fool. This is path of least resistance. Listen, Black mans walks into a shop and doesn't teef shit don't matter.

CHRIS What moist shit you pontificating on now–

MISHECK We enter the shop we've good as teefed shit anyway, even if we ain't. These people's synapses already played out what they think we gonna do in milliseconds. Even if I walk out the shop and not done noffink–

CHRIS Double negative. You lean?

MISHECK   Listen! The fact they've already played out what I was gonna do remains … Trace trauma bruv. We already teefed it, in their heads, even if we didn't teef it, which we could've been there to do, which we ain't, cos you're lame. Chris! Come!

CHRIS   Mish, you always on some … Dem security guards are black!!!

MISHECK *(over it)* Nigerians tho! You don't get it … Again.

CHRIS   I get these tings. Projections.

MISHECK   So fuck it innit.

CHRIS   Why you talking about teefing shit Mish? We ain't here cos we jacked stuff. We're here cos—

MISHECK   Same principle applies to acts of violence Chigga. They put all that and all us in the same box.

CHRIS   And I'm not black.

MISHECK   But you wear a hoodie innit.

Ophelia comes out.

OPHELIA   Wha' you do?

MISHECK   He's making you a brick wall innit. What's with all the walls man.

OPHELIA   Who are you and what are you doing here?

MISHECK   Can't I chat with a bruva?

OPHELIA   No! You cyant. Rules of community service. G'warn now.

MISHECK   Fuck you bi—

Ophelia goes for Misheck who bolts. Chris looks lost in the commotion.

OPHELIA   Idiot pickney. Trespassing too.

CHRIS   What the fuck are you doing?

OPHELIA   Clearing away the strays. You. Know. The. Rules. Now I need you to run some errands. *(Handing him a list)* Soy Sauce, Garlic, Ginger, Spring Onions, Chicken Breast and—

CHRIS   Think I'm your slave?

OPHELIA   I thought you could—

CHRIS   Wanna make up for the past.

OPHELIA   What do you know about the past?

CHRIS   This is community service … not some plantation ting.

OPHELIA   What nonsense you talk?
CHRIS   Taking out your black anger on me.
OPHELIA   Oh no my youth! You cyan gwarn like that–
CHRIS   I cleared your shit. I did what you said. I filled them bags with rubbish and you still up in my business like a Wendy Williams interview.
OPHELIA   Wendy What? Look. Chris.
CHRIS   You wanna treat me like a dog–
OPHELIA   Christian!
CHRIS   I could complain you know. I got rights.
OPHELIA   Christian. *(Beat)* I thought I could cook for you tonight.

Beat.

CHRIS *(disarmed)* Don't like Chinese.
OPHELIA   Try it.
CHRIS   It's bad for you. Oestrogen. Soya. Soya and Oestrogen. Makes you a batty man. It's gay.
OPHELIA   Lord have mercy! *(Beat)* Your ingratitude is beneath contempt bwoy.
CHRIS   Fry cats and dogs tho.
OPHELIA   Please. You talking some Fu Manchu complex right now.
CHRIS   Saves them money. Reuse oil for years ... like you can cook Chinese food.
OPHELIA   You want it or not?
CHRIS *(puts hand out)* Whatever. Cash. *(Ophelia slips him £20. Chris makes to go then turns)* What's Fu Man Chu?

SCENE FOUR

1960's JAMAICA – Rocksteady music. Jolly and cheerful. Fade out. The store. Ophelia is packing up. She's chuffed. She's saying bye to some customers and counting her takings. Enter Snitch.

SNITCH   Where's your brother?
OPHELIA   Out back. Ordering more bananas. Wholesale.

SNITCH   Miscalculate di stock I presume? *(Ophelia ignores him. Continues counting the money. Snitch continues to hover)* You looking chirpy. Radiant in fact. You got any?

OPHELIA *(handing him a fritter)* Last one. We almost sold out. Word got round. Phone burning up.

SNITCH *(munching)* I could get sick of these after a while.

(He checks out the garish sign) The Original. Chinese. Jamaican. Banana Fritters. You know this sign is pretty big. Imposing. Make you all know about it.

OPHELIA   Excellent marketing.

SNITCH   How all this all work then?

OPHELIA   We rent this lickle patch, we use Chong's goods. Set up is good.

SNITCH   So optimistic. So hopeful.

OPHELIA   How could anyone be too optimistic with you around Snitch.

SNITCH *(starts to rhyme)* Me talk di truth cos me have di proof–

OPHELIA   Don't start all that up again Snitch. It's so irritating.

SNITCH   I like it when you're irritated. Reminds me of my mother. It's sexy.

OPHELIA   Ergh!

SNITCH   Hold on to the money you made today. Don't tell Chiney bwoy exactly how much you make. It's only what they'd do to us anyway. *(Ophelia ignores Snitch, continues to pack up)* So what are you going to do this evening? I thought maybe you and I could–

Clinton and Chong enter. Chong continues into the store.

CLINTON   This evening we celebrate! Snitch you coming too.

SNITCH   Actually I wondered if you wanted to come to a meeting with me.

CLINTON   I'm going to the shebeen, celebration.

SNITCH   Make a bit of money and blow it. Just the stupidness me expect from a black man.

Chong comes back out.

CHONG   Creating a successful partnership is not stupid. Better than selling trinkets to tourist pon di beach. It's dignified.

SNITCH You getting a good cut out of all this I am presuming? The lion's share.

CHONG They rent this space at $4 a day. Similar set up would be $10. So no. The ingredients they use are from my shop at half the usual price. So no. And for the first day's work I'm not even charging them.

SNITCH So what do you get out of it?

CLINTON What?

CHONG You heard me.

SNITCH Control.

CHONG Keep today's cyash Clinton. Celebrate.

(Just at that moment Lim enters, grumpy and sweaty. He drops his suitcase on the ground. Wipes his brow. Takes off his hat) Lao Ba.

It's dead silence. Lim slowly looks about the place.

LIM A'what dis?

CHONG *(showing the sign)* New business venture father!

The silence is awkward. Lim goes up to the huge Banana Fritters sign.

OPHELIA Hello Mr Lim.

Snitch kisses his teeth.

CLINTON Good evening Mr Lim.

LIM There doesn't appear to be anything good about it. *(They all start talking at the same time explaining what is going on apart from Snitch who remains observant and silent. Lim silences them all)*

(In Chinese) Ga ma? [What are you doing?]

CHONG *(positioned between Ophelia and Clinton)* Lao Ba, you always talk bout I don't have a business mind and I should be better at all of that.

OPHELIA It's a collaboration Mr Lim—

LIM Did I ask you anything?

OPHELIA No sir.

LIM What's the name of this store?

CHONG Ba.

LIM What's the name!?

CHONG Lim Dry Goods.

LIM So why is there a huge sign about some Chinese and Jamaican and Bananas and Fritters?!!

CHONG *(swallowing)* It's about the marketing you see–
LIM Mi cyan't see the entrance for Bananas every which way!
OPHELIA Uncle Lim please give it a few days so we can prove–
LIM How this all work then?
OPHELIA Well–
LIM Chong?!
CHONG You see, I charge them each day for this space and the condition is they buy the ingredients from our shop. Simple.
LIM How much?
CHONG *(in Chinese)* $10 kuai qian.
LIM *(scoffing)* It should be $20. And the ingredients?
CHONG Half price. Cos they using our stock?
LIM *(laughing)* What di' … It should be more cos they using our stock. Have the privilege of being connected to this front, this here business, my name. Association with di Chinese.
CLINTON Mr Lim sir, please.
LIM Typical Jamaican. No business sense whatsoever. As a Chinese I expect you to make proper business style. Instead you waste the stock and make me look like a idiot fool!
CHONG Lao Ba.
LIM No! You hear my conditions? $20 a day and ingredients… a third off.

He picks his stuff up and walks up the steps to the store. Moving a box of bananas out the way.

CLINTON Even the money we made today won't make no profit for that.
SNITCH Clinton?
CLINTON A waste of time and money.
CHONG I don't know what to say Clinton.

Lim comes out again. Silence.

LIM So?
CLINTON So what?
LIM The money you owe me. For today?
CLINTON Chong said …

LIM I calculate the amount to be $20 plus *(he quickly calculates the amount)* Plus one third of the profits.

OPHELIA That's not actionable.

LIM This is my business. These are my terms.

SNITCH Clinton man?

OPHELIA I mean something mutually beneficial?

LIM Excuse me?

OPHELIA Chong and I were discussing how an alignment of forces could increase the profit margin if given time to– *(Beat)* Chong!

LIM Why you talk to my son so? *(Beat)* You owe me twenty-eight dollars.

SNITCH Clinton don't–

CLINTON Here.

SNITCH Clinton. *(Lim takes the money. He goes back in)* Clinton?!

CLINTON WHAT?!

SNITCH Seeing as you're not going out to celebrate now–

CLINTON How can I with no money!

SNITCH Come with me. They have free food and drink. Maybe more of a reorganization than a celebration you could say.

Clinton starts to leave. Snitch follows.

CLINTON Ophelia. Go home.

Ophelia looks at Chong, then she leaves. The space is dead quiet. Chong contemplates. Lim comes out again.

CHONG Me nah know why you didn't let me explain my business plan. I had big plans to expand, I wanted to surprise you and show you I–

LIM Idiot pickney.

CHONG They made money today.

LIM Typical Jamaican. *(Chong goes to walk inside, but stops when Lim continues–)* In China. We lose everything after your Yeh Yeh died. My mother your Yan Yan struggled to make money. To feed me. Washing clothes, iron, sewing for hours for nothing just so we are able to eat. Me and your grandmother. Two people depend on each other. We had nothing but the family's three Qing Dynasty vases. Assets. Worth much. First vase your grandmother sell to pay off grandfather's debt to loan shark, then they kill him anyway. Second vase my mother give me before she died so I could sell it and afford to come here. Set up business. She told me many Chinese already here for years in Jamaica and I can join the existing clan.

(Beat. Lim looks about the place) They help me because I am Chinese. Help with di set up, feed me.

CHONG Ba–

LIM One person helped me the most. Your mother. She showed me how to organise, create a plan, execute. Beautiful. She did the bookkeeping, I ran the shop. We employed others from the clan and everyone make it happen. But she was the beautiful brains behind it all. Then we had you, and she lost too much blood in the birth, stupid doctors couldn't save her.

CHONG You never told me this.

LIM You need to think like a Chinese bwoy. Do the plan, execute, properly like your mother. Don't do things without me. This here is a family business. Things changing around here bwoy. The gwai lo [white ghost] so high you can't see him no more. The huk gwai [black ghost] starting to eat bitterness over it.

Lim goes to walk inside.

CHONG Where's the last vase?

LIM I keep it in back of store under the safe. If anything ever happens to me, you take it. Family. Asset.

CHONG I'm sorry.

LIM Lock up store. I'm going home.

SCENE FIVE

PRESENT DAY LONDON – Traditional Chinese music blends into the sound of the inner city. Chris and Ophelia in Garden.

OPHELIA These are long lasting bulbs. Hyacinths, tulips, daffodils–

CHRIS You want them over there then?

OPHELIA They will look better here.

CHRIS Sun shines over there tho innit.

OPHELIA I suppose you're right. Maintaining a continuously flowering garden is a strategic operation. We want sixty to eighty days of colour from these bulbs.

Ophelia potters about.

CHRIS Don't mess up that area please.

OPHELIA *(moving stuff)* Developing manners I see. Right, I'm off to a community meeting now. So please don't brok up me garden digging for China.

Ophelia messes up a patch of the garden with her curiosity.

CHRIS Don't mess it up.

OPHELIA I think you may have found your calling Christian. What about that patch over there?

CHRIS Gonna grow vegetables there. I've been reading up on it on Google.

OPHELIA A cottage garden? I guess you want some money to buy the seeds?

CHRIS Yea.

OPHELIA I'll get some money out while I'm gone tomorrow when I go see Doctor Ram. You sure you don't want to do it over there?

CHRIS Nah. Leave that area man.

OPHELIA You want me to cook tonight?

CHRIS No.

OPHELIA Suit yourself. *(Ophelia goes to make her way back in with her bag and coat)* You sure you don't want me to cook.

CHRIS Chinese?

OPHELIA Wasn't that bad was it?

CHRIS A bit gooey. But okay. *(Beat)* How about I cook?

OPHELIA Oh no no no my youth!

CHRIS I could do laz agg nee.

OPHELIA Can't even pronounce it.

CHRIS It was a joke. You think I'm stupid?

OPHELIA I don't think you're stupid Christian. Look what you've done to the garden. Divided up the place nicely. Mathematical. Always good with the numbers you lot.

CHRIS I'll do jerk chicken.

OPHELIA   Oh and how do you make jerk chicken?
CHRIS   Google.
OPHELIA   You're not messing up my kitchen bwoy.
CHRIS   Not allowed inside anyway.
OPHELIA   That too.

Chris gets out a black and white photo of Ophelia and Chong from the past.

CHRIS   Who's this?
OPHELIA   Where you find that?
CHRIS   Shed. *(Beat)* I was looking for spades and stuff.
OPHELIA   It was locked.
CHRIS   It was. He looks Chinesey like.
OPHELIA   He is 'Chinesey like'. Like you.
CHRIS   My mum was Irish.
OPHELIA   Your name is Chiang Weng–
CHRIS   It's Christian!
OPHELIA   But the force is strong in you bwoy.
CHRIS   You some Jamaican Yoda?
OPHELIA   You are Chinese.
CHRIS   Half.
OPHELIA   Yes. Half Chinese. *(Chris is irritated)* I know you are half Irish.
CHRIS   Yea.
OPHELIA   Just like I know that you are half Chinese.
CHRIS   So?
OPHELIA   I know that you are petulant.
CHRIS   You said I developed manners–
OPHELIA   And I know that you are making me late for my meeting. Give me that! *(The photo)* Stop snuffling about my tings or you'll get another strike on your form.
CHRIS   Another? What was the first one?
OPHELIA   I was in a bad mood.
CHRIS   That's dark. You can't give me strikes for no reason.
OPHELIA   Watch me.

Exit Ophelia. We enter into a dreamscape flashback. The past. Chris is talking to Pyro who we don't see yet.

CHRIS Yea. Half Chinese.
PYRO Ni Hao Ma?
CHRIS What's that?
PYRO Ni Hao Ma? You should know. You're half Chinese.
CHRIS Happy New Year?
PYRO No that's Gong Xi Fa Cai. But you gotta pay attention to the tones. It's tonal. Four tones and a neutral tone.
CHRIS How do you say "I am Chinese"?
PYRO Wo Shi Zhong Guo Ren. Try.
CHRIS *(badly)* War shur Zong Gor Ren.
PYRO You keep looking round.
CHRIS Mish and my boys coming soon innit.
PYRO *(mocking)* Oh. So, like just gotta keep it real like.
CHRIS Affirmative.

They laugh.

PYRO Wanna go to Littleheath Woods later? Pretend we're in the holodeck. Or we could go Forbidden Planet? Gonna order the NCC 1701.
CHRIS Come on man. We're too old for that shit. *(Beat)* Anyway, NCC 1701 is gay bruv. You know it's all about the NCC 1701-D.
PYRO Negative.
CHRIS Positive.
PYRO Neutral.
CHRIS Zone. *(Beat)*
  (Smiling) You're a dickhead.
MISHECK How can an inanimate object have a sexual orientation?

We hear the arrival of Mish and friends.

CHRIS I'll tell you later. You best dust.

SCENE SIX

Ophelia is on her way to the meeting and runs into Misheck. Misheck tries to ignore her.

OPHELIA You think I don't know where you're going?

MISHECK Don't watch that.

OPHELIA You better not even try trespassing. I'll call the police.

MISHECK Don't get para. Fucking old bitch–

OPHELIA Cos that would jeopardise Christian and his attempts to improve his situation.

MISHECK *(stung with envy)* I'm going to the shops.

OPHELIA You got choices. Use them.

MISHECK Fuck you.

SCENE SEVEN

1960's JAMAICA – Ophelia is setting up for the next day. Chong tries to comfort Ophelia.

OPHELIA Don't.

CHONG I'll talk to him.

OPHELIA His terms is not doable. $20 a day.

CHONG Ophelia listen.

OPHELIA We already invested all the money. You said your father would be impressed. He didn't even give us a chance.

Chong tries to help her set up.

CHONG Where's your brother?

OPHELIA He went with Snitch last night, never came back.

Lim comes out.

LIM Chong! There's boxes of bananas in here been ordered from the cash and carry. Too many. Blocking the aisles in here. Move dem.

Chong goes inside and starts bringing out boxes of bananas.

CHONG Let's just see how today goes. Sell as normal, I'll talk to my father.

Ophelia heats up the oil and starts preparing knowing it's a futile task. Lim comes out with more boxes of bananas. Notices Ophelia.

LIM Where di gas from?
CHONG It's ours.
LIM Who pay?
CHONG I paid.
LIM Hrm.

Clinton arrives. He has a trolley load of even more bananas. A gas cylinder.

CLINTON TURN THE GAS OFF!!!
LIM I'm drowning in bananas.

Lim goes back in.

CLINTON Turn it off Ophelia, now.
CHONG Listen to me.
CLINTON You listen carefully to me Chong. I realised that I have been taking you for granted. Not allowing myself to see the opportunities that you could reveal to me.
CHONG Clinton let me talk.
CLINTON As the old saying goes "If you want something done, you haffi do it yourself." So that is exactly what I am going to do.
OPHELIA Why all those bananas?
CLINTON I got them direct from a warehouse in Tivoli.
OPHELIA We got too many. You bought this all with what money?
CLINTON We are using these for today and from now on. Ophelia turn it all off.
CHONG *(getting involved)* Clinton listen. We can split this business three ways. I'll be a proper partner with you. A three way.
CLINTON You think I'm stupid? You think we are all stupid. You see me pon di side of di road with my lickle Black Banana Fritters store and you see it and you want it.
CHONG What stupidness you talk bout?
CLINTON You see it and you want it. So you say you want to help me out.
CHONG I've been your friend for years Clinton.
CLINTON Fuckries! You want it pure and simple. You want for incorporate. Have control. Control it.

CHONG No–

CLINTON And then profit from our hard work.

CHONG I am helping you.

CLINTON Fuckries! Your inherent nature is to take it over. Conglomerate it. Absorb it.

They scuffle. Clinton gets Chong in a neck hold.

OPHELIA Get off him!

CLINTON You know how much my sister and I struggled. So much to try and just get by. I see you were using us as an example to your father. Using us to show him you know business. That you can do what all the Chiney man dem do.

They fight.

OPHELIA CLINTON! CHONG! Stop it. *(They stop fighting)* You spend one night with Snitch and he gets inside your head like this?

CLINTON Me realise. All I wanted was to raise ourselves out of this here shitty life we live. No mother. No father. No family. Just us. Just our common sense. But it wasn't common sense was it. Typical Jamaican business ways. Fuck up and get fuck over by others. Dutty sneaky Chiney man wid him ulterior motive. Dutty sneaky Chiney man–

CHONG Me a Jamaican!

CLINTON Ah ah.

CHONG Me a Jamaican man. Me born and raise here. I am just as Jamaican as you. You say you stupid then I am too.

CLINTON We di black man, di original.

CHONG Chinese Jamaican. We came here as slaves too.

CLINTON Your father came here to make money. Him born in China man. He came here for exploitation. Read your book bwoy.

CHONG Chinese people been here from centuries ago.

OPHELIA Clinton. You've gotten all twisted in your thoughts.

CLINTON Hush Mouth.

OPHELIA Chinese people came here as labourers.

CLINTON Black people were slaves. Labourers got paid.

CHONG …

OPHELIA Jews came here when they were banished from France, from Spain from Portugal. Lebanese came. We all came from somewhere else.

CLINTON	But who sufferin?
OPHELIA	The Carib Indians, the Arawak. They the original. They suffered first.
CLINTON	So wha' you say is no one is a Jamaican?
OPHELIA	We are all Jamaican. Out of many one–
CLINTON	Him a Chiney man. It's in the blood. Jamaican or not his blood corrupted.
CHONG	My blood? Mr Beadle who sell you the canisters for the stall. You don't think him corrupt? Him a famous money launderer. Him a whitey.
OPHELIA	Him mixed.
CHONG	Good as white as look at him. Him corrupt.

Clinton starts to move parts of the fritter stall to the other side where it existed before. Simultaneously mumbling a mantra while the others keep talking.

CLINTON	Black Man, Black Power, Black Business. Jamaican reach!
CHONG	Mr Polanski from James Street got done for extortion. Him corrupted. Him white. Mrs Johnson from the brothel down at Sun Square. She in jail. She black.
CLINTON	Black Man, Black Power, Black Business. Jamaican reach!
CHONG	Don't do this.
CLINTON	Black Man, Black Power, Black Business. Jamaican reach! *(He moves most of the stuff and takes down the big sign. There is a standoff between Clinton and Ophelia)* Ophelia! *(Ophelia is torn. Looks at Chong)* Ophelia!

She moves to Clinton's side.

SCENE EIGHT

PRESENT DAY LONDON – Chris is in the garden with Misheck.

MISHECK	Is it ready?
CHRIS	You ain't smokin my weed bruv.
MISHECK	To sell, you dickhead. Sample.

CHRIS You're not wasting product. This is capital. Ain't ready. *(Misheck look confused. Chris ushers them over to the weed plant)* I gotta check if this is male or female. She needs to be alone to produce the buds. The male plant just confuses her like.

MISHECK ...

CHRIS You looking lost Mish. If it's male I gotta take it away from the female else it could turn it into a hermaphrodite.

MISHECK What the– Hermaphrawhat?

CHRIS Not male, not female ... sort of being both at the same time like.

MISHECK This is some Caitlyn Jenner shit.

CHRIS It ain't ready.

MISHECK Where you learning all this man and woman and hermaphra-greek-ting from?

CHRIS Google innit.

MISHECK Nah nah nah, Miss 'Jamaica Jamaica' schooling you isn't it. She's like some proper hydroponic ting?

They laugh.

CHRIS She don't smoke. She just watching me through the nets.

MISHECK You been inside yet?

Mischeck makes for the door.

CHRIS Don't.

MISHECK Chill chigga. I won't touch nothing. Just a bit of recon you see meh?

CHRIS Community service remember? You're jeopardising me.

MISHECK Jeopardising? Dictionary bwoy now is it? She teaching you English Clit now is it?

CHRIS You're gonna get me in shit.

MISHECK *(incredulous)* You fucking planted a weed plant in her garden! *(Misheck goes to the door. It's unlocked)* You see meh? ... Didn't even break in.

Misheck goes in. Ophelia arrives through the back way. Carrying shopping.

OPHELIA Chris can you help me with this.

CHRIS *(improvising)* Oh. Miss Randles, check this ting out.
OPHELIA What ting?
CHRIS I planted chillies yea.

Chris distracts Ophelia away from the back door.

OPHELIA Good. I need to put this in the kitchen.

She goes to walk in the house.

CHRIS Miss Randles.
OPHELIA Call me Ophelia.
CHRIS The guy in the picture yea, was he your friend? Or colleague?
OPHELIA He was a–
CHRIS What's his name like?
OPHELIA His name was 'like' Chong. Well, actually it was Chong, no 'like' about it.
CHRIS Was he the one who taught you how to cook gooey Chinese food?
OPHELIA He couldn't organise a cup water.
CHRIS So he spoke like Chinese innit?
OPHELIA Occasionally yes but he was Jamaican.
CHRIS So he spoke like you?
OPHELIA Of course.
CHRIS That's fucking funny man. I'd love to see that.

Beat.

OPHELIA The way you speak is funny man ... like. *(Misheck sneaks out as Ophelia talks, oblivious, distracted)* You changed your tune Christian. Seeking your roots all of a sudden. You have to know where you came from to know where you're going. I'm full of pearls of wisdom like that.
CHRIS I'm from Croydon.
OPHELIA Your family? Your heritage? Your background? Your blood?
CHRIS Mum's Irish ... was Irish, Dad left.
OPHELIA He ever speak Chinese to you?
CHRIS *(pondering)* He tried. Then he left.

OPHELIA And you never tried to contact– *(Ophelia smells a rat. Notices the patch where Chris is growing weed. Misheck sneaks out but observes them from afar. Chris can see Misheck escape)* What dat?

CHRIS What's what?

OPHELIA You think I'm stupid? That looks like a ganja situation right there.

Misheck enjoys watching Chris getting caught.

CHRIS Nah negative. It's not! It's the geraniums and I just gotta–

OPHELIA You're doing it all wrong.

Beat.

CHRIS *(gobsmacked)* What?

OPHELIA It need sunlight. Proper sunlight light. You need to cover it up with a plastic box.

CHRIS And punch holes in it?

OPHELIA Affirmative.

CHRIS And you gotta put chopsticks like a support.

OPHELIA Correct. *(Beat. Ophelia goes to go inside. Stops. Misheck looks on enviously)* Your mother was Irish then?

CHRIS I ain't chatting about that.

SCENE NINE

1960's JAMAICA – Clinton and Ophelia are at the banana fritter store which now exists on the other side from the dry goods store as before. Lim is working outside.

LIM Sorry your little business idea didn't work out. My son is not the business man I expected him to be. Always dreaming about some fantasy and stupidness.

OPHELIA We can just go on as we did before and put this episode behind us.

LIM Indeed. We live, we learn. We move forward right. Onwards and upwards.

Lim shuffles back inside.

CLINTON It's better like this. Independent. I never liked him. So sly. His teeth grimace like a cyat. How did I not see him for what they always was? Me blind.

OPHELIA Enough Clinton.

Lim comes back out with boxes of bananas.

LIM Here you go Clinton.

CLINTON What's this?

LIM Surplus. Chong must have stupidly ordered too many. They blocking every which way.

CLINTON We don't need them.

OPHELIA Clinton wait... Mr Lim, you don't have to.

LIM I want to. For all the inconvenience from Chong. You don't want to waste them now. That would be stupidness.

CLINTON Why don't you sell them?

LIM They're nearly off anyway.

Clinton suppresses incredulity.

OPHELIA Thank you Mr Lim. Thank you very much.

Lim drops off the boxes of bananas.

LIM Chong! Sweep the front!

Lim goes back inside.

OPHELIA Better than to waste them.

CLINTON Nearly off?!

OPHELIA A three-way partnership would have worked out better in the long run. You blinded by rage in the moment. Better like this? This is what wasn't working in the first place. Our lickle ramshackle fritter store. It's laughable.

CLINTON Snitch said Business is Bigness, Fearless and–

OPHELIA Since when you listen to his clap trap? Him let off from Fort Clarence Hotel for not being able to organise a glass of water. Now he sells bracelets on the beach.

Chong comes out to sweep the front. Brings out more unwanted bananas.

CLINTON We don't want them.

CHONG Clinton man.

CLINTON Me say me nah want them!

CHONG   Take the bananas na'man.

He goes back in and gets a big can of oil out places it in sight.

CLINTON   You think I don't know what you trying to do?

OPHELIA   Chong just go.

CLINTON   You want to ingratiate yourself. Get involved. Dem rotten *(indicating bananas)*. Yellow and rotten.

LIM *(off stage)* Sweep the front bwoy!

Chong reluctantly does so. Oil gets left. Snitch arrives.

SNITCH   Jamaica's finest? Chinese? Jamaican? Banana? Fritters. It never felt right to me you know. Something about the syntax.

OPHELIA   What do you want?

SNITCH   See how things are going.

CLINTON   Better.

OPHELIA   We haven't sold anything yet.

CLINTON   It's still early.

SNITCH   Soon come, soon come.

CHONG *(giving a box of bananas to Clinton)* You know three people called the store. Want to order some fritters for lunch. I can sell some for you. Through the store.

SNITCH   Keep your dutty fingers out of our stall.

OPHELIA   It's not your stall Snitch. Clinton, let Chong sell through the shop. *(To Clinton)* Who calling us with no phone?

SNITCH   Business is business and–

OPHELIA   Hush Mouth!

CLINTON   You forgot your bananas.

Chong goes and dumps the box outside the stall downstage. Downstage Ophelia goes to give the box to Chong. They meet in the middle.

CHONG *(sotto in Chinese)* Wo Ai Ni. [I love you.]

SNITCH   What you talk? *(Chong leaves and Ophelia starts to leave)* Ophelia! Ophelia! Wherefore art thou Ophelia?

OPHELIA   That's the wrong play ya dyam idiot.

SNITCH   But you still the beauty.

OPHELIA *(kissing her teeth)* You make me want to throw myself in the river so. Ergh! I'll be back.

She walks out.

CLINTON   Where you go?
OPHELIA   We need more oil.
CLINTON   Go down to Tivoli and get some.
SNITCH   I'll take you.
OPHELIA *(surly)* No. I wanna be alone.

She leaves. Snitch looks about the stall and notices the oil Chong left.

SNITCH   The oil right here! *(Ophelia is gone and didn't hear. Clinton picks up the oil and places it at the steps of the dry goods store)* So we have another meeting tonight. Discussing how to integrate marketing and promotions.
CLINTON   I'll be there. Need fi strategise.
SNITCH *(looking at a box of bananas)* Clinton you need to learn how to order stock properly these bananas are overripe.

Clinton sighs exasperated. Lim comes out.

LIM   Chong? You seen him?
CLINTON   Oh I see him all right.
SNITCH   See right through him.
LIM   Chong?! *(In Chinese)* Lay Hai Pin Doe? [Where are you?]
SNITCH *(to Clinton)* Why you still using this big sign? Ain't right.
(*Snitch paints a big cross through the word Chinese. Looks at Lim who chooses not to react*) JAMAICAN Banana Fritters. Much better.

SCENE TEN

Lights now on Lim. On the phone.

LIM   Ah hello officer Blagdon. I wanted talk to you about something... There's these people you see... I think they are trying to monopolise the area around my store... I want good competitive market and things. But I feel like you need to check this lot out. See if they have a license to be there.

SCENE ELEVEN

PRESENT DAY LONDON – A wall. Chris and Misheck bowl on.

MISHECK Old people never have shit. Don't do tech innit. Like I was expecting some curved flat screen hi def type ting. That vayse looked antique tho.

CHRIS It's called a vase dickhead.

MISHECK Could be worth money. Door just open. How stupid is that?

CHRIS Can't you just go jacking shit somewhere else?

MISHECK ...

CHRIS You just making shit complicated. Go teef some other granny.

Beat.

MISHECK I can't believe she's letting you grow weed in her garden.

CHRIS She understands these tings you get me.

Chris laughs about the situation. Misheck doesn't.

MISHECK You two a proper unit is it?

CHRIS No.

MISHECK Is. Well, you just get proper close. I'm off to get some proper pussy you get me?

CHRIS Oi!

MISHECK There's a ting called loyalty bruv. Hoes before bros. No grannies involved.

Misheck kisses teeth, leaves.

SCENE TWELVE

1960's JAMAICA. The curtain goes down. We are in a back alley somewhere. Ophelia walking forlorn. Chong rushes up behind her.

OPHELIA Don't try it Chong.

CHONG Ophelia please. I never realise it would work out like this. You have to understand me. I only wanted the best for you all, for us.

Ophelia turns round and they kiss passionately, feverishly, surreptitiously. Ophelia begins to slap Chong harder and harder.

OPHELIA What are we gonna do? It's a mess. *(They kiss again)* No business, no money, no nothing!

They kiss.

CHONG I'll sort it out. I promise.

OPHELIA I'm drowning in your promises.

CHONG I'm trying to think of something.

OPHELIA I thought I could smell burning.

They look at each other. A smile.

CHONG I love you.

OPHELIA What are we going to do Chong?

CHONG Me fix up. This is what we a do. First me a go to every place I know and tell them all about the banana fritters. Make everyone buy them. Business will grow. Advertise in the paper. Advertise on the radio. Rejuvenate the stall and get my friend back. When Clinton sees the business booming with my help maybe him trust me again and we can be partners. A three way. Set up new stalls all over Kingston. Two at the Shabeen, three at the promenade, open one in Fort Clarence, then we start with the smaller islands dem–

OPHELIA Stop! Head in the clouds again. We can't advertise. We don't even have enough money to keep the stall open as it is.

CHONG Work in the store for a bit. Earn some money.

OPHELIA Your father won't allow that. He can barely stand me.

CHONG He'll have to once I tell him you're my gyal.

Beat.

OPHELIA You would tell him?

CHONG I'm gonna fix dis! Me ah do anything for you.

They kiss.

OPHELIA He'll kill you! Or Me.

CHONG I throw caution to the wind?

OPHELIA *(in Chinese)* Wo Ai Ni [I love you]

SCENE THIRTEEN

PRESENT DAY LONDON – Ophelia is sitting in a deck chair. Chris is looking in a box of medicine he's collected on her behalf.

CHRIS They said I gotta go back for the rest cos they were out of stock.

OPHELIA Thank you Christian.

CHRIS I ain't stupid. These ain't no hayfever tablets that's oramorph. That shit's harsh.

OPHELIA You a doctor now?

CHRIS My mum took that shit.

OPHELIA Must have had a strong constitution.

CHRIS She hated politics. She just drank.

OPHELIA When she pass?

CHRIS A year ago.

OPHELIA I'm sorry.

CHRIS Why all the meds?

OPHELIA My lungs.

CHRIS Asthma?

OPHELIA Just some thing from when I was young. It won't leave my system. It's no matter.

CHRIS Ophelia?

OPHELIA What?

CHRIS Lock your door yea.

OPHELIA I have nothing anyone wants.

CHRIS Anyway, lock your door, this ain't Jamaica.

OPHELIA What do you know about Jamaica.

CHRIS I know they do gooey Chinese food.

OPHELIA Like you know what good Chinese food is? You and your Morley's fried chicken and chips sodden in tomato sauce.

CHRIS What you know about Chicken?

OPHELIA I know you can do more than just fry it. *(They both laugh)* Let me tell you something for nothing. You wanna impress a girl? Cook good good. Non' of this Morley's or Nando's. Cook her up a meal and impress an empress. Show her you can create from scratch. Not short cut it with take out.

CHRIS   Tell me about this Ching Chong guy.

OPHELIA   Who you calling Ching Chong? You di Ching Chong. Char!

CHRIS   Where is he?

Beat.

OPHELIA   In a vase in the living room.

Ophelia bursts out laughing.

CHRIS   You have been smoking I know it.

OPHELIA   It's not ready yet.

They laugh more.

CHRIS   Those tablets making you loony. This ain't so bad you know. Cos the weather good innit.

OPHELIA   I'm going in for a nap. Just go when you done. No need to call me.

Ophelia goes inside. Chris is looking into space. He turns around, and is startled to see Pyro standing there.

CHRIS   What the fuck–

PYRO   I forgive you.

CHRIS   Go.

PYRO   I forgive you.

CHRIS   I said go. I ain't doing this. I don't need this.

PYRO   I need this Chris.

CHRIS   …

PYRO   I needed to come here.

CHRIS   Fuck off now! NOW!

Ophelia hears the commotion and comes out.

OPHELIA   No no no. Christian you can't exploit it when tings was going well. Rules is rules. No friends allowed. G'warn now.

Beat.

CHRIS   Pyro! Go!

PYRO   Hi Mrs?

OPHELIA Randles. What are you doing inna my yard? Chris is not allowed visitors. Rules.

PYRO You're right Miss Randles. I should've knocked on the front door.

OPHELIA The whole world back to front these days. I turn my back for two seconds and you got your nay do well friends come inna my yard.

CHRIS Tell him to go!

PYRO Chris, I forgive you.

OPHELIA G'warn now.

PYRO I just wanted to have a word with Chris if that's okay.

CHRIS I don't want to have a word with, with this batty man! Fuck off! Go!

OPHELIA *(to Pyro)* I think it's best you go.

PYRO Yes. I'm sorry do disturb you.

Pyro leaves.

SCENE FOURTEEN

1960's JAMAICA – Snitch and Clinton are at the stall.

SNITCH The Original. Jamaican. Banana. Fritters! Pure! Sweet! Ripe and clean! Get them while they're hot.

Chong comes out.

CHONG *(enthused)* I got an order for twenty fritters for the shebeen. Here.

Offers the money but Clinton refuses.

SNITCH What this?

CHONG They ordered it man. Phone burning up.

CLINTON Twenty fritters?

CHONG Yea man.

SNITCH You an agent now? Middle man. Want a cut?

CHONG Clinton take the money. I'll deliver them.

CLINTON We are not business partners.

CHONG They're ringing my phone for dem. Take the money na man?

Clinton reluctantly takes the money. Chong goes back inside. Snitch is singing.

SNITCH Come now, come now, Banana fritters sweet! Come get your portion you know you want fi eat! *(He walks about the place)*
Come now, Come now eat them while dem hot. What we got, what we got... *(he's trying to think of the rhyme).*

CLINTON Enough, Snitch. Your stupidness not gonna help. Talking into thin air.

SNITCH It's still early days Clinton. The school rush soon come.

CLINTON No it's not. We've been here. We've done this.

SNITCH We need to think outside the box.

Chong comes out again.

CHONG I need an order for St Aiden's church. I'll bring them on the way to the shebeen. *(Chong gives more money. Beat)* Clinton?

Clinton takes the money. Chong goes back in.

SNITCH Relying on his telephone–

CLINTON He's paying for the fritters up front.

SNITCH Him marking up the price when him reach. When will you realise?

CLINTON Start making the fritters.

Snitch tries to make fritters. Some hot oil spits at him.

SNITCH Ouch! Where's Ophelia? We would be selling more if she was out here.

CLINTON What?

SNITCH Utilize, capitalise, moisturize!

CLINTON What you talk 'bout?

SNITCH When your sister prance about the place, you know all the men come buy the fritters.

CLINTON Don't you talk about my sister–

SNITCH No body care about some margar, dry foot bottom, man folk!

CLINTON I'm not margar.

SNITCH You not curvy either. Whereas your sister now. She has the angles that be making the men dream of juk juk! Receptacle!!

CLINTON Eh!?

SNITCH Listen to me now. What mi a say is. We need to get her out here wearing some sexy clothes. Entice the mice! Entice the critters! Then them buy the fritters.

CLINTON Prostitute my own sister?

SNITCH Business is business and tings is tings. It's not prostitution. It's marketing.

CLINTON It's low.

SNITCH Low is you broke and hungry and undignified sitting in the corner scratching ya dry foot bottom and dusting the sun flakes from your eyes. You've seen the way men look at her. Talk to her, she'll understand.

CLINTON Where is she anyway? Something not right with her. Always running off. Get this get that.

SNITCH This is about making the family business work. She'll be safe. You here. Me here. Don't give up the good fight. Keep hope and you can prevail.

Chong comes out.

CHONG Dem ready?

Beat.

CLINTON You marking up the price?

CHONG Of course me not markup the price!

Chong takes the fritters and leaves. Lim comes out but Clinton and Snitch don't notice.

CLINTON I never thought it would be like this.

SNITCH Don't trust them Clinton.

Lim walks towards them.

LIM Clinton! Sorry to be the bearer of bad news but some officer come today and give me this.

CLINTON What?

LIM It says you're unlicensed.

CLINTON Chong said we didn't need a licence here.

LIM You don't need a licence to rent space outside my store. That's my tings. Yes you're correct. But here you do need a licence.

SNITCH They didn't have a licence before they moved to your Chiney shop, why this now?

LIM	Perhaps the government trying to be more proper proper. Crackdown on rogue business.
SNITCH	I see through you! You see through him?
LIM	This here is an official notice stating that you have to remove yourselves from the premises immediately. You see through that? *(Clinton reads it)* I'm sorry Clinton.
SNITCH	Listen up, brain storm ideas. We can work this out some how.
CLINTON	No, no, no, no, no, no! Everything's brok.
SNITCH	It's not. Don't doubt the power of critical mass.
CLINTON	Shut up!
SNITCH	This Chiney shop like some curse over you.
CLINTON	Go! Leave!
SNITCH	Clinton brother!
CLINTON	You're not my brother! I'm done listening to your stupidness. G'warn now! *(Snitch gets burnt by another spit of oil. "Ouch!" It spits again. He leaves)* Why can't I just make a living. I put all my energy into these things and they fail.

Lim looks touched. Guilty.

LIM	I had it hard too.
CLINTON	It's not a competition.
LIM	You were too hot headed to just suddenly leave when you were using my store front.
CLINTON	You created impossible conditions.
LIM	Things take time.
CLINTON	…
LIM	I sense you have a business mind. Determination. Sense of competition.
CLINTON	We did very well on our first day on your side. Phone burning up. Orders coming in fast.
LIM	Maybe I was being hot headed too. Come back and see Ah Chong re-arranging my business. No respect. No notice. I'm not just his father. I'm the boss.
CLINTON	He wanted to show you he can do business.

LIM   Chong got no business sense. Always dreaming. No focus. But you. I see you are willing to make this work. Listen. Pack up all this stuff and let's talk.

SCENE FIFTEEN

PRESENT DAY – Chris is working in the garden. Ophelia is filling out a report.

OPHELIA *(side eye)* Has the parolee been punctual? Hrm. Well, seeing as on time is late in my book I would say no.

CHRIS   Aww leave it out yea. I'm early if anything.

OPHELIA   When it suits you. But you have improved me must say.

CHRIS   I planted you a whole aubergine patch. Put that in your report?

OPHELIA   Is the parolee courteous? Hrm.

CHRIS   Do what?

OPHELIA   Do nothing. On a scale of one to ten, with ten being very satisfied and one being very dissatisfied. How happy are you with the parolee's conduct so far?

CHRIS *(under breath)* For fuck sake.

OPHELIA   Well, he's a potty mouth, him confuse my gender, insults my cooking.

CHRIS   But it is gooey!

OPHELIA   And growing illegal substances inna my yard. *(Beat)* Has the parolee showed violent and negative tendencies. Well, you'll have to tell me?

CHRIS   Course not!

OPHELIA   What a relief. Cos I would kunk ya head into next week if you so much as laid a finger on me you know.

CHRIS   I don't do violence to old people.

OPHELIA   But you do do violence.

Beat.

CHRIS   Depends innit.

OPHELIA   So if someone is putting violence on you and you defend yourself then that is acceptable?

CHRIS   Or if someone disrespects me or steals from me. Or tries to hurt someone I care about.

OPHELIA   What if they were just being themselves? Just being a person in the world? Would you be violent to someone just because they were different to you?

CHRIS   I know what you're getting at. Don't know what things you read about me. Some case file written by some pig. Doesn't know me. Doesn't know the ins and outs. Don't claim to know me from a case file.

OPHELIA   I don't claim to know you Christian.

CHRIS   Always going on about I'm Chinese this I'm Chinese that, you just know these things and ting and ting.

OPHELIA   If you don't feel safe telling me that's fine. *(Beat. Chris sits)* Can I ask about your mother?

CHRIS   What?

OPHELIA   You miss her?

CHRIS   Dunno. I kinda got used to her not being around the last few years. Like she was dead already. House empty.

OPHELIA   Where was she?

CHRIS   Some place called Weston-super-Mare. Rehab innit.

OPHELIA   And your father?

CHRIS   I told you he left, I never knew him. Talking of Chinese tings yea. Who is this guy in the picture with you?

Chris takes out the picture.

OPHELIA   I took that off you! Why you got it again?

CHRIS   I found it again.

OPHELIA   Keep out of the shed. Out of bounds.

Ophelia tries to get the photo. They fight but it becomes playful.

CHRIS   You can be all busy body with me but when I wanna arks a few questions you dry up is it?

OPHELIA   Only thing that's dry is your foot bottom and your ashy knees.

CHRIS   Oh insults now?!

OPHELIA   Give it back or you'll get a strike in your report!

CHRIS   Oi! You can't do that!

SCENE SIXTEEN

1960's JAMAICA – The Banana Fritters store is gone. Lim is talking business to Clinton.

LIM What we have here is a system that will really work. None of this half wit nonsense that Chong setup.

CLINTON It could've worked if we had–

LIM Your little banana stall has potential but first we need to know if we can work together.

CLINTON How do I do that?

LIM You are already doing it Clinton. You're here. Listening to me. Learning from me.

CLINTON What do I do next?

LIM Agree with me. Work for me. Promote me. Promote my store.

CLINTON Promote it?

LIM I've been thinking about doing a special offer on goods and so I want you to go out and give these flyers to people. *(Hands him flyers)* Telling them about Lim Dry Goods and that no one can beat our prices.

CLINTON I was thinking we could come to some agreement with getting my Banana Fritters Stall back at yours. Not being some flyer boy.

LIM Jumping the gun as usual. This is sort of a trial to see if we can work together.

CLINTON But for now you my boss?

LIM There is only one boss Clinton. The customer. And he can fire us simply by taking his money elsewhere.

CLINTON But me doing this feels like some sort of failure.

LIM Very honest of you. Don't be put off by failure. Good business is the result of hard work and learning from failure.

CLINTON How long the trial for?

LIM However long it takes.

CLINTON But eventually me and Ophelia can organise our fritters stall here?

LIM Possibly.

CLINTON But your conditions were not doable. Is there room to negotiate?

LIM Maybe we'll go into it as partners.

CLINTON Really?

LIM All lasting business is based on trust. I need to trust you first.

CLINTON So you, me and Ophelia as partners?

LIM Not Ophelia. Just you.

Lim dresses him in a big cardboard sign that hangs off his shoulder and written on it LIM'S DRY GOODS.

CLINTON Why leave her out?

LIM Sacrifice, Clinton. Chong is my son and he's not a partner. *(Lim hands him a big sign that says 'SPECIAL OFFER NOW ON AT LIM DRY GOODS')* An entrepreneur always searches for change, responds to it, exploits it for its opportunity.

CLINTON Yes. Yes. It's just this is so far from the vision I had for myself.

LIM Willingness to change is a strength.

CLINTON I feel stupid like this Lim.

LIM The man who uses his skill and imagination to see how much he can create from a dollar, is bound to succeed. Go downtown to the shebeen and promote the business.

CLINTON The shebeen?!

LIM Is there a problem?

Beat.

CLINTON ...

LIM Then make your way along the tourist areas. Where they drink Pina Colada. Go now.

Clinton leaves looking silly. Chong come running in out of breath.

CHONG Father, I have something to tell you.

LIM What?

CHONG I want Ophelia to be a partner with us.

LIM *(laughing)* You must be out of your mind.

CHONG Not at all. I also need you to know that–

LIM We can't have two huk gwai [black ghosts] working here. You have to be careful with who you keep in the fold.

CHONG Two?

LIM I just employed her brother?

CHONG *(hopeful)* You did?

LIM I did.

CHONG How much are you paying him?

LIM No pay for trial period. If he proves himself I'll pay him.

CHONG That's slave labour!

LIM This country was made up of slaves. When they were freed – Chinese people came over looking for work to fill the deficit of labour in the fields. When they completed their contract they stayed, created business. The blacks didn't. Because the Chinese have a history of being entrepreneur. Blacks don't have such a thing. They are young in the head. Simple. No skills in the blood. They were sold by their own people into slavery to the gwai lo who use them on the plantation. Black selling black.

CHONG The same thing existed in China, Father. You just selecting parts of history that serves your conscience.

LIM You wouldn't understand.

CHONG You're not listening to me!

LIM Black people should know their place. You see how they were failing before. Brother and sister, banana and fritter. Silly.

CHONG When they were on our side they did okay. That was my idea!

LIM Of course they did. Association. Anything linked to anything Chinese is going to be seen in a good light. The huk gwai don't have such things. So when they exist as a banana fritter stall with us, people come and buy and have confidence, they make money from association with us ... but alone? People just fear food poisoning. You understand? We are two different types of people who can only co-exist in harmony if we know our station in life.

CHONG ...

LIM It's nature, history. When I first started business with your mother, we had to jump through hoops. The disorganisation, the ramshackle administration, the corruption. All sorts of foolishness because the huk gwai don't know how to do these things. They nearly brok up my business many times. Luckily I had your mother to help me sort it all out. What have you got? Some brok lickle black gyal with no business sense.

Chong is taken aback that his father knows.

CHONG We love each other.

LIM *(laughs)* They'll love us when they want something from us. Still dreaming Chong. Blacks will never love you. I love you and I'm trying to teach you how to succeed in the world. What I say is di truth.

CHONG I respect you father but I don't agree.

SCENE SEVENTEEN

Chris is in the garden. Pyro is back.

CHRIS Pyro! You can't just come back like this. There are rules. Now bounce!

PYRO I wanted to see you. Sort things out.

CHRIS Pyro!

PYRO I think it would be a good thing. To sort things out. I am gonna talk to Misheck too.

CHRIS *(menacing)* Are you fucking dizzy?

PYRO For a few months I was yes.

CHRIS You know what I mean. You can't do this.

PYRO Put you in a difficult position? What? Like face up to things?

CHRIS …

PYRO What about me? The things I gotta face up to? The things I had to face? You should know about face, saving face, it's a Chinese concept innit.

CHRIS You don't get it.

PYRO I do. You were saving face and I got my face smashed.

CHRIS You're gonna get me in trouble.

PYRO Already did.

CHRIS *(unravelling)* Fuck off, fuck off fuck off!

Ophelia comes out.

OPHELIA Why another ruckass inna my yard?

CHRIS   Tell him to go. He shouldn't be here. No friends allowed remember?
OPHELIA   Friends? This don't look too friendly to me.
CHRIS   Anyone.

Ophelia ponders a moment.

OPHELIA   Talk.
CHRIS AND PYRO *(both speaking at once)* What? / Okay.
CHRIS   No.
OPHELIA   If you two don't talk it out. Chris you getting a strike.
CHRIS   That ain't fair. You can't–
OPHELIA   Three strikes and your community service order is extended and reevaluated and you end up washing walls at the back of the Whitgift centre.
CHRIS   You can't do that.
OPHELIA   You already got two, Christian.
CHRIS   For what?
OPHELIA   Cos I felt like it.
CHRIS *(under breath)* Fucking bitch.
OPHELIA *(about to write)* Umhrm.
CHRIS   Okay!

Awkward silence. No one wants to talk.

PYRO *(out of the blue)* Basically Chris is a closet homosexual trapped in a straight, pussy aspiring, grime, street, road man persona and extremely unhappy about it–
CHRIS   Oi!
PYRO   We were having an under cover bromance where I was teaching him Chinese and gently encouraging him to lift himself out of a ridiculous reality he'd created for himself.
CHRIS   Not that simple–
PYRO   All the while we were both secretly bonding over the fact that both our mothers died a year ago, mine from suicide and his from a drug overdose. As time went on it was pretty clear that Chris has a proclivity … towards Star Trek … and also liking members who are born and labelled XY if you know what I'm chatting about … like.

Beat.

OPHELIA Is it?

PYRO Is. I just came to say hi really. It was nice meeting you again Miss Randles. Bye Chris.

Pyro leaves.

OPHELIA He seemed nice.

CHRIS You don't know what you're fucking with.

Chris goes inside the shed and gets his stuff.

OPHELIA Er, didn't I tell you not to go inside there?

CHRIS Where else I gonna keep my stuff?

Chris goes to leave.

OPHELIA Er, I said you could put it inside, it's not time yet. You getting a strike.

CHRIS Give me one then.

OPHELIA Don't forget to pick up my prescription. Chris! Chris?

SCENE EIGHTEEN

1960's JAMAICA. A secluded area near Fort Clarence beach.

Chong meets Ophelia.

OPHELIA How did it go?

CHONG It's not happening.

OPHELIA What?

CHONG My father will never accept you.

OPHELIA You didn't tell him?

CHONG He already knew. Him and his racial pecking order. I can't stand his ignorance.

OPHELIA Chong.

CHONG I'm not Chinese enough for him, I'm not Jamaican enough for my own friends. My own people. I feel like we can't belong no where.

OPHELIA We belong together.

CHONG ...

OPHELIA You're my Jamaica Boy Chong. I love you.

CHONG I dream of big things for us Ophelia. I don't want my father to get in the way of any of that. I'm not the son he wanted. The only option I can think of is … disappear. Leave this place.

OPHELIA Why should we? We belong here. If they can't see that then that's their problem.

CHONG Your brother will not see this.

They kiss passionately. They hear Snitch sing from afar. Drunk.

SNITCH I hereby decry the black man's fight!
The Chiney Shop and its economic might!
Me walk thru di door and me wonder what right?
Domineering over us like dem white!
(Chong hides. Ophelia tries to follow but Snitch catches sight of her.)
Why you run so? *(Ophelia doesn't answer)*
Your brother vex me. Him disrespectful you know.
After all the things I help him with?

OPHELIA He's stressed. The business tings dem change every second. He running around like some headless chicken.

SNITCH Lately, you also rushing around here there and everywhere it seem.

OPHELIA Well, business is business and–

SNITCH Don't think I don't see it. Me notice these things. Cos I got a good eye for these things.

OPHELIA Ya' drunk?

SNITCH It no matter.

OPHELIA You stink.

SNITCH Clean me.

OPHELIA Ergh. You think I would go near you with your picky nastiness.

SNITCH Ophelia me very much like it when you talk dirty to me.

OPHELIA Move from me. Me said move from me.

SNITCH Come gyal let me stab out the meat!

He goes for her. Grabs her.

OPHELIA NO!

Snitch goes for her again. She struggles. He tries hard. Ophelia fights him off. Chong comes out and drags Snitch off Ophelia.

SNITCH *(frothing excitedly)* I knew it! I knew! I knew it! I can smell it in the air.

CHONG You talk nonsense fool.

SNITCH I can smell the juices. The garlic—

CHONG Shut your mouth.

SNITCH The soy, the opium. *(Chong goes for Snitch. Snitch wriggles out, laughing)* Oh it's all coming out now. It's all coming out!

Snitch runs off. Ophelia and Chong look at each other.

CHONG Let's just go, Ophelia.

OPHELIA Where?

CHONG Far away. Anywhere.

OPHELIA I can't leave Clinton. We are family. I'm all he's got.

CHONG Not after Snitch tells him. Mi know dat for sure.

OPHELIA Running away is not the answer.

CHONG Till it calm down. We go down south. Rent a place. Sort out a plan.

OPHELIA Rent a place? Who's gonna rent to us.

CHONG Listen up. I got some savings in a vase in the back of the store. And the vase is also worth a lot I know it. Come all the way from China, we can sell it.

OPHELIA It's a family heirloom.

CHONG You're my family now. I'm getting it.

OPHELIA Let me just try talk to Clinton.

CHONG No. Go pack Ophelia. Wait for me at the bus station.

He runs off. Ophelia shouts after him.

OPHELIA Chong wait!

Ophelia runs off.

SCENE NINETEEN

Misheck is snooping about Ophelia's yard. He looks like he's casing the joint. Checking the windows. He considers the shed but it's locked. Ophelia comes out of the back door and catches him.

OPHELIA He's not here.

MISHECK Oh hey.

OPHELIA *(wry)* Oh hey.

MISHECK When is he back?

OPHELIA You know he's not allowed people come and visit him. You trying it again. I don't know when he's back.

MISHECK He needs friends innit. Hanging around you ain't good for him. Inter-generational. Unhealthy.

OPHELIA You expect me to believe you got his best interests at heart? Good for nothing.

MISHECK …

OPHELIA What did you do today that was constructive? Productive? Inspiring? Something to work towards in terms of your future?

MISHECK I see how you work. Getting in people's mental. Fucking with their heads. Fucking people psychological style.

OPHELIA You're a lost cause.

Beat.

MISHECK That hurt … Bitch.

Misheck goes to leave.

OPHELIA Why can't you be more like that other one?

MISHECK …

OPHELIA Skinny, spectacles, awful posture. Pirate I think Chris was calling him.

MISHECK Pyro?

OPHELIA They seem a good match. A bit of a fiery duo but he made a good impression on me.

MISHECK Pyro came here?

OPHELIA He didn't stay long. Rules is rules. *(Chris arrives)* Chris, he can stay for five minutes. Then he has to go.

Ophelia goes inside.

CHRIS *(about Ophelia)* Must be in good mood.

MISHECK *(nesting)* Yea. We was talking. She ain't that bad.

CHRIS She didn't tump you upside your head then?

MISHECK No, we was talking.

CHRIS Okay.

Chris goes to move some stuff.

MISHECK We was talking about stuff.

CHRIS *(trying to be funny)* Socio-economic classifications? Sounds exciting. Can you pass me that black bag.

MISHECK Gay stuff. *(Beat)* You chilling with that dutty chi chi man innit?

CHRIS No.

MISHECK You think I'm dumb?

CHRIS Why would I chill with some batty man? You know I don't deal with that narstyness. I'm here cos I don't deal with that.

MISHECK Not some batty man! That battyman.

CHRIS What the fuck she been telling you?

MISHECK That you and that nature offender kotching like.

CHRIS You think of all people I'd speak to him again?

MISHECK Cockcroach.

CHRIS Faggot.

MISHECK Should get burnt like wood.

CHRIS Ain't it obvious she's trying to mess with your cranial.

MISHECK How she know about Pyro then? Said he was here.

CHRIS She got my history written down. On file.

Misheck is not sold.

MISHECK I know you met him. I can smell it when you lie blud. Something ain't right, your facial muscles. You met up with him didn't? Didn't you?!

CHRIS He came looking for me. I told him to dust. I don't want no narsty batty man hanging around me? I said I'd comatose him again.

MISHECK He still has the gall to come say hello after–

CHRIS Listen–

MISHECK It's dodge bruv. It's proper dodge. I know something ain't right. I can smell it. I can smell it. Same smell. It's the same smell from before and it's the same smell I get now with you! With you and her!

CHRIS Misheck! What the fuck–

Ophelia has come out.

MISHECK With her!

OPHELIA   Chris.

MISHECK   Her! And him and I know you're gay! Say it! Say what I know blud. I can smell it in the air. The lube the narstyness. The offence. Say it blud!

CHRIS   Okay I'm gay!

MISHECK   What?

CHRIS   Yea.

MISHECK   I don't believe it.

OPHELIA   Oh lordy, make up your mind bwoy.

Ophelia chuckles. Starts laughing hard. Chris and Misheck baffled.

CHRIS   It ain't funny.

OPHELIA *(to Misheck)* You looking lost bwoy. So what? He's hummersexual, so what? 2020! And you young tings all agog about it.

MISHECK *(befuddled)* You think it's alright?

OPHELIA   All I'm thinking is now I know a little bit more about Christian. I just know a little bit more.

Misheck fumbles for his phone and starts looking through it.

CHRIS   Mish. For real yea.

OPHELIA   You young people. Really just need to–

MISHECK   Wanna know a bit more? *(Misheck places the phone in front of Ophelia. We can hear the sound of a homophobic attack. "Fuck him up Chris", "Stamp on his head", "Fucking battyman", "Fuck him up"! "Aww shit", "World star". Beat)*

(Exiting) There. Now you know him better, innit.

Misheck leaves.

CHRIS   Ophelia.

Ophelia is horrified. Stunned, she goes inside her house and locks the door. The sound of the beating gets louder and louder.

SCENE TWENTY

1960's JAMAICA. The curtain is down and it's a wall. Clinton is walking down the street with his flyers and sign looking silly. Snitch runs into him totally out of breath.

SNITCH	Look where you're going idiot.
CLINTON	No matter boss. My bad.
SNITCH	Clinton? What the hell? *(Snitch picks up the flyer and studies Clinton's sign)* This here be a new low. What him got you doing right here?
CLINTON	Just a little trial period. Before we become partners.
SNITCH	It's 3am and you're dressed up with a sign giving out flyers to no one?
CLINTON	It's how we begin a business relationship.
SNITCH	Look at you. Lim Dry Goods. You are his dry goods. He got you all got up like him own you na man! *(Snitch starts to laugh)* Oh my lord. This a picture alright. Backbone brok. Dignity gone!
CLINTON	Snitch.
SNITCH	No man. You haffi listen to me now. This is an intervention of the biggest kind. Cos if I'm not mistaken you appear to have been bought and sold my friend. Bought and sold. Chiney man mugging you off. What a sight.

Clinton throws the flyers on the floor.

CLINTON	Them all down at the shebeen laughing at me. Calling me idiot pickney for looking so.
SNITCH	Yellow man done sucked the dignity from the black man with him serpent tongue. And now you're a laughing stock. Clinton. You really so weak? Chiney man done fucked you over. Taken your business.
CLINTON	Hold on.
SNITCH	Taken your pride.
CLINTON	No–
SNITCH	Taken your dignity.
CLINTON	No!
SNITCH	They even fucking your sister.
CLINTON	What you talk 'bout?
SNITCH	Me just caught Chong.
CLINTON	Chong? What?
SNITCH	Me caught him–
CLINTON	Do what!?
SNITCH	Do your sister.

CLINTON ...

SNITCH And it seem like she liking it.

Beat.

Clinton rips off the shawl and smashes the sign to pieces.

CLINTON No! No! No!

SCENE TWENTY-ONE

Ophelia's yard. The middle of the night. We hear a crash and bang from within the house. Misheck runs out with the vase. Chris is somehow there. Chris crashes into Misheck, they fight. Misheck screams. Chris has a knife pointed at him.

MISHECK For what? For what? For what? *(Realising it's Chris)* Chris?

CHRIS What the fuck?

MISHECK What the fuck are you doing here?

CHRIS Give me the vase now! Give me the fucking vase.

MISHECK I'm wetted up blud. You wet me up.

CHRIS Fuck. Give me the vase. Or I'll cut you. I don't give a fuck.

We see the lights go on upstairs. We hear Ophelia's voice on the phone. Misheck bolts. Chris remains. Blood stained. He wipes his hands on himself. Ophelia comes out just as we hear the faint sound of the police sirens.

OPHELIA Jesus Christ Christian. What the hell?

CHRIS Are you okay?

OPHELIA If I knew it was you I wouldn't have called the police. Oh lord you done for now.

CHRIS It weren't me.

OPHELIA Why you here? Oh! – My lungs.

CHRIS You okay? Ophelia?

OPHELIA If you needed something I would've just given it you.

CHRIS Ophelia. I'll get it back.

OPHELIA What?

CHRIS The vase. *(The sound of the police siren gets louder and we can see the police lights)* You okay?

OPHELIA I'll be fine. Just go. Go!

Chris bolts.

Curtain down representing a London alley way. Misheck is running clutching the vase and is chased. We think it's Chris naturally but discover it's actually Pyro. Misheck runs out of energy. Stand off.

PYRO Resistance is futile!

MISHECK You!

PYRO Resistance is futile.

MISHECK I'm gonna fuck you up faggot! *(Misheck, still holding the vase, searches his pockets for a pen knife. He's in pain because he's been cut. Pyro gets his weapon out. It's a dagger but very odd looking and bigger than Misheck's)* What the fuck is that?

PYRO A highly desirable and hard to find special edition *Star Trek* Klingon Dagger. A must have for any collection. A bit like that vase I presume.

MISHECK That's so gay.

PYRO It's an inanimate object fool. Just like you're gonna be.

Chris catches up with them. Baffled by why Pyro is there.

CHRIS What's that?

PYRO Klingon Dagger.

CHRIS What?

PYRO *Next Generation*. Series 6 Episode 4? Worf's.

CHRIS Oh.

PYRO In *Star Trek: First Contact* Captain Picard gets revenge on The Borg who had previously taken his life away and abused him and took everything he had.

MISHECK ...

PYRO Just like me. And The Borg. A Homogeneous collective, No independent thinking, a bunch of brain dead cyborgs being told what to think ... like you and your road men folk, like society.

MISHECK ...

PYRO I had everything going for me. Good grades. Good marks. Good reports. I worked hard. I got scholarship to China.

CHRIS   Pyro.

PYRO   And you fucked it up! You stamped on my fucking head over and over and over again! Fulfilling your black, hood, thug aspirations. Reaching self actualisation. *(Pyro moves closer with the dagger and begins counting in Chinese)* Yi, Er, San, Si, Wu, Liu, Chi, Ba!

CHRIS   It wasn't just him was it!?

PYRO   But he deserves it.

CHRIS   Why?

Beat.

PYRO   Cos... I understand you Chris. I know why you joined in ... and ... I don't love him.

SCENE TWENTY-TWO

1960's JAMAICA – Chong runs along the wall (the fire curtain) It rises to reveal the Store and Chong runs into to it. Clinton arrives livid with Snitch and throws a wooden crate at the store.

CLINTON   Me look him dead in him slanty eye! As soon I as look me know him lie.

SNITCH   Dis ting we cyan sense ya know.

CLINTON   Di corruption stink up di place like somebody die. Me haffi tump him upside his face cos him too sly!

SNITCH   Call a coffin maker ya know. *(They look for more things to throw at the store)* Again! Again! You know they trash up a chiney shop across the town? We rising up against these people.

CLINTON   I hereby declare the black man's fight!

SNITCH   Tell him good ya know.

CLINTON   The Chiney Shop and this economic might!

SNITCH   Di unfairness reach you know.

CLINTON   Me walk thru the Chiney Shop me wonder what right?

SNITCH   These people have you know.

CLINTON   Domineering over us just like dem white.

SNITCH   Di social fairness broke up you know! This here be a patriotic act Clinton. Political.

CLINTON   Chiney man steal my pride and me him try mock.

SNITCH	Yes!
CLINTON	Chiney man take me business and teef all my stock.
SNITCH	Yes!
CLINTON	Chiney man dun me over so me holding this rock.
SNITCH	Yes!
CLINTON	To dash pon him face cos him my sister fock!

Clinton throws the rocks which smashes the window.

SNITCH   YES! YES! YES! YES! YES!

Clinton in a rage starts pouring oil about the store.

CLINTON   Lets see how big and proper you are when you have no business!

SNITCH   Yes! Clinton! Pour oil on di slippery devils dem. Pour de oil and show dem to be as greasy as you know they are.

Beat.

He sets it alight. He's overwhelmed by the brightness of the fire.

CLINTON   Let all the people know how we fight back!

SNITCH   Yes!

Ophelia comes running in.

OPHELIA   NO!!! Stop it, stop it!

CLINTON   You lying to me all this time. Sleeping with the enemy.

Ophelia desperately tries to get into the store but Clinton stops her.

OPHELIA   Chong is in there! Chong's in there! *(Snitch slyly disappears. Ophelia rushes into the store. Clinton follows. The fire crackles. After a short while they drag Chong out. He's dead. He's wearing a net carry sack which holds the vase. Money is spilling out of it)* Chong! Chong! Chong!!

SCENE TWENTY-THREE

Ophelia's garden. The vase is there pulling focus. Ophelia hovers over it for a good while pondering.

OPHELIA   I know you're in there. *(We think she's talking to the vase and has gone mad. Suddenly Chris comes out of the shed)* Made a nice little home I see?

CHRIS   I like it here. It's secure. I feel safe.

Ophelia notices his blood stained top.

OPHELIA *(making a fuss)* You hurt yourself. Come here.

CHRIS   Get off man. It ain't my blood.

Beat.

OPHELIA   You're late for your community service.

CHRIS   I had a reason innit.

OPHELIA *(regarding the vase)* You got it back.

CHRIS   I didn't.

Pyro comes out of the shed.

OPHELIA   Err!

CHRIS   No visitors allowed I know.

OPHELIA   No rumpy pumpy allowed!

CHRIS   Ophelia!

OPHELIA   No canoodling inna my yard!

PYRO   Morning Miss Randles.

OPHELIA   I hope you didn't hurt anyone Chris. You really could get into trouble. I could get into trouble.

PYRO   *He* didn't hurt anyone. *(Beat)* I didn't hurt him too bad like. Just. Well, I kinda speak Chinese, Miss Randles. I discovered … I kinda fight Chinese too.

SCENE TWENTY-FOUR

This scene alternates locations and times.

1960's Jamaica – The curtain is down. Sounds representing an airport. Ophelia is facing the audience.

TANNOY *(Jamaican accent)* This is your final call for British Airways flight 138 to London via Paris. This is your final call for flight 138 to London via Paris. Please make your way to boarding gate number 2. Thank you.

Present day. LONDON – Chris is at the wall. With his phone. He passes it to Pyro.

PYRO Wei? Ni Hao, wo zai xhun zhao yi ge ren. Ta Xing Wong. [Hello, I'm trying to find someone. His surname is Wong.] *(To Chris)* Weng? Or Wong?

CHRIS Wang? I dunno man.

PYRO Wang. *(To Chris)* So confusing you having the same name as your dad.

CHRIS You got the same name as your dad. Marlon. Marlon Junior.

PYRO Why do you think I'm called Pyro, dick head? *(To the phone)* Oh sorry! Not you, dui bu qu, dui bu qi. [Sorry, sorry.]

1960's JAMAICA – Lim and Ophelia at airport. Lim gives her the vase.

LIM Take it.

OPHELIA I can't.

LIM Take it please. I should have listened to my son more. And to you. I'm sorry.

Lim leaves. She walks off crying trying to take all her stuff with her.

Present day. LONDON–

CHRIS Hi, Yea is that Guangzhou Wang Association? Can I speak to Mr Chiang Wong please? ... Hello? ... English? Oh okay. Can you tell him I called please? Thanks.

1960's JAMAICA- Airport. Clinton is there.

CLINTON Ophelia.

OPHELIA Go!!!

CLINTON Please.

OPHELIA Get away!

1960's JAMAICA – The Airport. Ophelia is distraught. Cries into her tissue. Clutching vase.

OPHELIA Chong.

EPILOGUE

Present day. London – The curtain rises. Chris is in the garden with Ophelia and Pyro. They are helping Ophelia work a mobile phone.

CHRIS This way you can walk about when you talk innit. Cordless. You're mobile. Not trapped in the front room. No cords anymore.

OPHELIA Walk and talk.

CHRIS Or run and talk when some one try break in.

OPHELIA I'm not doing no running. I just smack 'em pon the head with it!

Hits the phone on Chris's head.

OPHELIA AND CHRIS Tonk! / Ow!

Pyro continues gardening.

PYRO That smart phone you're holding was inspired by Star Trek.

CHRIS You could communicate from the ship to the planet and back again.

OPHELIA But I can't beam you up from inna my yard when you vex me so can I?

CHRIS *(smug)* Nope.

OPHELIA I just smack you pon the head when you vex me so alright?

Ophelia smacks the smart phone on Chris's head again.

CHRIS Oi! Leave it man! *(Ophelia smacks him a third time)* For fuck's–

OPHELIA I am not a man ... man!

CHRIS It's an expression!

OPHELIA An expression of discombobulation of the gender binary constructs! Your words not mine! Char!

PYRO It's exactly how a smart phone works today. Signal communicates with a satellite up there and bounces back. Things have moved along since you were our age innit Ophelia. *(Chris and Pyro chuckle at their own joke)* Communication, it's the future ... innit.

Beat.

OPHELIA Chris did you Google how to bleed the radiators?
PYRO I did.
OPHELIA Would you two go and start on that now?
CHRIS You proper rule breaker innit these days. Weed plant, visitors, allowed inside the house.

Beat.

OPHELIA *(short)* Just go inside and make a start. There's something I need to do.

CHRIS *(defensive)* Alright! Chill girl, chill. *(Ophelia lifts the phone to strike Chris again. He flinches)* Come Pyro.

They both go inside. Ophelia types a number into the phone carefully. Waits.

OPHELIA Clinton? Is that you?

The end.

SPECIAL OCCASIONS

I wrote *Special Occasions* as a response piece to *The Pianist of Willesden Lane*, which played at St. James Theatre, London, in January 2016. My short play was subsequently performed again at the Arcola Theatre in March 2016.

In *The Pianist of Willesden Lane*, Mona Golabek dramatises her mother's story of being taken to London on the Kindertransport. Her mother Lisa Jura was the only one who survived the Holocaust, because her parents picked her to go to London in the hope that she could pursue her musical studies further. Lisa survives physically and emotionally through her piano playing.

I have long been fascinated by mother-daughter relationships, and was struck by the eerie spectacle of a daughter taking on the persona of her dead mother, impersonating her to tell her story. I also felt strongly that the relationship between art and trauma is not as linear as this redemptive story arc might suggest. I wondered at the depths of survivor guilt that must have driven Lisa Jura not only to achieve her own concert pianist dream, but to pass that dream on to her concert pianist daughter. I wondered about the inheritance of trauma by the second generation, as I marvelled that Mona Golabek would give up a successful concert career to tell the story of her mother, night after night, on different stages throughout the world. *Special Occasions* arose out of all this pondering and wondering – a stand-alone piece, about a fictitious mother and daughter, set against the background of the international settlement of Shanghai – one of the few places in the world that did not require visas, and to which European Jews fled the Holocaust.

Amy Ng is an Australia-born British-Hong Kong playwright. Her play *Acceptance* ran at Hampstead Theatre in March 2018. Her debut play *Shangri-La* premiered at the Finborough Theatre in July 2016. She is under commission to the Royal Shakespeare Company, Belgrade Theatre Coventry, iceandfire theatre company, Yellow Earth Theatre, and feminist theatre company Dangerous Space. *Tiger Girls*, a 45 minute radio play, will be broadcast 17 July 2018 on Radio 4. *Kilburn Passion*, a monologue performed by Daniel Mays, was first broadcast on 15 June 2017 on Radio 3. She was recently named to the BBC New Talent Hotlist 2017.

Amy is also a historian with a research interest in multinational empires, imperial decline, and nationality conflict, and is the author of *Nationalism and Political Liberty* (Oxford University Press).

Amy was educated at Yale University and at Balliol College, Oxford University, where she was a Rhodes Scholar. She graduated with a D. Phil in Modern History.

SPECIAL OCCASIONS

AMY NG

Characters
MOTHER   Viennese, Jewish. Age 41–66.
NINA   Her daughter. Age 16–41.

Time and Setting
The action of the play spans 1956–1981, and takes place in the Mother's living room in New York City.

SCENE ONE

1956. A living room in a New York apartment.

A table with a covered plate in the middle. Chinese teapot and two tea cups.

The Mother (41), glamorous with an elaborate hat, heels and dress, sits opposite Nina (16), sporting large schoolgirl glasses.

MOTHER   Sacher Torte was for special occasions of course. I'm talking about the original Sacher Torte in its wood box from the Hotel Sacher, of course. I'm talking about the original Sacher Torte from the Hotel Sacher next to the Musikverein, of course. I'm talking about the original Sacher Torte, the *musician's* Torte, because, for us, the Musikverein is Mecca of course.
(The Mother uncovers the plate, to reveal a Sacher Torte. She shows Nina the wood box) Don't ever get fobbed off by imitation sachertortes. You're looking for *this* seal, *this* box–

NINA   This came... from Vienna?

MOTHER   This very morning.

NINA   This... this must have cost a fortune!

MOTHER *(sings)* 'Im wunderschönen Monat Mai...' Happy birthday my darling May baby.

NINA   Mother you shouldn't have...

MOTHER   But your sixteenth birthday, darling! In Vienna you would have been a debutante this year – maybe even at the Opernball... *(sings a line from Strauss as she cuts the cake and serves it)*
I only ever had Sacher Torte that once in Vienna. My mother was determined my Bat Mitzvah should be every bit as elaborate as my brother's– which was radical, you've got to understand, for a girl! How she pinched the groschens, how we cried, nothing but bread and soup for months, but somehow she managed to get me a Sacher Torte! From the Hotel Sacher! I so wanted to get a Sacher Torte for your Bat Mitzvah but they raised the rent...

NINA   Don't worry, Mother. It's all rent controlled now.

MOTHER   To Rabbi Hirsch and his connections at City Hall! *(She lifts a tea cup)*

Nina drinks the tea.

NINA   It's different–

MOTHER   It is different. It's from Anhui province – the best kind– I was so excited to see it this morning in Chinatown. Old Mr Fu would always serve Anhui chrysanthemum tea when I taught his sons... sipping tea to the staccato of Japanese bombs, civilisation amongst the rubble. You should drink three cups of chrysanthemum tea daily until your audition – nourishes the throat – I've spoken to your head teacher. He says as long as you keep up with the work, you have permission to leave school by noon to practice /

NINA   / I got into the cheerleading team.

MOTHER   The what?

NINA   Cheerleaders are girls who – cheer – the football team. They also dance...

MOTHER   Why on earth would you want to do that?

NINA   It's a really big deal...

MOTHER   American football is so – vulgar.

NINA   It's just two afternoons a week.

MOTHER   We're talking about the Julliard auditions. We're talking about your future.

NINA   I'll make up the hours – I promise – I'll get up early–

MOTHER   I just don't understand you, Nina. At your age, I was wild with ambition. I worked ten, twelve hours a day – singing jazz in those smoky nightclubs in the international settlement – then I'll come home to that wretched hostel room and pore over the scores of great operas till dawn – such fire in my belly – I'd promised my mother I'll make something of my life. *(Jumps up)* Does this sudden desire for cheer-leading have anything to do with this? *(The Mother pulls out a yearbook and turns it to a page where Nina has drawn a heart around one of the photos.)* Who's this?

NINA Who?

MOTHER This no-neck muscle man–

NINA That's Jake. The football captain.

MOTHER Nina, you're much too young–

NINA Don't worry, Mother. He hasn't noticed I exist. *(Touches her glasses)* If I wake up at 5am every day could I–

MOTHER I'm sorry, Nina-leh – maybe after the auditions.

SCENE TWO

1962.

Same room. Sacher Torte and Chinese tea on the table, alongside a letter.

The Mother (47) straightens out cushions, singing the Erlkönig. Nina (22) bursts into the room with a stack of papers.

NINA Sorry Mother, the trains weren't running from the Bronx so I had to take a bus and–

MOTHER I don't know why you're bothering with these Yiddish fiddlers.

NINA My professor says the line between high culture and popular culture is arbitrary–

MOTHER That's ridiculous.

NINA But Mother, even Mahler used Yiddish folk tunes–

MOTHER But he elevated it to Great Art.

Nina notices the Sacher Torte.

NINA Oh wow. *(Beat)* What's the occasion?

The Mother hands her the letter, beaming.

Nina opens it and reads, while the Mother cuts the cake and serves.

NINA	Oh.
MOTHER	Isn't that wonderful! A full scholarship, to Columbia!
NINA	Mother, I'm not sure I'm smart enough to–
MOTHER	Nina-leh, of course you are. You can do anything if you put your mind to–
NINA	No I can't.
MOTHER *(beat)* You didn't have enough fire in your belly. The Chinese would say you have too cool a nature. Maybe it was the chrysanthemum tea.
NINA	I'm not sure about history of music /
MOTHER	If you can't make it as a musician, at least be a professor – Professor Mannheimer – your grandmother would have liked that.
NINA	Mother, an opportunity has come up. I can apply for a Ford Foundation fellowship to go to Japan for a year. I could record the music there /
MOTHER	Japan?
NINA	You've talked so much about Shanghai – this is the closest I can get /
MOTHER	Japan was the enemy, girl! Nazi allies! Do you know what they did to China–
NINA	Hitler was Austrian. And you import Sacher Torte from Vienna.
MOTHER	That's different. This is about culture, tradition – not letting them rob me of my own tradition–
NINA	I just want to study Japanese music–
MOTHER	This is about that soldier, right?
NINA	Who?
MOTHER	Mrs Cohen saw you with a soldier–
NINA *(beat)* He's just a friend.
MOTHER	And is he going to Vietnam? Is that why this sudden interest in Asia–
NINA	No. He's not frontline, he's military intelligence.
MOTHER	Where is he going?
NINA *(beat)* Okinawa.
MOTHER	I'm not having you turn up here with a big belly – do you know what children do to your dreams /

NINA	/ Not all soldiers are like Father. *(Pause)* *(Whispers)* Sorry.

MOTHER	You'd better write a thank you card to Rabbi Hirsch. His cousin got you into Columbia.

NINA	Mother, the Ford Foundation /

MOTHER	I just don't understand you, Nina. I've handed you a second chance to make something of your life – an Ivy League scholarship – if I had the opportunities you had – what's wrong with you?

Nina eats her Sacher Torte.

SCENE THREE

1980.

Same room. Sacher Torte and Chinese tea on the table.

The Mother (65) looks on while Nina (40) cuts the torte. The Mother hums Mahler's Kindertotenlied.

MOTHER	What's the occasion?

NINA	Mother, I've got a project – with Jakob Zweig! I'll be filming him rehearsing the world premiere of his new piece at the Met!

MOTHER	Oh.

NINA	Mother! Jakob Zweig!

MOTHER	And so?

NINA *(quietly)* This is a really big deal for me, Mother. A potential game-changer.

MOTHER	I suppose for someone who's failed her auditions, dropped out of Columbia, flitting from project to project /

NINA	/ If it weren't for people like me, documenting, explaining the music to young people – I mean, what's the average age of classical music audiences – because people don't want to just hear museum pieces. Jakob Zweig is revitalising /

MOTHER	He's killing classical music.

NINA	Jakob Zweig studied with Weber who studied with Mahler – you can't get more /

MOTHER	This atonal, twelve tone, randomised, this sprechstimme screeching– it's not music /

NINA / It's squarely descended from the Second Viennese music school–

MOTHER It's a betrayal of Vienna! Of my Vienna, the Musikverein, the Opernhaus, the Hotel Sacher–

NINA Jakob told me what your Vienna was like. The refugees. The impoverishment. The inflation. The anti-Semitism. The Hotel Sacher – bankrupt. You wouldn't think he grew up in the same city.

MOTHER I was a child.

NINA Jakob's the same age as you.

MOTHER I had a good mother! She created an intact world, a beautiful world, at home.

NINA She lied.

MOTHER No! It's called civilization. My father, unemployed, but dressed impeccably every day; my mother in her hat and her heels and an empty belly; the lighting of shabbas candles. And the singing. Always. Schubert lieder, Schumann lieder, the great arias, holding on to beauty, no matter what. And your Jakob dares trample all that with his /

NINA / And your parents sang Schubert lieder all the way to the gas chambers, did they?

The Mother slaps Nina.

MOTHER They picked me. They should have picked Isaac but they picked me – maybe Isaac's children would have made something of themselves... look at you! Look at me! And Mother thought I would make something of my life, because I was talented, had drive–

NINA What are you talking about?

MOTHER Even Jews didn't need visas for Shanghai in 1938. But ocean liner tickets were so expensive – my family could only afford one. And they picked me. Not Isaac.

NINA You never told me that bit.

MOTHER I can't leave you, Mama, I said, I won't leave you, but she said "To save you, I have to say goodbye." She loved me – that much.

Pause.

NINA Then say goodbye to me, Mother. To save me. Say goodbye.

Nina exits.

SCENE FOUR

1981.

Nina (41) and the Mother (66) sit next to each other on the sofa.

Nina stares into space. The Mother cuts some Sacher Torte.

MOTHER I had such a craving for Sacher Torte when I was pregnant. Of course I couldn't afford it then...
(The Mother serves the torte to Nina, who refuses) Poor pet! Morning sickness is horrible.
(The Mother pours some tea and serves it to Nina. Nina turns away) Did you really expect him to leave his wife for you? *(Pause)* He's old enough to be your father!
(Pause) It's better this way, Nina-leh. Just listen to his 'music'– suicidal. Nihilistic. We can't afford nihilism. It was us, us in the ghetto, who clung on to hope and beauty, who needed to dream–
(The Mother spoons more cream onto the rejected slice of torte and tries serving it to Nina again) It'll go down easier with cream.
(Nina refuses the torte) You've got to eat. I couldn't afford to buy good things, nourishing things when I was pregnant – no vitamins, no minerals, nutrients, protein – maybe that's why you turned out so–
(Nina dashes the torte onto the floor. The Mother gets down on her knees and cleans up. Nina gets down on her knees to help. The Mother helps Nina up gently) Hey. Take it easy.
(The Mother pushes the tea towards Nina, who turns away) Ever since I heard I would have another sweet little girl to cherish and to guide, to nurture, to instruct – another May baby!
(The Mother sings 'Im wunderschönen Monat Mai') It's much much better this way. Growing up, just you and me, what times we had, didn't we, Nina-leh? I gave up hope when you turned 40, I was so sad thinking my mother would never have a great-grandchild, that her line would die, that it would all have been in vain, and then suddenly, like Sarah–

The Mother sings 'Wenn ich in deine Augen seh'.

Nina presses both hands forcefully on her belly. From her expression, it is impossible to tell if this is a protective or threatening gesture.

The end.

CONVERSATIONS WITH MY UNKNOWN MOTHER

This dramatic conversation between the adoption triad (birth mother, adoptive mother, adoptee) takes place in between the reflections of reality and veiled memory. Is blood thicker than water? This work has been under development since 2014 with the assistance of Theatre Exchange (Birmingham), The British East Asian Artist Development Writer's Lab and SEA Arts Fest 2014. In March 2017 the RSC funded and facilitated a days' paid R&D on this play.

Lucy Chau Lai-Tuen wrote and performed *There are Two Perfectly Good Me's: One dead, the other unborn*, in 2011. Since then writing commissions include: *Ungrateful: A Paper-Daughter, Restrain Your Grief and Adapt to the Mishap* and *Come To Where I'm From: London*.

Lucy's short play *Waiting* was selected for the REDfest 2012 new writers competition at The Old Red Lion Pub Theatre. It was staged again at the UntoldArts 2 event in December 2017.

Re:Play a writing bursary from Nimble Fish and mentorship from Inua Ellams – *Ungrateful: A Paper-Daughter* which she performed to a sold out performance at the Southbank as part of Poetry International 2015 and *Restrain Your Grief and Adapt to the Mishap*, a short play for The Royal Court Theatre and the return of Live Lunch – Hidden a series of six short plays challenging the established view of what it means to be a British East Asian, produced and directed by Lucy Morrison. Longlisted for the OldVic12 2015. Published in *Foreign Goods* (Oberon, 2018).

In 2016 she was commissioned by Paines Plough/Tamasha for *Come To Where I'm From: London*. Her play *Comfort Women* about what happens to the survivors of war was developed by Papergang Theatre Company and given a rehearsed reading at The Tristan Bates Theatre 2015. It was then invited to show at the Women and War Festival in June of 2017.

My England (2018) is a Young Vic short monologue commission not yet performed.

Lucy's debut documentary, *Abandoned, Adopted, Here* which she wrote, produced and directed has won global acclaim and won a Golden Oniros for best screenwriting 2017.

CONVERSATIONS WITH MY UNKNOWN MOTHER

LUCY CHAU LAI-TUEN

"Dedicated to all transracial adoptees – hoping that you have found your own identity, your own family, are happy and at peace."

Characters
MICHELLE CARTER-CHUNG
FEI YEN   Michelle's birth mother.
MARY   Michelle's adoptive mother.
BETTY   Mary's mother; Michelle's adoptive grandmother.

PROLOGUE

Fei Yen, an old East Asian enters the auditorium – she could already be sitting / pre-set in the auditorium or she could walk into the space greeting people, chit-chatting. She makes her way to the stage and squats / sits down and takes out a small camping stove. Then she begins to make dumplings.

FEI YEN   There is a Chinese proverb–
Eat first, talk later.
(Fei Yen gathers what she has been cooking into a large dish and offers the dumplings to members of the audience)
Good, hah?
There is also another proverb–
Talk doesn't cook rice.
But it makes a good companion for any story.
And you are here for a story, aren't you?
Enjoy the appetiser, it's on the house...

Fei Yen packs up her things and disappears.

ACT ONE
SCENE ONE

Each act is set in both a simplified reality and a modernised version of one of ten Chinese courts of Hell. Hell is a white space, internal or external. Domestic or corporate, public or private depending on the Hell that you find yourself in. Hell therefore is a state of suffering. Inhabited by the dead who are 'expiating their sins' before, hopefully, going to heaven. They suffer mental anguish. Torment, torture, misery, affliction, agony, woe. It is an ordeal. A waking nightmare between realms, between death and life.

Projected title appears:

MAGIC MIRROR OF RETRIBUTION OR HELL IS WHERE THE HEART IS

Early morning, urban flat. Michelle Carter-Chung is getting ready.

Michelle sits, sideways on looking at herself in a dressing table mirror.

Michelle talks to herself, to her reflection. The reflection answers, but the voice we hear is not Michelle's. It is the voice of Fei Yen.

Michelle is dressed in black, the Western colour of mourning.

MICHELLE   I hate funerals.

FEI YEN   I should have buried you, mourned for you.

Michelle pauses and inspects her own reflection watching herself in the mirror performing simple actions. Raising an eyebrow, frowning, smiling. On the other side of the mirror a back light slowly reveals Michelle's reflection, it is the face of Fei Yen looking intently at Michelle. Initially Fei Yen is Michelle's reflection but as the conversation progresses Fei Yen becomes an entity in her own right.

MICHELLE   Funerals. The only time I ever think about family.

FEI YEN   How do you mourn for a child that's lost?
  I couldn't grieve for my daughter. She had no grave.

MICHELLE   Why is it that death always gets me thinking about a past that I never had?

FEI YEN   Were you a happy child?

MICHELLE   I haven't thought about my childhood in ages.

I guess – one someone dies – you do.

I was neither a happy or sad child.

FEI YEN Sounds more sad than happy.

MICHELLE *(pause – looks at her reflection which is still following her movements. Laughs)* Cardboard sliding, tree climbing, fishing for minnows.

Fei Yen separates from Michelle.

FEI YEN To eat...
MICHELLE No! *(Is taken aback by her 'reflection')*
FEI YEN What's the point in that?
MICHELLE *(with caution – while Michelle moves, Fei Yen indulges her and plays along, mirroring her movements)* It's what children did then for fun.

Building dams, riding back and forth on a tyre swing.

Blackberry picking...

Fei Yen stops mirroring Michelle and turns to face her head on.

FEI YEN Picking berries, for fun?
MICHELLE *(turns to check that there is no one behind her or–)*
We picked the blackberries to eat.

Fei Yen is now her own woman – no longer Michelle's reflection.

FEI YEN Yet you caught minnows for fun?
MICHELLE Who – what – where did you /
FEI YEN The people who...
MICHELLE Wait a minute – who /
FEI YEN I have no right...
MICHELLE Right to what–
Who the hell?
FEI YEN I have no right...
MICHELLE No you don't!

Pause.

FEI YEN Your parents /
MICHELLE Adoptive /
FEI YEN Your adoptive parents.

They treated you well?

MICHELLE *(beginning to take the situation in – though still incredulous about what she is seeing)* I had a roof over my head. Food in my belly, clothes on my back /

FEI YEN That's not what I meant...

Did they love you?

Laughs gently at Michelle completing the separation and the pretence she, Fei Yen is Michelle's reflection. Fei Yen emerges dressed all in white (the Chinese colour for mourning.)

MICHELLE Who...?

You're talking to the wrong person.

FEI YEN I'm talking to the daughter I lost... *(Pause)*

(Michelle looks intently at Fei Yen, scrutinising her face) They raised you as one of their own?

MICHELLE I'm sure they thought they did.

It was all very 'English'.

Very undemonstrative /

FEI YEN My parents were the same.

I don't mean English.

They weren't ones to show affection.

MICHELLE A child needs to feel love as much as they need to know love.

FEI YEN What did they teach you about China?

MICHELLE *(snorts)* Nothing.

FEI YEN How can this be?

MICHELLE Easy – you grow up alone.

As one of a kind and not in a good way.

The 'kind' that no one really wants, at least not in their back yard.

I was four before I realised that I wasn't white.

Just me and the local Indian restaurant.

The only two non-white things in the entire town.

Being Chinese was not something my adoptive parents were prepared to talk about.

In those days, you obeyed your elders. If something was forbidden, that was that.

FEI YEN They say,
'When children travel far from home, mothers never stop worrying.'
MICHELLE Did you?
Never stop worrying?
FEI YEN Never.
MICHELLE Words! Easy to say.
FEI YEN You think it was easy leaving you?!
MICHELLE You didn't 'leave' me.
You abandoned me.
You set me adrift.
FEI YEN I walked away from you.
I turned my back and I left you!
My flesh, my blood.
I could have been selfish. I could have kept you.
I would have hugged you and never let go.
And within a day, a week, a month, you would have died.
(Beat) Gone to join all the other young souls–
I would have killed, murdered my own child!
(Beat) How could I, a Mother, chose between death and loss?
What choice is that but a death sentence,
A death sentence for two!
MICHELLE They flew me thousands of miles away into the arms of a stranger.
FEI YEN How could I have known that they would send you away? That they would give you to the gwai los?
MICHELLE Ironic.
Westerners are called foreign devils. But in the end it was me that was the foreigner.
FEI YEN I want you to know that abandoning you and learning that you had been adopted, altered my very being, forever.
I did not want to abandon you. I wanted only to protect you.
To love you and give you the beautiful life you deserved.
You should know how much I loved you.
How much I still love you.

(Beat) I was a frightened young mother with no money.
No home and no family for support.
No one offered me any hope that I might be able to raise you.
That you might not die as so many other babies had died on the streets of Hong Kong.
I want you to know that if I could change that day I would.
I lost a part of myself when I left you.
I can cope with that loss, just.
But I want you to know I am not a criminal...
(Pause) Through my blinding grief, I picked the stairwell with care.
One that was busy.
One where you would be found.
I didn't know the depth of love I would feel for you, my first child.
(Beat) The day you was born, I held you, talked to you, kissed you, hugged you and never wanted to let you go.
It was only later that I felt it... overwhelming unconditional love.
But you were gone and I couldn't get you back.
I love you deeply. It is the one absolute truth of my life.
Those feelings don't go away over time.
I have four surviving children, since you, my first daughter.
I want my children, my cousins, friends, aunts and uncles to know that I have another child; my first child.
My children deserve to know the truth, to know their older sister and to share in her friendship and love.
What kind of monster am I that I deprived them of my first beautiful child?
You deserve to know me and I deserve a chance to know you!
I know I don't have the right to call you my child.
My daughter, but what other word expresses the closeness, the importance and the bond that you are and always will be to me?
(Pause) You're angry with me.

MICHELLE Of course you told your other children about their older sister.

(Silence) I see.

Michelle scrutinises her reflection – Fei Yen.

FEI YEN I could never find the right words, the right time. Weeks fell into months, months tripped over into years.

MICHELLE Who promised me a tomorrow?

No one, so I make the most of today.

When we are born, we cry, and the world rejoices.

When we die, we rejoice, and the world cries – we hope.

Slowly Fei Yen's face disappears and Michelle sits staring at her own reflection.

Blackout.

SCENE TWO

Michelle is busy packing boxes in a an empty old house. Michelle walks in and out of the room carrying bits and pieces and places them next to a pile of boxes, screwed up newspaper and bubble wrap. Upstage left is an old fashioned full length dressing mirror. In the mirror an older English woman appears. This is Mary.

MARY What are you doing here?

What have you done with my things?

My beautiful expensive furniture?

MICHELLE Knick-knacks... *(Pause)* Why do we call them knick-knacks?

Michelle continues to walk in and out carrying ornaments, small boxes, bags.

MARY Who gave you permission to touch my private, personal things?!

Michelle starts to wrap and pack away the ornaments and objets d'art.

MARY You disappear without so much as a please and thank you!

Then you turn up like the proverbial bad penny.

Touching, snooping, going through my things, without even so much as a please or thank you!

Michelle drops an ornament and it shatters.

MICHELLE Don't you hate that when it happens! *(Looks at the mirror)* I could have sworn I covered that mirror.

Michelle walks towards the mirror and starts to inspect it. She turns away from her own reflection and when she turns back she is looking into the face of Mary.

MICHELLE Shit and derision! I buried you yesterday!
MARY You did no such thing!

Michelle stands there staring at herself-Mary. Michelle walks round the back of the mirror and then out to the front. Michelle stands in front of the mirror again. Looking at her own reflection-Mary.

MICHELLE First sign of madness talking to yourself.
  Second sign of madness...
  Is there a second sign to madness?
MARY It's talking to inanimate objects!

Michelle carries on with her tasks and walks away.

MARY Are you listening to me?
  I said it's talking to inanimate objects!

Michelle comes back into the room with a box full of stuff and sits on the boxes, using them as a make-shift sofa. She stares at the mirror. Looking at her own reflection-Mary.

MICHELLE I never thought I'd see the inside of this place again.
MARY No, neither did I!
MICHELLE I thought, if I clear out the house, open the cellar–
MARY Should have kept you down there longer!
  Spare the rod spoil the child.
MICHELLE Let some light in–
  I could finally draw a line.
  Place that full stop.
MARY You don't place a full stop.
  A grown woman!
  And still you have no grammatical sense!

Michelle gets up and continues to walk about picking up more knick-knacks and placing them into boxes. She walks back into the room carrying a copy of the complete works of Shakespeare.

MICHELLE *(looking at the book)* Shakespeare – the only thing we had in common.

MARY How sharper than a serpent's tooth it is
To have a thankless child!

MICHELLE Wonder what my therapist would have to say about me talking to myself.

Talking to people who aren't there.

Dead people.

MARY Our Nellie knew someone, who claimed they could talk to the dead. Stuff and godless nonsense, if you ask me. If your 'therapist' is any good he'll have you committed. *(Sniffs)*

If I'd have known at the time Chinese people are more prone to being mentally unstable I'd have never agreed to taking you on. All that touchy-feely nonsense. Just another excuse to wheedle money out of people who have no common sense!

MICHELLE The writing desk, it's the only thing I want. All those years, not all of them were sad. All I want is one old fashioned out of date, writing desk. How pathetic is that?

MARY What was that?!

MICHELLE Wonder why number one son Donald didn't show.

MARY What's that about my son? What did you say about Donald? Speak up!

MICHELLE I hope I get a better send off when I go. A few distant relatives, only there for the reading of the will. *(Beat)* Not even her own son – that's harsh.

MARY I see you still have the same bad habits! Slouching and mumbling. No one has time for a mumbler!

Michelle uncovers a few Kodak brownie pictures of her as a child. Michelle rolls her eyes.

MARY Don't you roll your eyes at me!

MICHELLE *(looking at a stiff lifeless photograph portrait of Mary)* I think you would have lived a better life if you'd been born in the Victorian or Edwardian era.

MARY Cheeky monkey! I saw what happened to the nice working class people. Trodden on. Ground underfoot.

Whilst the haves made merry on the broken backs of people like my mother. She worked hard all her life, not because she wanted to, but because she had to. *(Sniffs)*

I did love my mother in my own way. But I wasn't going to settle for just being her when I grew up. Dignity without brass?

Why shouldn't I have some of what the folks up the hill had? I toughened up, became more pragmatic, less woolly, no touchy-feely nonsense. If you want summit then you have to make sacrifices along the way. I got the home, the security, the family and status that I'd always yearned for. So I lost out on popularity and friends, both over-rated if you ask me.

People always want something from you. Life is not free. Life is grim if you don't have money and status. All I wanted was to be in a better position, to be one of those that had, not one of those that didn't.

(Pause) I gave you everything that you could want for, clothes, food, a home, I even gave you my name and what do you do as you grow up, you kick up a fuss and throw it all back in my face with nonsense about, 'wanting to find yourself' and feeling excluded. If you'd learnt to stop slouching and mumbling maybe you wouldn't have been ignored.

Try dressing properly and...

MICHELLE *(her mobile goes off)* Hello... speaking...

Hi yes that's right...

MARY 'Hi' what have things come to!

MICHELLE *(still talking on the mobile)* It's an old writing desk a bit bulky...

MARY You leave that desk be.

You have no right putting your smutty hands on my furniture!

MICHELLE No real value, it's the only piece I'm interested in.

MARY How dare you! Do you know nothing! That was a very expensive piece. Top of the range in its time...

MICHELLE Everything else is hideous...

MARY You never did have any taste!

MICHELLE Yes you could say that...

No that's fine well when you come to pick up the desk you can have a look at the other pieces...

Fine you get first dibs, you'll be doing me a favour taking stuff off my hands... It's all big bulky and hideous, I don't have the room even if I did want the rest of the stuff...

Okay someone will let you in tomorrow.

Thanks.

MARY Michelle Carter – I demand to know what you've done!

Michelle freezes, looks around at her reflection which is Mary and then continues going about her business.

MICHELLE *(laughs to herself)*
   Almost told the removal man he'd gotten the wrong number.

   Michelle Carter? You've got the wrong number mate!

   (Pause) Michelle Carter-Chung – well there is nothing to stop me now from changing my name is there?

MARY Don't you dare! We gave you a name – our name.

MICHELLE Michelle Chung – I could get used to that.

Michelle continues to pack away the remaining things. The last thing she picks up is an ugly vase. She pulls a face.

MARY Don't you turn your back on me!

MICHELLE *(Michelle has her back to the mirror. She deliberately drops the vase)* I never did like that thing – hideous, what a shame, oh well.

Mary fades away. Michelle stands up and faces her own reflection. She smiles. Throws a dust cover over the mirror and then goes back to closing the boxes. She picks up the broken pieces of the vase, the other broken ornament and walks out of the room switching the light off as she goes. The front door slams, the dust cover flutters to the floor and Mary appears in the mirror.

MARY I can't be dead! I refuse to be dead, I am a god-fearing woman! A good woman!

Blackout.

SCENE THREE

Michelle's flat. Evening. Michelle settles down for an evening at home. An empty plate and a half-empty bottle of beer sit on a low coffee table. Michelle slumps onto the old sofa. She stares at a modern flat screen TV which is off. Michelle searches for the remote. She gets up and walks to an open window and closes it – as soon as Michelle closes the window Fei Yen appears as Michelle's reflection. Michelle uses the closed window as a mirror to 'straighten' out her hair.

Michelle walks back to the sofa, Fei Yen turns and she fades away leaving just a closed window. Michelle continues to search for the remote. She finds it, switches the TV on and flicks through some of the channels. Finding nothing she switches onto a rolling news channel and turns the sound down. Flops back down on the sofa, picks up a tablet from the coffee table and starts reading but can't concentrate. Michelle stands the tablet up on the coffee table. The newscaster on TV slowly morphs into Mary.

MICHELLE *(looks at the TV screen)* Oh for the love of...

Will you leave me alone! You're not real, I buried you, you're dead!

MARY How sharp it is to have a thankless child!

MICHELLE Or in your case two?

MARY What did you just mumble? Out with it!

MICHELLE I'm ignoring the ghost in the room now...

Silence.

Michelle closes her eyes. In the window another face appears one that we have not seen before – an older Caucasian woman in her late 70s, possibly older.

BETTY Well this is a fine to-do isn't it?

MARY *(looking about from within the TV screen)* Who said that?

(She looks at Michelle – who is now asleep – and emerges from the television screen) Who's there?

BETTY Keep your knickers on and stop fussing. *(Betty emerges from the window. The two women stand and stare at each other)*

I've never been one for standing on ceremony, especially when there's a perfectly good seat to be had. *(She walks over and sits down next to the sleeping Michelle)*

Oh for heaven's sake stop standing there gawping like a flayed[1] fly catcher. Shut your mouth and take weight of your feet! *(Mary reluctantly does as she is told)*

What has thee gone and done now?

MARY Mother – it's really you?

BETTY What of it? You look like you've seen a ghost.

MARY You're dead.

BETTY Tell me summit I don't know.

MARY What are you doing here?!

BETTY I could ask thee the same.

---

1. Flayed – (Yorkshire) frightened

MARY — I asked first.

BETTY — What are we, six years auld? *(Pause)*

I was doing quite well, no thanks to thee. Suddenly without a by your leave I'm catapulted down here. They don't like trouble-makers upstairs. *He* doesn't take kindly to wayward spirits...

MARY — What on earth are you going on about?

You're still addled...

BETTY — Of course I'm addled. So would you be if you got dumped in an auld people's home.

(Beat) Do you know the only one out of family that came to visit me regular, wasn't even me ain flesh and blood?

MARY — I meant to visit. It was difficult to find the time and then life just got busier and busier.

(Beat) What do you mean the only one out of the family...

BETTY *(tapping Michelle gently on the leg)* This one here. The only one that came to see me.

She did all the things – Alive or dead you'll always be my daughter. We forget what people did, what they said, but we never forget how a person made us feel, do we?

You came out all higgledy-piggledy. There was a felted[2] dark restlessness in thee. Never satisfied, always chasing after more. Maybe that's what happens when you lose so many bairns. Eventually the spice runs out and there's nowt left but sour.

MARY — How can you say such awful things about your own flesh and blood?

BETTY — Truth has sharp teeth.

MARY — You never loved me. You always pined for the runts that you'd lost. I was the one that survived. I was there in front of you. You should have loved me.

BETTY — I did love thee, I just never took to thee. You were lost the moment you mistook money for affection.

MARY — I saw what poverty did. I ate, slept and grew up on poor people's fare. I wasn't going to live my life bobbing at the knee for others.

BETTY — I never raised thee to have champagne tastes on a lemonade income!

---

2. Felted – (Yorkshire) hidden

MARY And I wasn't going to settle for a low income and low life. I heard the whispered secrets through the cracked doors at night. I wanted more. What was wrong with wanting to be more, to better myself, eh?

BETTY Nowt wrong wi' it, it's how you went about it. You were always brussen.3 Even as a child there was a ruthless, loveless, cruelty within thee.

MARY You may have been content to eat other people's insults but I wasn't.

BETTY As a mother I'll always love you. There's just different metal in thee.

(Beat) Should have said no, that's on me. That's my sin.

MARY And mine was being the daughter of a Jesus killer.

(Pause) You thought I didn't know. I heard your secret mumblings.

BETTY It was what it was. It were better in private behind closed doors.

MARY You lied!

BETTY I never lied, I just didn't say out loud. In my heart I never changed. Doesn't matter what others think. As long as you can stay true to thee sen.

MARY Hypocrite!

BETTY It was for your protection. Those days people were not known for their patience. I didn't want you to suffer, to have to face the daily obstacles that I had. I wanted you to be free. I wanted the best for you...

And while we're at it, I never hated you...

You weren't an easy child. You made it very difficult for anyone to be fond of thee. You always chose your own path.

MARY I refuse to believe any of this nonsense.

BETTY It doesn't matter whether you believe or not. It won't change the fact that both thee and me are dead. Let me give you one piece of advice, stop blaming everyone else for what went wrong in your life. Stop transferring your wrong doing and wrong thinking onto others.

You played your tune now's the time to pay the piper.

We've had our time. We had our chances. It's out of our hands, it's up to others to judge.

---

3. Brussen – (Yorkshire) bad, bad-natured

MARY	I've done nothing wrong.
BETTY	Then you've nowt to worrit about.

Just go on about your business.

(Michelle stirs. Betty stokes her forehead)

You can cover shit with as much sugar as thee wants, but you'll still be walking in muck.

MARY	I don't have to sit here and listen to this!
BETTY	Neither do I lass. I just wanted to see for me sen...
MARY	To gloat, to say, "I told you so."
BETTY	I just wanted to see how you'd turned out after I'd gone.
MARY	And?
BETTY	Better than I expected.
MARY	Thank you.
BETTY	That was nae a compliment...
MARY	What's that supposed to mean?!

(Betty gets up and walks back into the window and disappears) Walk away, Mother!

(Turns to look at Michelle) This is all your fault!

She digs Michelle in the ribs, then gets up and walks back into the TV and is gone.

MICHELLE *(wakes up with a start)* Don't you just hate that when it happens?

(Michelle stretches) At least I didn't drool!

She turns off the TV.

Blackout.

SCENE FOUR

Morning. Michelle is seated on a bus, staring out of the window through her own reflection in to the middle distance. Michelle's reflection slowly morphs into Fei Yen who appears in the reflection to be seated on the bus where Michelle is seated. Fei Yen stretches out her arm and hand so that it goes through the reflection to lightly touch Michelle's arm. Michelle freezes.

FEI YEN   I wanted to see the woman you had become.

Michelle looks about her. She checks the seat next to her – empty – so looks back at the window to see only her reflection. Then she turns back to be faced with an old woman, Fei Yen, sat next to her. Michelle turns back to the window to see only her own intermittent reflection.

FEI YEN It's been a long time since I was last sat on the top deck of a bus, well it would have been a tram. Hurtling along at speeds I'm sure were unsafe even then.

MICHELLE So you don't get about much?

FEI YEN I'm getting about now more than I used to. I'm quite the jet-setter these days.

MICHELLE So you fly a lot then...

FEI YEN *(smiles)* Yes. *(Beat)* I suppose I do.

MICHELLE I'm sorry have we met before – you seem very, familiar.

FEI YEN *(beat)* I don't think that we have ever met before. Not in the conventional sense.

MICHELLE So we've met in the 'unconventional sense'? *(Laughs)*

There is something about your face... I'm sorry you must think me so rude. I'm Michelle C– *(Pause)*

Chung. Whereabouts do you live?

FEI YEN I lived in Hong Kong. I'm no longer restricted by borders or countries. I see myself more as a global citizen.

MICHELLE You'll be pro-Europe then. Bit of coincidence, I was born in Hong Kong. Didn't stay for very long.

FEI YEN That's a shame.

MICHELLE These things happen.

FEI YEN Yes I suppose they do.

MICHELLE Do you have family over here in the UK?

FEI YEN I'm not sure, it's rather complicated.

MICHELLE Is that why you're over here? Searching?

FEI YEN Yes, yes that is exactly why I am here.

MICHELLE These days most people would have done an Internet search, good for you. Next stop is me. Good luck, hope you find what you're looking for. *(Michelle holds out her hand. They shake)*

What cold hands. My Gran used to say it was a sign of bad circulation and a warm heart. *(Michelle gathers herself together, ready to get off the bus. She bends down to pick up her bag)*

Any way it was nice meeting you. I'm sorry but I didn't catch your na– *(Michelle looks about. There is no-one else there. She looks around again, then looks out of the window and realises she has missed her stop)* Oh for feck's sake!

Sound of the a bell being rung impatiently multiple times.

Blackout.

ACT TWO
SCENE ONE

Michelle's apartment, the doorbell goes. Michelle opens the door to reveal Fei Yen standing in the door way.

MICHELLE   You!

FEI YEN   Yes, me– Can I come in?

Michelle hesitates, then gestures Fei Yen into the apartment.

Fei Yen enters and looks around. She sits down on the sofa.

FEI YEN   You asked me if we had met before...

MICHELLE   You said no, not in the conventional sense.

FEI YEN   That's the truth...

MICHELLE   I'm sensing a 'but'.

Pause.

FEI YEN   Do you think I might have some tea?

MICHELLE *(beat. Michelle looks at Fei Yen)* Tea it is.

Michelle goes to the kitchen. There are sounds of water being poured, cups clattering etc.

Fei Yen get up and looks about the flat at the ornaments, the flat screen TV, laptop and tablet on the old writing desk (it's the desk we saw earlier). Fei Yen stands looking out of the window. Michelle re-enters carrying cups and tea on a tray. She places everything on the coffee table.

FEI YEN   What a pleasant surprise. I wasn't expecting green tea.

MICHELLE   I'm lactose indignant.

FEI YEN *(frowns)* Lactose?

MICHELLE   Indignant.

It's a joke, people often say they're lactose intolerant.

(Michelle looks at Fei Yen) It means that they are allergic to diary / milk products. I'm not strictly 'allergic' to milk, I just don't like the stuff. Hence, I'm lactose indignant, rather than intolerant.

(Beat) Not the best joke – it's almost as bad as I'll have a white tea but without the milk.

Beat.

FEI YEN   Shall I be Mother and pour–

Awkward moment – Fei Yen begins to pour the tea.

MICHELLE   I've been very British about all of this. But now I'd quite like to know, who you are. And how you found me. *(Beat)*

And what are you exactly?

FEI YEN   What do you mean?

MICHELLE   Are you a ghost?

I've lost it...

FEI YEN   We don't talk about such things. Ghosts are respected! If you were– *(She stops herself)*

MICHELLE   Really Chinese, then I would have known that.

FEI YEN   I didn't say that...

MICHELLE   You didn't have to. It's what you thought though, isn't it?

FEI YEN   I'm the person who gave you life, who bore you, who–

MICHELLE   I'm supposed to accept that you're the ghost of my birth mother, just like that?

FEI YEN   Yes. *(Pause)*

I'm only here because you summoned me.

MICHELLE   Oh so I 'summoned' you. I mentally forced you to come and haunt me. Funny but I don't remember writing that one into my diary.

FEI YEN   Please– You needed my help. It was invitation enough. I've always been with you, watching over you.

MICHELLE   Great! How long have you been a stowaway in my head?

FEI YEN   Ancestors can be very helpful to their descendants, if properly respected and rewarded.

MICHELLE   Ancestors? I don't have any ancestors! I have borrowed relatives who disown me because I look the way that I do. What do you want from me?

FEI YEN   Does it matter? What matters is I'm here with you... in a manner of speaking. Past ones of the family have a right to enjoy the offerings from the living.

MICHELLE   Would you please leave me alone and get out of my head? Maybe if I chucked some fruit in a dish?

FEI YEN   I thought that you'd be pleased. Pleased to be able to see your own flesh and blood. To look into the eyes of your mother and see yourself in me.

Pause.

MICHELLE   This is beyond weird.

FEI YEN   Is that so wrong?

MICHELLE   Why couldn't you have appeared when I was younger?

FEI YEN   I don't think that it works like that...

MICHELLE   Then how does it work?

FEI YEN   I was living then. I had my own children...

MICHELLE   'Your own children'? What the hell does that make me then?

FEI YEN   I didn't mean...

MICHELLE   When I needed you most. When I cried for a mother that I couldn't remember. When I was desperate to hold onto someone. You weren't there.

FEI YEN   I torture myself over and over. What was done was done. I can't change that.

MICHELLE   When I was six, eight, eleven, where were you?

FEI YEN   Haunted by the reflection of your face in the faces of my other children. Each living child a torturous joy made all the more bitter by my loss.

MICHELLE   Your loss... what about my loss? *(Pause)* How long have you been...

FEI YEN   Dead? It feels like forever, to be honest. I can't remember. Time has a way of bending, of always being just out of sight, just over the hill or round the next bend.

(Beat) As children we were taught that new hells with new punishments are created to mirror the world as it changed.

(Pause) There is a City of Innocent Deaths it is there that I hope I will find my other lost children.

MICHELLE How many children did you lose?

FEI YEN No more than most families.

MICHELLE How many children survived?

Pause.

FEI YEN Why do you need to know? How many children were there in your family?

MICHELLE Two.

FEI YEN That's not a family! That's an excuse. (Pause)

I'm in a hell of my own making. What's her excuse?

MICHELLE 'Her?'

FEI YEN The Mother you grew up with.

MICHELLE Mary. Perhaps she's in a hell of her own making too.

(Beat) At least you might both have that in common.

FEI YEN You shouldn't make fun of things like that.

Death is no laughing matter.

MICHELLE In the West death can be very comical.

FEI YEN In the West I discover that many things are 'comical.'

I'm considered 'funny'.

People like me make others laugh.

Why are we the mirth makers?

Is it our fine wrinkles, our short stature, the way we speak?

It's not a generous laughter.

Lurking in the shadows, it comes out only in the darkness of cold thoughts.

(Pause) I would have clung to you. I know things change, so holding on would not have been possible. But I would have tried.

Life slipped through my fingers again and again. So many sisters and brothers that were never fully born.

At first I was the woman who revealed her age, because I was too young to have anything to lose. As the years wrapped themselves around my body,

I became the woman who stopped talking about age. I'd become too old to have anything to gain.

MICHELLE If you'd been wealthy would you have gotten onto a plane and flown half way around the world to search for me?

FEI YEN Had your life been filled with gold, would you have gotten onto a plane and searched for me?

MICHELLE I don't have pots of gold and I did get on board a plane.

FEI YEN You came to Hong Kong?

MICHELLE I didn't find you, just piles of rubble, bamboo scaffolding and burnt records.

FEI YEN I'm here now – in a manner or speaking.

Pause.

MICHELLE I flew five thousand and nine-hundred and ninety-eight miles – Longest haul flight I'd ever taken. *(Pause)* Mad!

FEI YEN We could have passed each other...

MICHELLE But we didn't.

(Silence) So why are you haunting me now? Or have you just run out of things to do in eternity?

FEI YEN Death is not a disembodied experience. We don't float around and moan. If I didn't know that I was dead I might almost think I was alive. Some do, you know.

It can take a while to adjust. Then there are those that refuse to accept things as they are. It never ends well for them.

(Looks at Michelle who is patiently waiting for an answer) I was forced to come. It's part of my penance, embracing my mistakes. Not that you were a mistake. I should never have abandoned you. I was too weak willed. And then when they advertised you in the local paper. My next mistake was not claiming you when they advertised in the local newspapers that you'd been found.

MICHELLE A Celestial Alcoholics Anonymous.

FEI YEN I was not an alcoholic!

MICHELLE I'm not saying that you were an alcoholic... What the feck am I doing?!

AA – they have a philosophy, part of which is accepting the things that you've done wrong. Embracing the people that you've hurt or damaged because of what you've done. That's all I meant–

FEI YEN Up there, or is it down there, I suppose it depends on your point of view. What religion you subscribe to, your ethnicity, your race, but everyone goes through central booking.

MICHELLE Central booking?

FEI YEN They go through your file, your life. You're cross-referenced. After that you're sent to where you need to be. To do whatever it is you need to do, before you're moved on. *(Pause)*

I'm sorry.

MICHELLE For what?

Having me?

Abandoning me?

Setting me adrift?

FEI YEN For everything.

Blackout.

SCENE TWO

Lake of Blood And Terrible Bee Torture

Lake of Blood and Terrible Bee Torture. Ruled by Wu Guan Wang. The Pool of Blood is always hungry, so Wu Guan Wang also takes care of family matters. Disrespectful daughters and rude sons are mashed into their component parts with great gusto.

Projected title appears:

THE HELL OF FAMILY TIES

Michelle and Therapist:

MICHELLE I guess I'm still anxious, not sure why the funeral came and went. I'm still standing. I cleared out the house–

THERAPIST / MARY You sound uncertain of that – is there something you would like to share with me?

MICHELLE It's nothing…

Whilst I was clearing the house I kept getting flashes of my adoptive Mother. She was there standing talking to me.

Well more telling me off, shouting at me.

THERAPIST / MARY Why would your Mother do that?

MICHELLE Adoptive dead Mother.

THERAPIST / MARY Yes.

One thing that has always puzzled me, why do you insist on referring to your Mother as your adoptive Mother?

MICHELLE Because that's what she is – she was.

My adoptive Mother.

Maybe if she'd have bonded with me, been more emotionally supportive and sympathetic–

THERAPIST / MARY I supported you for eighteen long years.

Eating my food, being kept warm at my expense, clothed by me, educated by me. You would have been worthless if it weren't for me.

MICHELLE Mothers are supposed to love you unconditionally aren't they?

THERAPIST / MARY In life nothing is free. If you want something you either have to work your backside off for it or you buy it. That's fine if you're rich and idle but for most folks it meant sweat and elbow grease. I wasn't having any of that. That's why I trained to be a teacher. I stupidly thought I'd be able to teach maths, geography and general science. Women were only supposed to teach art, music and religious studies.

Mary sits side on to a small dressing table reading a letter. Michelle sits side on to an old writing table (the one we briefly saw in Act I, Scene Two), her back to Mary's back.

Michelle is trying to write a letter.

MARY Everyone said, "It'll complete you, giving birth will complete you as a woman."

(Pause) I hated IT. I detested all of IT! Mother tried to tell me about married life. I didn't want to listen. I thought, 'I can get through this,' keep him at arm's length. How anyone can think... IT can be enjoyable.

If you could have children, without doing IT, I would have had three, four, even more. Now that would have completed me.

(Pause) I just couldn't, do IT.

Messy, painful, heavy.

All that hot breath, sweaty body weight bearing down on me.

Once was enough. I let him do IT a couple of more times and then banned him from my bedroom. He said that 'I'd led him on.' That I was frigid. I ought to go and talk to someone. I wasn't going to do that! Talk to a total stranger about IT. Have a stranger judge me because I refuse to open my legs for my husband. I wish he'd left me. I kept to my side of the marriage bargain. I did my duty. He stayed, to spite me. To punish me. I didn't care as long as he left me alone at night. We spent the rest of our married lives, apart. At night I could hear him through the walls, disgusting! After enduring IT, he had a son, what did I have? Nothing. I suggested that we adopt. He was happy with that suggestion. I'd have a little baby girl.

The perfect daughter I'd always pictured. All mine. He had his son and I would have my daughter. She'd do all the things that I did but better and even some of the things I couldn't do. The perfect solution. A baby without the mess. An instant family.

A perfect family. And then this— *(looks at the half opened letter)*

"Dear Mrs Carter, it is with regret that I have to inform you, that you are not suitable for a domestic adoption.

However might I bring your attention to a very special adoption program. I enclose information. If you would like further details or to discuss your options, please don't hesitate to contact me directly via the telephone my number is also enclosed. Or if you prefer you can write to me at the above address.

Sincerely Dr P Francis."

I was so angry. What did they mean, I wasn't suitable? They hadn't said, you and your husband aren't suitable. It was I wasn't suitable. I flicked through the brochure and the enclosed papers. Do you remember Sunny Smiles? Those little books full of pictures of smiling children?

You bought a smile for charity. The Brownies and Sunday school children went door to door selling smiles. It was a bit like that, only it wasn't just the smile, you got the whole baby.

I don't mean you bought the baby. Gracious no, you applied to adopt it. All the babies were Chinese, they were adorable. Just like those China dolls. So I applied, the perfect solution.

MICHELLE   Dear…

Why am I writing this letter?

(Pause) I'm a mature adult with a life of my own…

(Pause) All those 'conversations' come flooding back.

Drowning the adult in me.

I feel like a six year old being sent to sit outside the headmistress' office.

What's the point?

I'm free at last.

(Pause) There is one thing I want to know.

Why?

MARY Why? Why?

Why do you have to ask questions?

Always asking questions you were.

MICHELLE The first time I asked about adoption you slapped me across the face.

Silence.

MARY You caught me off guard.

(Beat) Why did you have to spoil everything?!

MICHELLE Spoil?

MARY Why couldn't you have been a good girl. A quiet girl. They told me that Chinese children were no trouble. They did as they were told. They made the perfect daughters. Trust me to get saddled with the one contrary child out of the bunch. I should have had them up under the Trades Description Act.

You were anything but– It wasn't supposed to be like this.

(Beat) Any of it...

MICHELLE Be like what?

MARY *(silence)* Having a baby was my duty. It completed the home. I thought I'd done that, but one child wasn't enough. They expected at least two. I couldn't go through *it* again.

His sweaty fumbling, groping hands all over me – Then it came to me. Dr Francis' letter. That was the answer to all my prayers. A child without having to...

God was talking to me. Telling me to respond. A boy for my husband and a girl just for me. The perfect family.

MICHELLE I was adopted because you didn't want to have sex with your husband! I wish I'd never asked.

(Pause) When I buried you I thought everything else would be buried with you.

But here I am, still tormented by the past. By a mother who used adoption as a sex substitute.

(Pause) Just because you 'chose' the child doesn't mean you get the perfect daughter.

There is no such thing as the perfect family.

Just as you can't make an omelette without breaking eggs, you don't get to make a family without fertilising them.

MARY Marriage makes you unclean! Men sliding, breathing, fumbling all over you. Adopting you was my reward for putting up with my husband. Babies aren't supposed to remember.

Right from the start you defied me, clasping your hands together and bowing like the heathen that you were. You got excited at the smell of cooking rice. You mocked me. You laughed at me from the moment you entered my home. I wasn't going to stand for that. You were even speaking your own language! How could you! You were supposed to belong to me. You were my retirement policy. You were supposed to be the dutiful daughter who would do everything for me, love me and never leave me. I rescued you, I gave you life. You were my second chance.

MICHELLE And you were supposed to be my first.

Blackout.

SCENE THREE

An urban Michelle sits on a bench, day-dreaming.

MICHELLE I know this place, I know this...

Harper's Common! I haven't been here for – years.

The last time...

Betty appears on the bench next to Michelle.

BETTY *(finishing Michelle's sentence)* ...Were, when you were just short of me knee-caps!

MICHELLE Gran?

BETTY Aye I'm here.

MICHELLE Have I died?

BETTY Give over you daft apath.

Have thee died!? I don't know what's happening with folks these days.

MICHELLE Then I've really lost it. I went to your–

BETTY Spit it out lass, spit it out!

Thee went and saw me off and a very nice do it was an' all.

Wasn't so sure about those round spice things.

Indian if I'm not mistaken.

MICHELLE Pakoras, Gran. Sheila made them, you remember Gita?

BETTY Sheila, which Sheila? Lez and Julie's?

MICHELLE No Gran – two doors down from the Hardy's. You know, Sheila, the one with the colic baby...

BETTY *(beat)* Oh you mean Gita, Gita-Rita!

MICHELLE Gran! Her name's Sheila!

BETTY Get away with you! I know who you mean Gita. Feisty thing she was. Like her Pooh-kor-ahs. *(Beat)*
I don't hold with regrets. Regrets are for those that have wasted time. I'm sorry I couldn't have stuck around for a bit longer.

MICHELLE You and me both, Gran.

BETTY I never did quite know how to talk to me ayne daughter. It were always skew-whiff. Awkward like – whereas along comes thee, funny little thing that thee was, but it were like butter melting across a hot crumpet.

MICHELLE Death hasn't changed you at all Gran. I'm so glad.

BETTY Why would death change a person? In't more likely to make you more of who you really are?

MICHELLE So you do, 'go on' even after death?

BETTY Some folks do, some folks don't – it's all up here. *(She taps her temple)*
I just like watching folks. Seeing you grow, the changes – ee it's all out there in't it. I'm glad that you let things go. Getting shot of things. I know it's never been easy.

But look at thee, successful, popular, your ayne place to live.

Human beings were an odd lot. We flock together and huddle for comfort with what we know, what makes us feel safe and lord help you if you're not that. Well I does nae need to tell you that.

I was brought up with deep roots and a faith that ran through everything like a stick of Blackpool rock.

You've been an' grown up backwards. You've learnt, you've back-tracked and found your ayne roots.

(Beat) Our Mary, well the type of roots Mary wanted well... Even if we could've I doubt either of us would have.

Sometimes even children that are born are abandoned, orphaned within themselves. A mother can't always love every child that she has. Maybe I just ran out of love. Child after child was either dead before they say the light in the world or didn't reach past five and then Mary she fought every moment, in the womb, at birth, when she was being nursed, even in her sleep she fought. We all want a good life.

Mary, she wanted perfection. Life without bumps; it's not life, it's hell and it never works out.

MICHELLE   Don't mean to be rude Gran but why are you here? Why am I seeing – things?

BETTY   So you've chatted then, you and she. You mun be vexed. It were different times.

Different way of looking at things.

MICHELLE   I'm not daft Gran. You taught me better than that.

BETTY   But?

Your head's having a banter wi' your heart.

Let it, they'll sort thi'selves out in their own time.

Past is done and int' ground. You move on – you cannot but help move.

Only those that have nowt to worrit or wonder about stay still.

Those that have sorrow are always ont' go.

I have to make this brief – time's getting short.

MICHELLE   You were the only one that ever understood me. You were the first grown up that talked to me. I wish you could stay Gran.

BETTY   Lass, I'll always be wi' thee. *(She touches Michelle's heart)* Just keep in mind what I taught you. No one can ever take away what's in here *(she taps her temple)* and what's in here *(she taps her heart)*. Stay true to those two things and you won't go far wrong.

MICHELLE   I remember being at school, then running all the way home. Chased by a group of bullies. They'd cornered me and given me a really good hiding. Thrown sticks, stones, mud, cow dung – the works. Somehow I always managed to get away.

Mother tore into me. I'd ruined my new school uniform and new shoes.

You found me in the cellar blubbing like a trouper.

Took me back to your house. Cleaned me up and put plasters on my cuts. Didn't tell me off, in fact you hardly spoke at all.

You gave me a hug and asked, what I'd learnt.

I remember thinking at the time, what an odd question to ask. I said something like, I can run faster than most.

You smiled and said, there you go.

BETTY   Just remember that you can run in both directions.

Betty gets up and disappears.

Blackout.

ACT THREE
SCENE ONE

Taking into account your crimes and repentance, Zhuang-Lun-Wang (ruler of the tenth and final court of hell) will decide what form your next incarnation will take.

Once Zhuang-Lun-Wang has decided your fate, along comes Meng-Po with her Tea of Forgetfulness. One sip and you lose all memory of your previous life. You also forget your time in Hell, which means you are free to make the same mistakes all over again in your next life.

Projected title appears:

TAKING TEA IN HELL

A white room, a waiting room with chairs, a table, magazines and leaflets.

Fei Yen sits sipping tea observing Mary.

FEI YEN   There are so many platitudes about being a good Mother, even ones about being bad Mothers. Though why you would want to immortalise being a bad Mother I really don't know.

MARY   Sons are three times more trouble than daughters that's what I was taught. I should have gone with my gut feelings. I was cheated. They told me that Chinese girls made the perfect daughters. Why did I listen. I found out too late that daughters do nothing. They are expensive to educate. Expensive to keep.

And give back nothing but lip! I should have known! Women don't need the protection of men. We need protection from ourselves, from each other.

FEI YEN   My husband was a good worker, a good son to his parents, a good father to his sons, but a terrible husband. Girls were always looked upon as a disappointment. In the early days we scavenged amongst the refuse dumps in Kowloon. From time to time we come across the baby girls that had been dumped amongst the stinking refuse. Sometimes there would still be life left in them. Their little naked limbs twitching trying to reach out, to grab for a phantom breast. Other scavengers having stripped the littleness clean of clothing and dignity. A boy brought status. Sons continue the family line. Boys are the best, because they can work. They were thought of as stronger. If my first born had been a son, everyone would have celebrated.

MARY I knew they'd had a harsh life. They'd had to move suddenly from Glasgow, which is how I ended up being born in Yorkshire. I can't fault my parents. They worked hard. Some might say that they did the best with what they had. I wasn't the first, not sure that I was the last. But I was the only child that survived. I couldn't help myself. But I clocked what others had and I wanted the same and if that meant subbing out where I'd come from, then so be it. I always felt that my mother spent more time and energy missing and mourning for her dead children more than loving and paying attention to me. I wasn't like my mother. I didn't have the patience, strength or calmness that she had.

Neither did I share her deep religiousness.

Of course I'm a practicing Christian, what else was I going to be. When I found out about my Mother's past, I was shocked. How could she be this foreign, this alien thing?

The bond was always weak between me and Mother. That was the straw that broke us.

How could she have kept this from me, not only kept it from me but she never really recanted. She'd never embraced being a Christian she just played at it, deceiving everyone, even her own daughter. I felt so ashamed. Such a betrayal...

FEI YEN At dusk near the harbours and the outskirts of the towns we'd discover the remains of babies underneath the river bridges.

Bodies of babies, maybe from the local orphanages, or local hospitals. Some had been stillborn others had been thrown away. Medical waste. The bodies had already begun to rot. I felt the life growing within me and I vowed that I would not allow my baby to become one of these bloated, abandoned pieces of festering flesh.

MARY Nearly eighteen hours of excruciating pain and my son was born. They handed me an ugly misshapen, mewling and whimpering bundle. I looked at this slimly crying wrinkled, 'thing'. I felt – absolutely nothing. There was nothing to see of me in this miniature. What I held in my arms, this thing that I was supposed to suckle looked more like Winston Churchill than me. Wrinkled, old and unpleasant to look at.

A constant reminder of having had to endure IT and my husband's needs. Perhaps if he'd been a bonnie baby with bright blue eyes and fine blond hair maybe I would have felt otherwise. But ugliness begets ugliness. My husband had his son and he was welcome to him. I wanted a daughter, but there had to be another way. If there was, I'd find it.

FEI YEN We were young and without hope or money. We couldn't return to mainland China. That was out of the question. My husband was doing the best that he could. For the time he was very modern and forward thinking. Let's wait and see, he said, maybe fate would be kind to us. In my heart and in my belly I knew fate would not be kind. The signs of life that I felt were not male. I knew that it was a girl. We got so used to seeing bundles in alleyways, behind piles of rubbish. Bundles of fabric bound with string that screamed but as the days went by silence and stillness came. Till at last the bundle was just a bundle. The one thing I noticed with all these bundles, they were left in carefully chosen spots. Never far from the footfall of the wealthy. A hotel, a British club. The Chinese version of the stork myth was to tell our children that they were found in a trash can.

A week before my time, my husband rushes home. He's crying, cradling a red package. He places it on the floor and unwraps it carefully, it's a baby girl. The cord still attached to the placenta. She was blue and her throat had been cut. But somehow she was clinging on to life. We tried, we held her for what seemed like an age, until finally she let go.

We say that raising daughters is watering another man's garden, that daughters are thieves. Women are referred to as maggots in the rice. Back home the city was filled with wagons making rounds in the dark. Collecting the corpses of unwanted daughters. Soundlessly drowned as the mother gave birth into a bucket of water.

MARY My daughter will be everything that I wasn't and more.
FEI YEN My daughter will survive I'll make sure of that.
MARY I will love my daughter like no other.
FEI YEN I love my daughter as only a Mother can.

Blackout.

SCENE TWO

Fei Yen and Mary are seated in a kind of waiting area. Very modernist, Spartan and pure white. They are having tea.

FEI YEN This is different.

MARY I wouldn't know.

Awkward pause as they sip their tea in silence.

FEI YEN I never thought hell would be so pleasant.

MARY *(sotto voce)* A ridiculous notion!

FEI YEN I can't speak for Christianity, but Buddhists, they know their hells. *(Laughs to herself)* I think I've been put through all ten Hells, or is it twelve? I never could remember.

MARY Must you go on and on about death?
I really don't understand why I'm here… stuck with you…

FEI YEN You really have no idea, do you?
And there was I, having been taught that the West had all the answers.
It was bigger, smarter and richer…

MARY I'd rather not 'talk' to you anymore.

FEI YEN You're dead.

MARY Can I call someone for you…
A doctor?

FEI YEN I don't need a doctor.
I'm dead too. *(Laughs)*
(Mary moves to sit further away from Fei Yen taking her tea with her) The sooner you come to terms with your own death the easier it will be.
I wasn't expecting death to be quite so – life-like.

MARY Stop talking to me now, please.
I don't talk to mentally deranged people.

FEI YEN I know all about you, I've seen your records.

MARY What do you mean you've seen my records, what records? If they're mine they should be private not for the likes of… you to be looking at.

FEI YEN I thought you weren't going to talk to me anymore?

MARY I'm not…

Where is everybody?

What is this place?

FEI YEN Hell.

MARY Hell isn't an empty white room!

FEI YEN This hell is.

MARY Hell is hot, dark and full of brimstone...

And, I can't be dead,

Why only this morning I...

FEI YEN You found yourself in someone else's home talking to a daughter you haven't seen in over forty years?

You might not think you're dead, but you're certainly in your own hell, which right now happens to be an empty white room talking to someone you think is mentally deranged.

MARY Stop talking to me!

I don't know you.

I've never laid eyes on you before.

(Beat) You go over there and stay there.

I'll move further over there...

FEI YEN We're both stuck here for however long they see fit.

As small as she was my daughter still had all her vital organs . . . when I placed her on that stairwell, I thought she'd be going to a better life, a better home.

MARY When we applied for the court order, for the adoption I never thought it would be so hard. You take a baby, they know nothing. Easy. A mother is a mother after all, isn't she?

FEI YEN Outside it's noisy, inside I'm empty.

Two failures, like two lost twins.

They talk much but arrive nowhere.

I might as well be climbing a tree to catch a fish!

MARY I can't be expected to hang about here. I'm going to find the person who's in charge. I demand answers!

Mary storms off, first in the wrong direction and then exits with purpose.

Fei Yen watches with amusement.

Blackout.

SCENE THREE

Fei Yen and Betty are waiting. I's a kind of nondescript waiting room. Projected onto the wall behind them is one of those Ticket number waiting displays that you see in Hospitals and Doctors' Surgeries. Fei Yen paces up and down. She appears to be in distress.

BETTY Pacing up and down won't make things any better.

FEI YEN You're right but it's one of those things that you do. It's better than doing nothing.

BETTY Aye that it is.

FEI YEN Are you here for your final meeting? I feel so nervous...

BETTY What's thee got to be nervous about – you're dead! *(Giggles)*

FEI YEN You never think about your own death, it's like seeing yourself in a mirror, you're always selective about what you look at.

BETTY True – funny isn't it?

FEI YEN Do you have people waiting for you?

BETTY I had my final meeting years ago – time isn't the same here is it? No, I was asked to go visiting.

FEI YEN I see – I just didn't want to leave. I think I got stuck, so they let me go – for a little while.

BETTY You get all sorts here. Lost, angry, in denial, restless, rebellious and unrepentant souls. Some never leave – they can't let go of what's gone. And can't get their head round what's about to come. So they end up wandering, carrying around their anger or whatever it is that's eating away inside.

FEI YEN Sadness is always moving, it never stays still.

BETTY I'm curious who had such a tug on your heart, you couldn't leave them be?

FEI YEN My daughter.
A daughter of just five hours, maybe less.
The child I spent the least time with but have never forgotten.
Not one day has gone by when I have not thought or cried over her. I have lost and cried over a handful of children that the world could not embrace.

BETTY Children should never go afore the parents but in my day it were the norm. I had six kinder but only one survived. Maybe I paid more attention to the stillborns than the child that survived. Sometimes the apple just doesn't land that close to the tree.

FEI YEN In giving her life, I took away all that she should have had.

BETTY You did what you thought was best, as Mothers do. You can't keep beating your sen around the head for that. For good or ill it's done.

FEI YEN I saw the mountains of refuse. Some of it was still alive. I didn't want my beautiful child to be any part of that.

BETTY I saw the hate in my neighbours' eyes as we ran from our home. I didn't want my daughter to go through that.

The Ticket number changes to 8888.

FEI YEN That's my number.

BETTY Good luck.

Blackout.

SCENE FOUR

Michelle sits in her flat in the dark. On the coffee table are three small incense burners. She's looking at a variety of old photographs. Her adoptive mother (Mary), her adoptive grandmother (Betty) and a crumpled faded photograph of an old building in Hong Kong.

MICHELLE I'm told that the dying often want to be comforted. Hearing, I love you, I forgive you and thank you is a very good way to allow them to go peacefully. You shouldn't miss out on a chance to say goodbye, you should be in the room and say what needs to be said. *(Upstage behind Michelle, Mary, Fei Yen and Betty appear each lit from above by a single light as if standing under an uncovered light bulb. Michelle lights the three incense burners and places one picture behind each burner)* Well here I am I'm in the room and I'm ready to say what needs to be said, slight deviation, I know you're supposed to do this before they die, better late then never, I say.

MARY You broke my heart.

MICHELLE Don't you mean dreams?

MARY	In my book it's the same thing.
BETTY	Oh give over and whist for once.
MICHELLE	Thanks Gran. What would I have done without you?
BETTY	Same as other folks, the best that you could, with what you had. You would 'ave been all reet wi' out me.
MICHELLE	You don't know that Gran…
BETTY	No, but you're still there aren't you?
MICHELLE	True – though sometimes I wonder what for.
FEI YEN	I never stopped thinking about you. I carried you here *(points to her heart)* Always.
MICHELLE	You arrive on my doorstep. You say that you're my Mother. I have no proof of this…
MARY	She's not to be trusted. She could be any has been, looking to profit from underhand dealings!
MICHELLE	She's dead for God's sake! How the hell is she going to profit from any of this?

(Looks at the picture of Mary) You're all dead! When will that sink into your ivory feckin' dome?!

MARY	How dare you talk to me, your Mother like that?!
MICHELLE	You're not my Mother!

Silence.

MARY	How dare you! Just because I didn't squeeze you out! Doesn't give you the right to take away my motherhood to you. Who fed, clothed, named, homed and rescued you? Gave you a place to be far from the squalor and dirt of Hong Kong?
MICHELLE	Just because you did all those things doesn't make you a mother. Any more than I'm your daughter because I lived under the same roof as you.
FEI YEN	I knew it! I knew that you felt…
MICHELLE	You're no more of a Mother to me than she was.

So you were having a hard time. Did you really have to abandon me?

FEI YEN	Yes I had to abandon you, I had no choice /
MICHELLE	You always have a choice /
FEI YEN	And it was the choice I made. The choice that gave you life instead of death.
MICHELLE	Leaving you free to start over again.

MARY What kind of Mother behaves like that?

FEI YEN The loving kind. At least I had children...

BETTY If I could grab hold of you and bash some sense into you I would *(Michelle laughs)*

And that includes you Mrs Woman *(Michelle stops laughing)*

Aye that's better.

We're being self-centred and selfish.

You– *(talking to Fei Yen)* You wrap yourself in a hair-shirt and bemoan that you gave up your little baby girl.

Tragic, but you're not first and sadly you won't be the last that's put between a rock and a hard place.

It's summit you have to live with. Be happy that your baby turned out as well as she did.

(Talking to Mary) And as for thee, daughter!

Mary, Mary quite contrary – that was always the trouble with thee. Living vicariously too afraid to actually get involved with life for your sen. Instead you wanted to be pulling strings.

MICHELLE Shut up all of you!

Sorry Gran, I didn't mean you.

BETTY No harm no foul. I'll leave you to it.

FEI YEN I should never have left you.

MICHELLE But if you hadn't I wouldn't be here. I wouldn't be me.

FEI YEN I suppose that will have to do.

MICHELLE That's all I've got.

BETTY *(to Fei Yen)* Come on let us get going. Always fancied putting my hand to a bit of Chinese cooking. You any good at schooling?

FEI YEN Teaching? I'm not sure. But I'm willing to give it a try if you are? *(They both laugh)* Bye daughter, I think this is the last time you'll see me. But I will always be with you whether you like it or not.

BETTY Remember what I taught you, you'll be just fine.

MICHELLE Thanks Gran, miss you.

Bye... Mother.

Betty and Fei Yen wave. The light on them fades and they disappear into the blackness.

MARY You can't leave me alone! Mam! Anybody?

You! This is all your doing!

MICHELLE   I can't take credit for any of this, this was all you.

MARY   You ungrateful child! After all that I've done for you!

MICHELLE   What exactly did you do for me – over and above what a Mother is expected to do?

MARY   Don't you get clever with me. You haven't outgrown me taking a hand to you to knock some sense and good manners into you.

MICHELLE   I'd like to see you try, with you being dead and all.

MARY   Was it too much to ask for a loving, respectful daughter?

MICHELLE   No it isn't too much to ask. It's just how you asked. You demanded, you controlled in order to get. Respect and love are earned. You can't bully, terrorise or buy your way into a child's affection. I was not a China doll to be posed and dressed as you saw fit.

MARY   What was the point of adopting you, if you weren't going to be the daughter that I wanted? Why did I bother?

MICHELLE   I can't answer why you did that. But from what I've learnt recently, to escape your marital bed? Because you wanted a newborn baby and that was the only way you could adopt one?

MARY   I have nothing but bitterness to show for all my effort, all the trouble that I was put through. But you, you're alright Jack aren't you? Even me own mother's gone off and left me. I'm all alone in the dark and there's none there to help me. I didn't want my mother's life, was that wrong of me, to want better, to want more? I wanted love, I wanted a car in the drive, the privet hedge and the brass door knocker on the stained glass windowed front door. I wanted two children neat, tidy, clever, clean and obedient who looked to me for their every need. A husband that was kind and understanding. I ended up with Douglas, a sex mad husband and you a queer little out of place adopted daughter.

MICHELLE   Life, sometimes isn't all that it's cracked up to be. Why don't you go and find your Mother? Better still why don't you go and look for your husband?

MARY   Why on earth would I want to do that?

MICHELLE   Because you're lonely, because you married him. You must have felt something? Because you can't stay here.

Because I'm not a frightened six year old. I've grown up and I'm moving on. I had no control over the circumstances of my birth and abandonment. But my life – that is my responsibility and no one else's. I can do something about that and live the best life that I can. It's not about what I lost or what I wasn't given access to. It's about me being happy with who I am, what I am or what I am not. And if other people don't like that then so be it, that's their right as long as they don't try and impose their beliefs on me.

Michelle blows the falling ash from the dying incense sticks and they finally burn out. The light on Mary dims slowly.

MARY You can't do this to me! I won't let you do this to me...

The light and Mary disappear together.

MICHELLE What a day! What a week – what a life!

Michelle tidies the incense away. She pulls out a box from under the table full of photographs and starts to look through them, [these should be projected behind Michelle so the audience can see] – old Kodak photographs of Mary and Michelle as a child in all sorts of places. Betty with Michelle as a child eating ice cream, laughing. As we watch and see the photographs, the lights fade up.

Fei Yen appears carrying the camping stove. She sets it up again and begins to busy herself.

FEI YEN Each family has its own difficult scripture,
Why should I be different?
My daughter leaves Hong Kong. I realise I lost the light in my soul.
Hong Kong was full of ghosts, day or night they were there. I was afraid that one day the reflection I'd see in my teacup would not be mine. Besides there was little work and even less food for people like me.
I thought I could start again...
Build a new family. Which I did but...
The family that I almost had haunts me still.
We all eat and drink, but who among us really appreciates the taste of food?

(Fei Yen gets up and makes her way through the audience, handing out what she has been cooking)

I never did care much for people handing out advice.
They were usually strangers who knew nothing themselves but think about this they say you should govern a family as you would cook a small fish – very gently.

Fei Yen walks through the audience and disappears. We hear an audio stream and see a projection of quotes from adult adoptees on what it means to be transracially adopted:

> *I've always known that I wasn't wanted, I was needed.*

> *Biological parents and 'real' parents are not always one and the same.*

> *Adoption is living a parallel life to a silent destiny unknown I used to think to myself, 'It's so strange, I do not know **one**, just one blood relative,' and feel very alone in this world even if I was among my adoptive family.*

> *I often think about my birth mother and what it would be like to meet her.*

> *I have been so fortunate in being adopted. I am so grateful.*

> *I will be forever grateful to my adoptive parents.*

> *Being adopted is like a lottery, you win some you lose some, depending where you're born, depending where you end up. I am so grateful that I won.*

> *Being adopted and how it feels is like peeling away layers of an onion. You move thru' life wonderfully for a while and then hit a new layer that might sting the eyes / heart. It takes time to absorb the meaning of one's abandonment / loss and our identity evolves slowly over time.*

> *Adoption is the good and the bad all wrapped in one but it's how we chose to deal with it that makes the difference.*

> *Adoption meant I lived, I survived, but at what cost? Everything that I should have had and known was taken away from me and what's worse I was lied to. And that is the one thing that I can never forgive and never forget, adoption turned me into an outcast, a cultural Frankenstein, shunned by the people who adopted me and shunned by people from my birth culture.*

> *Being transracially adopted is to be a tree without roots.*

> *Being a TRA means that you learn about your life (if you're lucky) backwards.*

> *I have no idea who I am – on the face of it, what does that matter? But believe me it does. You have no idea. It's not just a question of not*

knowing who your immediate family is / was. But things like health history – most people don't give those types of things any thought, you can just bowl up and ask Gran or Uncle Fred – adoptees can't.

They say you can't miss what you've never had, believe me that's utter crap. I miss not having a father and mother, not knowing, not being able to see, to touch.

I was asked once as an adoptee whether I would have preferred a life in an orphanage or life as an adoptee – knowing what I know now, having experienced what I have. I wish I'd been left in the orphanage.

I am without identity – well an identity that people accept. I am voiceless, homeless – soulless.

The lights continue to dim and the quotes fade out.

The end.

TANGO

Tango was based loosely on the experiences of Mark and Ed Koh-Waite, a gay couple looking to move to Singapore from London, where they got married, adopted two boys, and lived as a family for several years. I was introduced to the couple (who'd once lived in Singapore) through their friends, Tracie and Adrian Pang, artistic directors of Singapore theatre company Pangdemonium, who first approached me in 2015 with the idea of dramatising Mark and Ed's story.

Singapore has a bad track record on LGBTQ rights. Casual research easily turns up a difficult history of anti-gay legislation and an ongoing, very exhausting public debate about LGBTQ equality. Specific to Mark and Ed's situation, any attempt to transplant a non-normative family to the country comes up against a wall: no laws and policies exist that recognise such a family as a unit; and the social terrain, with its uneven levels of acceptance for LGBTQ lives, is tricky to navigate.

Of the many stories Mark and Ed told me about their attempts to move back, the one about the elderly waitress who unexpectedly lashed out at them for being same-sex parents to two young boys, hit me the hardest and became the basis of the play. This single, very complex confrontation pulled together so many of the layers I needed to tell this story: the class dynamics of discourse around LGBTQ rights; the difficulty of inter-generational dialogue in Singapore; and the politics of mobility, amongst others.

I was conscious that Mark and Ed's story represents a very specific strand of LGBTQ experience. The conversation became messier, more complex, indeed more urgent, when theirs was not the play's sole voice of persuasion. The 'tango' of the title therefore refers to the fiery dance between numerous parties in the midst of an ugly culture war; and the dance-music is the odd, horrible silence of a government that refuses to take moral leadership in one of Singapore's most pressing socio-political crises.

Joel Tan is a Singapore playwright and performer based in London, where he is pursuing the Masters in Dramatic Writing at Drama Centre London, Central St. Martins. Recent productions of his plays include *Tango* (Pangdemonium, 2017), *Cafe* (The Twenty-Something Theatre Festival, 2016), *Mosaic* (The M1 Fringe Festival, 2015), and *The Way We Go* (Checkpoint Theatre, 2014). His plays have received acclaim for their range and complex insight on contemporary Singapore, and several are collected in *Joel Tan: Plays Volume 1*, published by Checkpoint Theatre, where he is an Associate Artist.

Joel also creates performances with artists working in contemporary art, poetry, and dance. This most notably includes *The Nature Museum* (Singapore International Festival of the Arts, 2017; Fast Forward Festival, Athens, 2018), a museological performance tour created with visual artist Robert Zhao; and spoken word memoir *You Are Here* (2016), created with poet Pooja Nansi. Joel also writes non-fiction, and his essays have been published by *Art Review Asia*, POSKOD Singapore, *Esquire Singapore*, and *The Substation* Singapore.

TANGO

JOEL TAN

Tango was commissioned by Pangdemonium Theatre Company in Singapore, and was first performed at the Drama Centre from 19th May to 4th June 2017. The play was directed by Pangdemonium's Artistic Director, Tracie Pang; set design was by Kwok Wai Yin; lighting design was by James Tan; sound design was by Jing Ng; costume design was by Tracie Pang; the stage manager was Leah Sim.

This play was inspired by the Blog '4 Relative Strangers,' written by Ed and Mark Koh-Waite.

Characters
KENNETH WOON-BUTLER
LIAM WOON-BUTLER — Kenneth's husband.
JAYDEN WOON-BUTLER — Their adopted son.
RICHARD WOON — Kenneth's father.
ELAINE NARANDRAN — Kenneth's friend.
LEE POH LIN — A waitress.
BENMIN LEE — Poh Lin's nephew.
ZULKIFLI BIN RAZAK (ZUL) — Benmin's lover.

Cast
Koh Boon Pin	Kenneth
Emil Marwa	Liam
Lim Kay Siu	Richard
Lok Meng Chue	Poh Lin
Karen Tan	Elaine
Benjamin Chow	Benmin
Ruzaini Mazani	Zulkifli
Dylan Jenkins	Jayden

Notes

There are several split scenes in this play. Life goes on in these split scenes as attention is diverted to another, sometimes they overlap.

Each scene should only be partially realized: some furniture and props to suggest a much larger piece, when at any one time the audience only sees a slice of it.

The time-frame of the show is about three months from start to finish. Time jumps happen in sections marked by playbacks of snatches from news reports, Internet chatter and social media.

Dialogue markings

Slash (/)   Indicates the point of overlap with the start of the next line.

Double slash (//)   Used at the start of a line and the subsequent one to indicate that they play simultaneously.

Dash (–)   Indicates an abrupt interruption.

Ellipsis (…)   At the end of a line, indicates trailing off. Ellipsis used in place of a line indicate a silent reaction.

Backslash (\\ )   In split scenes, these are used to distinguish between strains happening in different scenes.

ACT ONE
SCENE ONE

A Chinese restaurant. Singapore. Elaine and Kenneth at a table for five.

ELAINE Her lipstick matched her red Lexus. I know 'cuz I was so stunned I just kept staring at her lips moving. "Nyeh-nyeh-nyeh, lesbian lesbian lesbian, nyeh-nyeh-nyeh".

KENNETH Oh my god.

ELAINE She's basically screaming at me. "Oh… kids won't understand that Chloe has two mums, how can I explain to my daughter…" And now she's throwing out facts and statistics…

KENNETH And Chloe was…

ELAINE Yah, in the car. Which is why I–

KENNETH You should've–

ELAINE Punched the bitch?

KENNETH   Did you?

ELAINE   No, drove off. When we were undergrads, I would've. Probably kicked her too.

Enter Poh Lin.

POH LIN *(to Kenneth)* 你还要花生吗？ [You want some more peanuts?]

ELAINE *(to Kenneth)* You want / peanuts?

KENNETH *(to Poh Lin)* Actually, do you mind speaking in English? My friend here doesn't speak Chinese.

POH LIN   Oh. Sorry. You want peanuts?

ELAINE   Oh. No, it's okay auntie, thank you.

Poh Lin exits.

KENNETH   When did everything become so cheena?[1]

ELAINE   Singapore, you dunno meh?[2] *(Beat)* Anyway, I understood her. So how. Suckling pig?

KENNETH   Suckling pig?

ELAINE   What? When a lesbian and two faggots sit at a table, it's a cause for celebration.

KENNETH   When did you start eating meat again?

ELAINE   Pregnancy changes your outlook. Where are your two men?

KENNETH *(checking his phone)* Lost in the Botanic Gardens.

ELAINE   So. Back for good. After ten years of avoiding / Singapore.

KENNETH   Haven't been avoiding Singapore. We went up to Singapore Day in London two years ago.

ELAINE   How's Dad?

KENNETH   You know about the stroke, right?

ELAINE   Yeah. / Sorry to hear.

KENNETH   Mild one. But, you know. With my mum gone and everyone else in Perth...

ELAINE   Yeah. *(Beat)* But you and your dad...

---

1. Cheena – (Malay) 'Chinese'
2. Meh – (Singlish) Like *lor*, *lah*, *leh*, *hor*, *and ma*, one of a range of Singlish particles used for emphasis

KENNETH End of the day he's still my dad and I'm still Chinese. Guilt runs in our blood. Anyway, the bank needed someone here, and the expat pay is nice.

ELAINE Good also lah. Change of scenery.

KENNETH Yeah. Liam really misses Singapore.

ELAINE And you?

KENNETH Well.

ELAINE Well.

Enter Liam with Jayden.

LIAM Sorry we're late!

ELAINE // *(Getting up)* Liaaaam!

JAYDEN // Hi Papa!

LIAM // Sit down, sit down, don't get up, don't get up.

ELAINE *(to Liam)* How was the old Unesco Heritage site?

LIAM Oh right, there's that now isn't there? Jayden.

ELAINE Hi Auntie E.

LIAM How was it, Jay?

JAYDEN Alright. We fed swans. Like Hyde Park but hot.

KENNETH It was probably modelled after Hyde Park.

JAYDEN This country doesn't look like Asia / at all.

ELAINE Is this your first time in Asia, Jayden?

JAYDEN Course not. We've been to Bali? Bangkok. / I liked Bangkok.

ELAINE Bangkok!

JAYDEN Hanoi, too. Phuket.

ELAINE All so nearby. And so far. / Avoiding Singapore, is it?

LIAM No fault of mine the only time we meet is in London.

ELAINE Liam, you've put on weight!

KENNETH // Elaine.

LIAM // Who says that?

ELAINE We're over forty now. It's fresh territory.

KENNETH Elaine isn't vegetarian anymore.

LIAM Shocking.

ELAINE Shock is what happens when you don't see your friends for so long.

No, Kenneth, let me order, I come here all the time.

KENNETH *(makes to leave)* Okay, then I'm going to the loo.

ELAINE Suckling pig, how?

KENNETH *(as he exits)* Yeah, yeah. Elaine, your pick, we're getting this.

ELAINE Nonsense. *(Calling to the waitress)* Excuse me!

Enter Poh Lin.

POH LIN *(to Liam)* Hi sir, ready to order?

ELAINE Can we get–

LIAM – wait let me, let me. *(In Cantonese)* Ngo oi yah-gor[3] suckling pig–

POH LIN – Wah, good, your Cantonese! Okay, one suckling pig...

JAYDEN *(to Elaine)* Cantonese is Dad's favourite party trick.

POH LIN *(in Cantonese)* 仲有? [Some more?]

LIAM *(lost)* Ah...

ELAINE One broccoli / cao garlic...

JAYDEN Dad that was pathetic.

LIAM Better than yours. How many languages do you speak?

JAYDEN My French is alright.

LIAM Your French is useless phrases. *(Rapidly prodding him)* // C'est le stylo de mon oncle, c'est une petite chat, c'est un gros cochon...

JAYDEN // Ow, stop it! Stop it!

ELAINE // *(To Poh Lin)* And one Yangzhou fried rice.

POH LIN Okay. So cute ah these two, both like children.

LIAM Jayden.

JAYDEN *(to Poh Lin)* Hello Auntie.

POH LIN Hello! *(To Liam)* So cute. This one your son?

LIAM Yes, this is my son.

POH LIN He don't look like you or you...

ELAINE Ah, no–

LIAM Oh,–

---

3. Ngo oi yah-gor – (Cantonese) 'I want one...'

POH LIN	– Oh adopt is it?
LIAM	Yes, adopted, but she's not my wife. My husband–
ELAINE	– Auntie, we finish ordering first can?
POH LIN	Oh, sorry, sorry. / Yes, anything else?
LIAM	No, Auntie, my husband–
ELAINE	– Wasabi prawns?
POH LIN	Repeat for you ah. Suckling pig, one, later how?
ELAINE	Cook in noodles.
POH LIN	Noodle. Okay, one broccoli, one Yangzhou fried rice, one wasabi prawn, okay.

Poh Lin exits.

JAYDEN	She thought you were my mum, Auntie Elaine.
ELAINE	Liam, I'm sorry, I shouldn't have–
LIAM	– it's okay, I'm not upset. It just takes some getting used to.
ELAINE	It's just, with Roxy and Chloe, sometimes we just don't bother explaining it.
LIAM	Oh of course, it's probably / easier...
ELAINE	The confrontations can get so... / you know...
LIAM	No, of course. I'm not / saying that...
ELAINE	I'm sorry.
LIAM	It's alright, it's nothing major.
ELAINE	Okay.

Beat.

LIAM	Just next time, maybe it's best if we handled it ourselves?

Silence.

//SPLIT SCENE//

The restaurant, back of house.

Benmin, a cook, is coming off his shift. He's packing away his work clothes. He sits down and types into his phone.

Enter Poh Lin, and Benmin quickly hides his phone. The exchange is in Singapore Mandarin.

POH LIN   回家啊？ [Going home lah?]
BENMIN   没有 la，去找朋友。 [No lah, meeting friends.]
POH LIN   很会花钱 hor? [Got so much money to spend hor?]
BENMIN   哪里有。你几点下班？ [Where got. What time do you knock off?]
POH LIN   今天做 double shift。 [Doing double shift today.]
BENMIN   Orh.
POH LIN   很累。 [So tired.]
BENMIN   休息一下啦。 [Take a break lah.]
POH LIN   今天那么忙，怎么休息？ [Floor so busy today how to take break?]
今天有很多 angmoh，我很紧张，我的英文那么烂。 [Today got a lot of ang moh[4], I very stressed, my English so bad.]
BENMIN   有 meh? [Is it?]
POH LIN   但是刚才有一个以为他会讲广东话 leh。 [But got one just now think he can speak Cantonese leh.]
BENMIN   哪里? [Where?]
POH LIN   四十六桌。跟那个 keling人. [Table 46. With the keling[5] woman.]
BENMIN   Eh，很 rude leh。 [Eh very rude leh.]
POH LIN   说真的吗！ [True what!]
POH LIN   胖胖还是 keling? [Fat or keling?]
BENMIN   两个啦。 [Both.]
(Peering out) 哦。哇，他们有儿子啊？ [Oh. Wah, they got a son ah?]
POH LIN   你去哪里？ [Where you going?]
BENMIN   Toa Payoh.
POH LIN   Toa Payoh 有什么？ [Toa Payoh got what?]

---

4. Ang moh – (Hokkien) lit. 'red hair', a mildly derogatory term for Caucasian people
5. Keling – (Singlish) Old-fashioned term of unclear origins, referring to Indian people. Considered by the older generation to be affectionate, but generally understood to be highly derogatory

BENMIN 去见人啦。跟他买东西。Internet 买的。 [Meeting someone lah. Buying something from him. From the Internet.]

POH LIN Chey，买东西去店里买啦。 [Chey. Buy things buy from shop lah.]

BENMIN Kitchen 在叫你啦。 [Kitchen calling lah.]

Exit Poh Lin.

//SPLIT SCENE//

JAYDEN Dad, why do they drop all their plurals. Dad?

LIAM *(distracted)* What?

JAYDEN The waitress, Dad. Why they drop their plural?

LIAM Jayden, don't / be rude.

JAYDEN But she does.

LIAM You sound funny to her.

JAYDEN Papa doesn't talk like that.

LIAM No, Papa has a different accent.

Enter Kenneth.

JAYDEN She still sounds funny.

LIAM Jayden, enough. We're going to be in this country for a long time. Stop playing with your chopsticks, it's very rude.

JAYDEN *(drumming chopsticks)* Dad, why is everything I do rude? *(As Kenneth sits)* Papa, is this rude in your culture?

KENNETH Yes, it's like drumming on the graves of your ancestors.

JAYDEN Bullshit!

LIAM Jayden!

KENNETH Jayden!

KENNETH Why're you being so rude?

JAYDEN 'Cuz everything I've been saying lately is just rude, / rude, rude…

KENNETH Stop that.

JAYDEN …

KENNETH So did I miss anything?

ELAINE Nothing.

LIAM	Nothing.

Beat.

ELAINE	So how have your first few weeks been, Jayden?
JAYDEN	Alright, I guess. Lots of shopping centres.
ELAINE	Sounds right. Bored?
JAYDEN	Yeah.
LIAM	It's not the shopping centres. He misses his friends. Back home they'd go to the same shopping centre every day and no one complained then.
JAYDEN	I'm alright.
LIAM	Got really emotional on the flight here.
JAYDEN	// Didn't.
KENNETH	// Oh yeah, we're staying near you Elaine. At Chancery, / my dad's place.
ELAINE	// Very fancy.
JAYDEN	// See, Dad? Chancery. Told you this place doesn't feel like Asia. Oh 'cept, Papa, why's the waitress got a different accent than you?
KENNETH	She just does. Florence back home has a different accent than you, and she was born in the UK, wasn't she?
JAYDEN	Suppose.
ELAINE	Who's Florence?
KENNETH	Our cleaning lady. Why're you so fascinated with that waitress, Jay?
JAYDEN	The waitress thought that–
LIAM	– Jayden, no.
ELAINE	– Oh dear.
KENNETH	– What's he talking about?

Elaine starts laughing, then Liam joins in.

LIAM	I'll tell you later. Really, darling it's nothing. Just... just now the waitress, she's a really sweet lady but, you know, very typical, she saw Jayden and thought Elaine was his mother! And I was going to explain to the waitress but Elaine–
ELAINE	– I swear I didn't mean to! It was just, she was taking so damn long–

LIAM	– and anyway, Elaine cuts me off. And that's really it.
KENNETH	Did anyone explain to her in the end?
ELAINE	Oh, no.
KENNETH	If she asks again we'll just tell her lah.

//SPLIT SCENE//

BENMIN (*noticing Kenneth*) 那个男的是谁？那个华人。 [Who's that guy? The Chinese one?]

POH LIN 不懂 leh，可能是他们的朋友。 [Dunno, their friend maybe.]

BENMIN Then 孩子是谁 [Means the boy is what?]

POH LIN 不知道啦。那个 angmoh 说 keling 女人不是他的老婆 [Dunno lah. The ang moh just now like say the keling woman is not his wife.]

BENMIN Yi Ma. Rude. (*Beat*) 可能是两个男的儿子。 [Maybe it's the two guys' son.]

POH LIN Chey，新加坡哪里有这种事的？ [Chey, Singapore where got such thing one?]

BENMIN 不懂。 [Dunno.]

POH LIN Chey，不是啦。 [Chey, no lah.]

BENMIN 你看他们… [You see the way...]

POH LIN 不要太晚回来啊，你知道我一点声音就会起来，我明天 morning shift。 [Anyway don't come home too late ah, you know a little bit of noise will wake me up, and I got morning shift tomorrow.]

BENMIN 今晚我可能很迟才回来，gate 你不要锁，我就不会吵醒你。Okay? [Actually tonight I might be back late, you just leave the gate open so I don't wake you when I come home, can?]

POH LIN 几点？ [What time?]

BENMIN 可能十点过后。去看戏。 [After ten, maybe. Watching a movie.]

Eh, 做工了，做工。 [Eh, back to work.]

POH LIN Orh. Bye bye.

BENMIN Bye.

Poh Lin exits. Benmin returns to his phone for a moment, then turns his attention back to the table, noticing that Kenneth has started holding Liam's hand.

Benmin exits.

//SPLIT SCENE//

Jayden has started drumming with his chopsticks again.

ELAINE ... *(to Kenneth)* See lah, who asked you to give up your citizenship?

KENNETH I didn't think we'd be back. And we wouldn't if my dad didn't keep driving those poor helpers out of the house. *(To Liam)* How many is it now?

LIAM Vinnie was the sixth in two years.

KENNETH She almost tried to–

LIAM Very ugly business.

KENNETH Moral of the story is make room in your life for elderly parents and sudden bouts of filial piety.

ELAINE Then Liam, what're you going to do?

LIAM Stay at home dad. That's the plan, at least. Kenneth's bank is applying for a long term visit pass for me, so I probably don't have to look for a job.

ELAINE Oh, didn't know we were that progressive.

KENNETH Well no. It's not for everyone. Mostly high level execs. CEOs. *(He notices Jayden struggling to eat)*

LIAM Kenneth's pretty high up, so we're trying to be optimistic. They've done it for other couples before. / Hush hush loophole.

KENNETH Jayden, do you want us to get you a knife and fork?

JAYDEN I'm trying!

KENNETH – You're holding it wrong darling, look, you don't cross them like this–

JAYDEN – I know, I just need to practice!

Enter Poh Lin, distributing food.

As Kenneth demonstrates the proper use of chopsticks:

ELAINE So legally whose son is he? Here, I mean.

LIAM   Ken's the one with the proper visa, so.

KENNETH   We cross a border and suddenly I'm a single parent and the stay-home dad is not a father anymore. *(Giving up, a little frustrated, Jayden has started drumming with his chopsticks again)*

Enter Poh Lin with the wasabi prawns. She looks disapprovingly at Liam, who by now has got his hands over Jayden.

LIAM   Jayden, please, stop.

POH LIN *(to Jayden)* Eh, boy boy, eh, cannot play with chopsticks, very rude.

LIAM   See?

POH LIN *(to Liam)* This one is your son?

Beat.

ELAINE   // Yes.
KENNETH   // Yes.

POH LIN *(food still in hand)* You and her?

KENNETH   No, me and him.

POH LIN   You and him.

KENNETH   Me and him.

POH LIN   两个男的？ [Two men?]

KENNETH   Yes. 你有问题吗？ [Yes. Do you have a problem?]

LIAM *(to Kenneth)* Ken, what's going on?

POH LIN   Sorry.

KENNETH   What's the problem?

POH LIN *(increasingly flustered, to Kenneth)* 两个大男人，这样跟一个孩子？你是变态啊？ [Two grown men with one young boy, like that? You are some kind of pervert?]

Stunned silence.

LIAM   What's she saying, Ken?

KENNETH   She's saying we're perverts, Liam.

LIAM   What.

POH LIN   这样不对。 / 真的很不对。 [It's not right. / It's really not right.]

LIAM *(politely, to Poh Lin)* Sorry, if you have something to say to us, could you do it in English please?

POH LIN 谁会让两个男人领养孩子？ [What kind of people will let two men raise a child?]
什么样的人？那么变态！ [What kind of people? So perverted!]
(Beat) Sorry，我不要再 serve 你们了。 [Sorry, I don't want to serve this table anymore.]

ELAINE What is she saying?

KENNETH *(to the others)* She says she doesn't want to serve us– *(To Poh Lin)* I want to speak to your manager, please.

LIAM – Let's not make a scene, please.

KENNETH I'm not making a scene.

POH LIN 不用找我的 manager。 / Please, 我去找别人来 serve 你… [No need to talk to my manager. Please, I'll get someone else to serve…]

JAYDEN Dad, people are staring.

LIAM Okay, we should just go, Kenneth.

KENNETH *(increasingly angry)* Guys, let me sort this out.

LIAM Come on Jayden. Let's go outside.

ELAINE Kenneth, it's not worth it. Come on.

Liam and Jayden go.

POH LIN Sorry，我不能 serve 你们，很不正常。 [Sorry, I cannot serve this table, it's not normal.]

KENNETH What?

POH LIN 你们是 gay 我不管，你们要怎样就怎样， [You all gay I don't care one, you can do whatever things you want,]
但是你们不应该连累小孩子。我不信这套。 [but you shouldn't bring a young boy into it. It's against my beliefs.]

KENNETH *(to Poh Lin)* 小姐我们没有 offend 你，你为什么那么 aggressive？ [We've done nothing to offend you, why are you being so aggressive?]

POH LIN Okay okay, 我去找别人 serve 你。 [Okay okay, I'll get someone else to serve you.]

KENNETH *(calling out angrily)* I want to see your manager now.

ELAINE It's okay. Let's go.

KENNETH Elaine, what the fuck! *(To Poh Lin)* Put down the food.

POH LIN 不 serve 你们是我的权利！ [It's my right not to serve you!]

KENNETH *(to Poh Lin)* I said put down the food!

ELAINE Kenneth, don't.

KENNETH *(to Poh Lin)* I said put it down!

Poh Lin, terrified, makes to leave.

KENNETH What have I ever done to you? What have we ever done to you? *(He grabs the plate, throws it on the ground)*

Silence.

SCENE TWO

Later that night. A coffee shop in Toa Payoh. Benmin and Zul are having canned drinks. Prelude to a one night stand, but Benmin doesn't quite get the picture. He's on edge, texting distractedly. Zul is languorous, at ease, eyeing Benmin curiously.

ZUL You want another green tea?

BENMIN No, it's okay.

ZUL You want something stronger?

BENMIN Uh.

ZUL Actually now almost eleven already, think they cannot sell alcohol also. You texting someone?

BENMIN Sorry.

ZUL You very shy ah?

BENMIN Yah.

ZUL So what does your username mean? Benmin.

BENMIN That's my name.

ZUL Your name is Benmin. Like Benjamin / without the 'ja'.

BENMIN Yah, without the 'ja'.

ZUL Your parents / gave…

BENMIN Ownself give.

Silence.

BENMIN You drink alcohol?

ZUL Yah why not?

BENMIN	...
ZUL	My place there got some vodka, you want?
BENMIN	No. Don't really drink.
ZUL	Yeah, no worries.

Silence.

ZUL	So you work in a restaurant?
BENMIN	Yah.
ZUL	Kay. *(Beat)* I'm an MRT[6] technician. So all the train breakdown is my fault.

Silence.

ZUL	Restaurant doing what?
BENMIN	Bit here bit there.
ZUL	Okay.

Silence.

Zul drinks the last of his green tea noisily. Benmin starts texting again.

ZUL	You really very shy ah. Sorry I talk a lot.
BENMIN	Yeah, sorry. Prefer to listen.
ZUL	You meet a lot of guys before?
BENMIN	Never.
ZUL	Never?
BENMIN	Only just download the app recently.
ZUL	Oh.

Beat.

ZUL	Am I your first?
BENMIN	Not say first lah.
ZUL	Second? Third? One point five?
BENMIN *(laughing)*	Yeah. Last time school got fool around lah, but...
ZUL	How old are you now?
BENMIN	30.
ZUL	Orh. Same.

Beat.

---

6. MRT – Mass Rapid Transport, the Singapore subway

ZUL	So right... you know on the app when people say 'meet up' it's usually, like, for fun?
BENMIN	For fun means...
ZUL	Sex.
BENMIN	Oh. Like...
ZUL	Fun.
BENMIN	Means sex.
ZUL	And it's getting late. You want to come up or not?
BENMIN	Oh.
ZUL	Nevermind you finish your drink first, take your time.

Silence.

//SPLIT SCENE//

Richard's Chancery Lane home. Richard is on the computer, something trips him up and he's annoyed. Enter Kenneth, freshly showered. He notices Richard's irritation.

RICHARD	Ahhhh! Come on!
KENNETH	What's wrong?
RICHARD	The bloody internet, it's on and off!
KENNETH	Nah. Like this. *(He demonstrates)* Just wait a while.

Long silence.

RICHARD	Nothing.
KENNETH	It takes time.

Silence.

RICHARD	Boy asleep?
KENNETH	Yeah.

Silence.

RICHARD	Weather alright?
KENNETH	Yeah.

Silence.

KENNETH	Okay try again.
RICHARD *(testing)* Ah.	

KENNETH Pa, why are you looking at the Caskets website?

Beat.

RICHARD Looking at packages.

KENNETH Why?

RICHARD Facts of life.

Silence.

KENNETH Pa. You don't need to plan your own funeral.

RICHARD What do you know about planning funerals. Last funeral you planned was your mum's / and that didn't...

KENNETH ...

RICHARD I mean. It was okay. Okay funeral.

KENNETH Okay?

RICHARD Could have been better.

KENNETH What?

Silence.

RICHARD Could be my turn soon, and you're busy adjusting and all that, don't–

KENNETH – it was a mild stroke, Pa.

RICHARD Mild stroke brought you all the way / from the UK?

KENNETH Not just that, told you, promotion opportunity and...

Beat.

RICHARD After Mum died, haven't seen you in what, almost ten years, and suddenly you're back here, got a job, husband and son in tow. Don't tell an old man not to read the signs.

Silence.

KENNETH Okay. Whatever makes you feel better. It's your funeral.

Silence.

RICHARD Sorry, I can be very tactless.

KENNETH It's okay.

Silence.

RICHARD You know I've always been very independent.

KENNETH Yeah. I know.

RICHARD	Just takes some getting used to. Having you around. And suddenly this ang moh…
KENNETH	His name is Liam.
RICHARD	And the boy.
KENNETH	His name is Jayden.
RICHARD	I know his name.

//SPLIT SCENE//

ZUL	So.
BENMIN	Maybe next time can?

Beat.

ZUL	Oh. You don't like Malays is it.
BENMIN	Huh, no lah.
ZUL	Not your type?
BENMIN	Uh…
ZUL	I don't look like my pic?
BENMIN	Huh, no. You actually look better in real life.

Beat.

ZUL	Thanks. So what are you looking for? I thought you wanted…
BENMIN	I dunno. I just thought maybe can meet up to talk lor.
ZUL	Okay.

Beat.

BENMIN	Sorry. I don't even know you, how to go and…
ZUL	Oh.

Beat.

BENMIN	Sorry.
ZUL	Sorry for what.
BENMIN	Wasting your time.
ZUL	No lah, what waste time. Sitting here with a cute guy drinking green tea is nice.
BENMIN	Thanks.

ZUL   Okay.

//SPLIT SCENE//

Jayden's room. Jayden and Liam on the bed, with Jayden's laptop.

JAYDEN   Dad, I've got to Skype Mel and Dan soon.
LIAM   I know. But answer me first. Are you okay?
JAYDEN   Yeah.
LIAM   You miss home?
JAYDEN   Yeah, 'course.
LIAM   Do you like it here?
JAYDEN   It's alright.
LIAM   You know, this is like my second home, and I know it's a little strange at first, but I really want you to like it here.
JAYDEN   It's not here, Dad. I dunno. Maybe it is.
LIAM   What do you mean?
JAYDEN   I'm not trying to be bad.
LIAM   No one's saying that.
JAYDEN   Just since we've gotten here you guys keep treating me like I'm five.
LIAM   That's not true.
JAYDEN   Are you kidding? Jayden, that's rude, Jayden, don't play with your chopsticks, Jayden say hello, Jayden, respect people's culture...
LIAM   All valid things.
JAYDEN   Valid how?
LIAM   This is a different country. They do things differently. We don't want to stick out more than...
JAYDEN   Is it the people staring on the street got you so worked up?
LIAM   Not worked up.
JAYDEN   I dunno. You guys don't have to pretend so hard that it's normal. It just makes people stare more.
LIAM   Well, 'cuz here there's a–
JAYDEN   – It's fine, whatever.

LIAM   Jayden, watch your attitude please.

JAYDEN   Sorry.

LIAM   Besides, it's a big move, we just want to help you adjust better. Like with that waitress just now…

JAYDEN   Dad, can you guys just chill? I'm fine. We deal with stupid people back home too. And the whole point of moving is so things are different, right? We don't have to pretend like everything's the same.

Silence.

JAYDEN   Okay.

LIAM   No. It's good. This is good. We are communicating. In a way that isn't passive aggressive and sarcastic.

JAYDEN   Uh huh.

LIAM   Okay. Good. Just checking in. Glad to hear you're okay. You cope in whatever way you need to.

JAYDEN   I'm fine. Can I go on Skype now?

LIAM   Shouldn't they be in school now? Tell them to stop being a bad influence from across the Atlantic. Don't stay up too late. Becomes a habit.

JAYDEN   It's jetlag.

LIAM   Jetlag? We've been here for two weeks already. When you start school, you'll regret it.

JAYDEN   Love you.

LIAM   Love you.

Liam makes to leave.

JAYDEN   Dad?

LIAM   Yeah?

JAYDEN   Why is Papa so weird around Grandpa?

LIAM   They haven't lived together in a long time, not since Papa was a young man.

JAYDEN   Did something happen?

LIAM   Nothing you should worry about. That was a long time ago.

A ping.

JAYDEN   They're online, Dad.

LIAM   Leave you to it. Night, then.

JAYDEN Night, Dad. *(To laptop)* Hey guys! Guess what?
Lights down on the room.

//SPLIT SCENE//

RICHARD Going to smoke. You smoke?
KENNETH Pa, you shouldn't be smoking.
RICHARD Liam smokes? The boy smokes? You know when I used to do business in the UK, boys younger than him / smoking on the streets like...
KENNETH No, none of us smoke.
Silence.
RICHARD I see the way you raise the boy. I wonder where you get it from.
KENNETH Mm.
RICHARD Your mother, obviously. Not me.
KENNETH Yeah.
Silence.
RICHARD I was younger and more stupid.
KENNETH ...
RICHARD Good to know, least I didn't pass it on.
Long silence, then Richard exits, packing his cigarettes. Liam enters shortly after, joins Kenneth on the couch. They share a quick kiss.
LIAM He smiled at me.
KENNETH Seriously?
LIAM That's progress.
KENNETH That's as good as it's gonna get. You think it's too late to abandon ship?
LIAM Jayden thinks we're smothering him.
KENNETH That's not new. He okay? About the restaurant...
LIAM He's being stoic about it.
KENNETH I'll have a chat with him later. I hoped it'd be easier. You'd think things would've changed after fifteen years.
LIAM It's not as bad as it used to be. City's so gay now.

KENNETH	You know I caught my dad planning his own funeral.
LIAM	Sounds like a nice chat. *(Starts rubbing Kenneth's back)*
KENNETH	Like shitting bricks. Ten years's worth of constipated shit.
LIAM	God, your neck's like wood. *(Beat)*

They lie quietly on the couch.

//SPLIT SCENE//

BENMIN	So, is this like a date?
ZUL	Can be whatever you want, man.
BENMIN	Thanks.
ZUL	For what?
BENMIN	Never really met guys before. Was quite scared. But you're quite nice.
ZUL	Ever got boyfriend?
BENMIN	No, not really.
ZUL	Just broke up.
BENMIN	Oh. What happened?
ZUL	Normal lah. Drifted apart. You from Singapore?
BENMIN	Born in Malaysia, but I've been here since young.
ZUL	Most Singapore guys are assholes. Got a lot of issues. Chinese guys especially. All don't like Malay one. Lu boleh cakap melayu?[7]
BENMIN	Sikit-sikit[8] lah, not really.
ZUL	You're nice. Bought me green tea, some more. Most guys won't even buy condoms. After sex also just wipe the cum off and go home, can't even have like a conversation. Sorry, too much? We don't have to do anything if you don't want. I'm okay one.
BENMIN	You and your boyfriend…
ZUL	Ex boyfriend. Five years. Five years is very long for gays. You know right?

---

7. Lu Boleh Cakap Melayu? – (Malay) Do you speak Malay?
8. Sikit-sikit – (Malay) A little

BENMIN Is it. Never really thought about it.

ZUL He wanted a lot from me lah. Wanted to get flat. Get cats. Dreamer, sial, macam[9] getting married. I'm a very simple boy, you know. Just want someone to talk to. Go dancing with. Watch movie. He feels old lah. Thirty-six already, I'm only thirty. Want to settle down. Maybe I just want to play some more. *(Beat)* Eh late bloomer, you got go clubbing before?

BENMIN Like nightclub?

ZUL Taboo? Tantric?

BENMIN Never.

ZUL Eh, what? You how old already, haven't been to Tanjong Pagar?[10]

BENMIN Got walk past before lah, never go in.

ZUL That's it, let's do it.

BENMIN Huh. Don't want lah, isn't it very ex?

ZUL My treat lah, since you bought me green tea.

BENMIN No lah, it's okay.

ZUL It's Friday night. Come on lah, I suddenly got feeling.

BENMIN I don't have clothes.

ZUL Come on. I like you. I think you're cute. You think I'm cute. Let's go somewhere we can get cute. Shake it off, man, you're not going to be thirty forever. Don't need to stay too long. Can get supper after that.

You hungry?

Beat.

BENMIN A bit.

ZUL Set. I Uber now. Okay?

BENMIN Okay.

ZUL Okay.

Lights down.

---

9. Macam – (Malay) As if
10. Tanjong Pagar – Singapore's gay strip

//SPLIT SCENE//

In Richard's living room. Liam is massaging Kenneth's shoulders. Moments pass.

Suddenly, a phone call.

//SPLIT SCENE//

Elaine, phone cradled in her neck, at her desktop at home.

ELAINE *(calling off)* Babe. Rox! Get the clothes from the dryer, can? *(Aside)* Come on, pick up, pick up, pick up the phone.

//SPLIT SCENE//

Kenneth and Liam stir.

KENNETH *(rousing, noticing the phone)* It's Elaine. *(Picking up)* Hey.

\\ **ELAINE**	Hey, are you online?
KENNETH	Online? / No, I'm getting a–
\\ **ELAINE**	Go on YouTube now. Go, go, go. Someone recorded it.
KENNETH	Recorded what?
LIAM	What?
\\ **ELAINE**	The waitress. And you. At Palace Kitchen, the, the... from this afternoon!
KENNETH	Why would–
LIAM	– Put her on speaker!
\\ **ELAINE**	Are you doing it?
KENNETH	Liam, go open YouTube on the computer...
LIAM	// Why?
\\ **ELAINE**	// Search "Palace Kitchen waitress / discriminates against gay couple".
KENNETH	Type "Palace Kitchen waitress discriminates against gay couple"...
LIAM	What? / What?
KENNETH	Someone made a video and uploaded it.

LIAM *(finding it)* Oh my god.

\\ **ELAINE** Found it? It's all over my Facebook feed.

Liam clicks and the video runs.

KENNETH Oh my god.

\\ **ELAINE** I can't decide if I'm horrified or if this is amazing.

LIAM Kenneth, this is horrible.

\\ **ELAINE** I mean, can't really make your face out, right?

KENNETH Yeah, kinda blur.

\\ **ELAINE** Read the comments.

KENNETH Read the comments, Liam.

LIAM "Disgusting behaviour. Waitress ought to be fired."

KENNETH // Wow.

\\ **ELAINE** // "Boycotting this shit restaurant. Welcome to the twenty-first century, fuckers." / My favourite one.

LIAM "LOL, the guy looks quite hot."

\\ **ELAINE** Did you see the "guy looks quite hot" one?

Jayden enters the living room in a fluster, brandishing his phone.

JAYDEN Dad! Papa! Oh my god, guys, / someone...

KENNETH Yeah, we just...

JAYDEN It's mad! Did you see the comments? Did you see the one – *(scrolling)* "This guy looks quite hot" –

LIAM – yes we've seen it.

\\ **ELAINE** Well. What do you think?

KENNETH I don't know.

\\ **ELAINE** Horrible or amazing right?

KENNETH Maybe both?

\\ **ELAINE** Yeah.

JAYDEN Wow. Fuck.

KENNETH // Jayden!

LIAM // Jayden!

The video plays on. Jayden, Liam, Kenneth and Elaine staring at their screens.

SCENE THREE

The next morning. Poh Lin's flat. Benmin enters. He's had one of the most transformative nights of his life. There's a song and dance stuck in his head, a giddy smile on his face. He goes to the kitchen, fetches some water, drinks it happily. He sits down on the couch. A text message from Zul. He texts back eagerly. Enter Poh Lin from her bedroom. A tense moment passes between them. Exchange in Chinese.

POH LIN 刚回来啊？ [Just got back?]

BENMIN Mm.

POH LIN 不会出声的 hor。 [Dunno how to call me ah–]

BENMIN Sorry. 我跟朋友比较迟 – [Sorry. Friends and I stayed out later than–]

POH LIN –你喝酒 ah? [–been drinking?]

BENMIN ...

POH LIN 你几时开始喝酒的？ [Since when you drink one?]

BENMIN 都没有喝很多。 [Never even drink that much.]

POH LIN 大了突然 pattern liao liao。 [Old already suddenly pattern all come out.]

BENMIN ...

POH LIN 下次跟姨妈讲就好了嘛。那个 gate 整个晚上没有锁 leh。 [Next time just let Yi Ma know ma. Means I left the gate unlocked the whole night leh.]

BENMIN Orh.

Silence.

POH LIN 有粥，你要吗？ [Got porridge, you want?]

BENMIN Orh.

She fetches him a bowl.

BENMIN Sorry.

POH LIN 哎呀，你都三十岁了，sorry 什么？ [Aiya, you thirty years old already, sorry for what?] 我还在想你那么老了才来出 pattern。 [I also wonder how come you so old then show pattern.]

人家到了三十岁都没有 havoc 了，你现在才开始 havoc [By thirty most people give up already, you now then havoc.]

BENMIN　　　什么 havoc？只是喝酒聊天而已 mah。[What havoc? Just chit chat and drink only.]

POH LIN　　　我以前也是很会 havoc 的，以为我不懂。[I last time also quite havoc one leh, think I dunno.]

以前马来西亚女生来新加坡都是 havoc 的。[All Malaysian girls come to Singapore used to be havoc one.]

不相信，给你看一些旧照片。[Don't believe, I show you some old pictures.]

(While she searches for the right album) 昨晚你跟谁？[Who were you with?]

BENMIN　　　朋友。以前 Greenfield 的同学。[Friends. Greenfield classmates.]

POH LIN　　　粥好不好吃？[Nice not the porridge.]

BENMIN　　　Mm. *(She finds the photo album, to Benmin's mild irritation. He's fighting a hangover)* 1978 年，我刚来新加坡的时候。[1978, I just came to Singapore]

这是你的 Auntie Alice。你看。我们以前是 Robinsons shop girl. [This is your Auntie Alice. You see. We used to be Robinsons shop girls.]

BENMIN　　　那么瘦。[So skinny.]

我去睡了啊。粥很好吃。[Going to bed. Thanks for the porridge.]

POH LIN　　　记得昨天那两个男的吗？[You remember yesterday the two men?]

BENMIN *(making to leave)* Mm?

POH LIN　　　46 桌？很夸张啊。骂我，把食物丢在地上。[Table 46? Big drama ah. Shouted at me, throw food ah.]

BENMIN　　　Huh，为什么？[Huh, why?]

POH LIN　　　我说我不要 serve 他们。[I said I didn't want to serve them.]

BENMIN　　　...

POH LIN　　　做么？这样看我。你知道那个 ah boy 啊？[What? Look at me like that. You know the young boy?]

那个华人和那个 angmoh，他们说是他们的儿子。[The Chinese one and the ang moh, they say it's their son.]

BENMIN   Huh.
POH LIN   两个男人怎么养一个儿子？哪里有两个男人有孩子的？ [Two men how to raise a son? Where in this world got two men have a child one?]
我问你，你告诉我，我做得对不对？ [I ask you, you tell me, am I right anot?]
BENMIN   什么对不对？ [Right about what?]
POH LIN   不 serve 他们啦！老板也说他支持我。 [Not serving them lah! Boss said he support me.]
BENMIN   你那么肯定，还问我？ [If you're so sure, why you ask me?]
POH LIN   因为我知道不好吗。可是真的嘛，他们说是他们的儿子，就真的是 meh？ ['Cuz I know it's not nice mah. But really what, just because they say the boy is their son means it's true meh?]
你知道外面有很多变态的男人。很变态的。 [You know there are a lot of perverted men out there. Very perverted one.]
BENMIN   Mm.
POH LIN   去哪里都看到，男的跟男的，女的跟女的，乱来的。 [Everywhere also can see one, men and men, women and women, anyhow one.]
非礼小孩子。连神父都非礼小孩子，知道吗？ [Molesting children. Even the priests molest small children, you know?]
BENMIN   …
POH LIN   你们这些年轻人，想法都很 funny 的。你最好小心点。 [You all young people got a lot of funny ideas lah. You better be careful.]
BENMIN   小心什么？ [Careful for what?]
POH LIN   出去喝酒，不要让这些人影响你啊。 [Go out drinking, don't let all of these people influence you ah.]
BENMIN   你以为我跟谁出去？ [Who do you think I go out with?]
POH LIN   我只是说说而已啦。 [Just saying only lah.] *(Beat)*
你都 30 岁了，一直没有女朋友。还是现在开始找啊，不要浪费时间去玩。 [You're already 30, until now don't have girlfriend. Better start looking now ah, instead of wasting time go and party.]

BENMIN		要找人，我也要先出去嘛。 [Find people also must go out to find right?]
POH LIN		是啦，你很聪明啦，你。 [Yah lah you very smart lah, you.]

Silence.

BENMIN		姨妈，你以后不要这样对顾客，知道吗？ [Yi Ma, next time you really cannot treat customers like that, you know?]
POH LIN		…
BENMIN		他们也没有麻烦到你，对不对？ [Not say they give you trouble also right?]
POH LIN		也没有啦。 [Not trouble lah.]
BENMIN		Then?

Beat.

POH LIN		哎呀，随便啦。不要讲了。 [Aiya, whatever lah. Forget it.]
BENMIN		Mm。我去睡了。 [Mm. Going to sleep.]
POH LIN		先刷牙。 [Brush your teeth first.]
BENMIN		Orh.

Benmin heads off to his room. Poh Lin, anxious, remains in the living room.

SCENE FOUR

Various snatches of dialogue, on the streets, and on the airwaves:

DJ ONE	Guess what, Prata?
DJ TWO	What, Kosong?
DJ ONE	Did you see that video on YouTube? Damn drama man, this Palace Kitchen waitress refuses to serve this couple at a restaurant, but you guess why, Prata…
DJ TWO	What lah, Kosong…?
DJ ONE	'Cuz' it's a gay couple lah dei, and not just that they've got a son, man, and she flips out…

YOUNG MAN	… You got see that video not, fuck sial, nowadays even restaurant also got homophobia lor…

YOUNG WOMAN ... 你看好那个 video hor, 虽然很模糊，不过那个男的，好像陈伟强… Channel 8 的陈 伟强 lor! [Eh that video if you look closely right, it's damn blur but the guy looks like Randall Chen leh... there Randall Chen 那个 Channel 8 的啦！]

YOUNG WOMAN ... Actually the food there normal only lor...

YOUNG MAN ... Oh my god, confirm the Christians going to kick up a big fuss one, better go holiday if not my BP sure kena ...

CHORUS ... Shit man, it's on Buzzfeed, HuffPost, Vice...
...Online Citizen...
...Mothership...
...Stomp...
...Newnation...
...晚报… [Lianhe Wanbao]
...BBC...
...Guardian...
...New York Times...
...Washington Post...
...Telegraph...

SCENE FIVE

Two weeks later.

Richard's home. Jayden at the dining table with Richard.

JAYDEN So that's it? Just let the eggs sit in there?
RICHARD Trick is in the time. Six minutes. No more no less.
Richard cracks an egg.
RICHARD Perfect. Just nice.
JAYDEN Just nice.
RICHARD *(finishing the eggs)* Some soy sauce, some white pepper. Toast. Coffee?

JAYDEN	I don't drink coffee.
RICHARD	Milo.
JAYDEN	What's that?
RICHARD	Horlicks?
JAYDEN	I'm alright with orange juice.

Silence.

RICHARD I used to work in the UK, you know. Very briefly.

JAYDEN Mm hmm.

RICHARD After my university in Singapore, I went on that all Europe trip. Worked in a hotel kitchen in London.

RICHARD Made these eggs, you call them coddled eggs.

JAYDEN We don't really have these back home, though.

RICHARD No? It's like poached eggs.

JAYDEN Oh awesome, I love poached eggs.

RICHARD You like to cook?

JAYDEN They don't let me use the kitchen at home. Say I'm too messy.

RICHARD Your parents... you like your parents?

JAYDEN Heaps better than my birth parents.

RICHARD Ah. You don't miss them?

JAYDEN I don't remember much of them. But I have these scars. And sometimes I have nightmares, though. When my dads first adopted me, I used to have to sleep between them in their bed or I'd have panic attacks. Now I don't have to. These eggs are really good.

RICHARD You know they say Hainanese[11] men like to cook.

JAYDEN What's a Hainanese?

RICHARD Me. Your dad. Hainanese. Means our ancestors come from Hainan Island. In China. Many years ago, they moved here. Known to be good cooks. Served you Brits.

JAYDEN Oh, like slaves?

RICHARD No! Respectable servants. Anyway, since your dad is Hainanese, that means you're half Hainanese. British-Hainanese. You like to cook, that's from the Hainan side.

---

11. Hainanese – Generally referring to the community of Chinese migrants from Hainan island

JAYDEN	Doesn't sound too bad.
RICHARD	Not bad at all. You ever poach an egg?
JAYDEN	No.
RICHARD	I'll teach you sometime. They teach you cooking in school?
JAYDEN	No.
RICHARD	School okay?
JAYDEN	Yeah. I guess.
RICHARD	No?
JAYDEN	I mean it's fun. *(Beat)* There's just this one guy.
RICHARD	Ah.
JAYDEN	Yeah, David, he's American.
RICHARD	Of course.
JAYDEN	It's nothing major, it's just he keeps...
RICHARD	Keeps what?
JAYDEN	Like whenever he sees me he suddenly goes all sissy?
RICHARD	Sissy.
JAYDEN	Yeah, making fun of my dads...
RICHARD	Okay. Should tell your–
JAYDEN	–Oh my god, no. Grandpa no, no, no.
RICHARD	No?
JAYDEN	No, that's the last thing... They'll come down to school, they'll drag him and his parents into the principal's office... I mean it's happened before. They overreact and make me look like such a loser.
RICHARD	They're your parents, of course–
JAYDEN	– yeah I know, but he'll go away, people like him always go away. It's only 'cuz I'm new. The other kids hate him too. Just need to put up with it till it does. Okay?
RICHARD	Okay.
JAYDEN	Don't tell my dads, seriously, Grandpa.

//SPLIT SCENE//

Elaine's flat. Kenneth and Elaine sit over a pile of old photo albums and other keepsakes from the 90s. They're musing over these.

ELAINE   Remember this? You made me this tape I think.
KENNETH   Oh my god. Paula Abdul. Sinead O'Connor. Janet... Whitney... Anita Mui? I don't think so.

Elaine inserts the tape and starts playing. Extreme's 'More Than Words' comes on.

They listen to it for a while.

ELAINE   Oh right, yeah. Robin made this one.
KENNETH   Yup.
ELAINE   Oh man, we used to listen to this in the honours room all the time remember? Skipping Prof Low's bullshit lecture. You, me, Robin.
KENNETH   ...

They listen to the track for a while.

KENNETH   Pretty sure I have a box like this back home. In my dad's place. Must have left it there when Dad kicked me out. *(Beat)* You think Liam would've liked Robin, or more to the point, if Robin would've liked Liam?
ELAINE   Robin hated everyone.
KENNETH   Would've hated Liam just cause he's British.
ELAINE   Silly Robin.
KENNETH *(finding a photo, examines it and passes it to Elaine)* Look at this photo. Three of us.
ELAINE   Campus Rainbow Connection.
ELAINE   Never took off did it.
KENNETH   With a name like that?

Silence.

\\ **RICHARD** *(making eggs)* You know, I used to be a bully when I was in school.
\\ **JAYDEN**   This guy isn't a bully, he's too lame to be a bully.
\\ **RICHARD**   Okay, but still. I know how these people think, you know.
\\ **JAYDEN**   Uh huh.
\\ **RICHARD**   They only pick on you 'cuz they think you are too yellow-bellied.
\\ **JAYDEN**   Yellow-bellied.

\\ **RICHARD** Weak, like a turtle, you turn upside down, yellow belly to the sky, and you can't / do anything.

\\ **JAYDEN** I'm not weak. I just can't give a shit about—

\\ **RICHARD** —You gotta show you're not weak then. *(Plating the food)* Nah.

ELAINE Can you believe we thought we were activists.

KENNETH We thought we were the only gays on campus.

ELAINE Do you think Robin would've understood the concept of a viral video?

Kenneth, growing moody, plays another mix tape. 4 Non Blondes's 'What's Up' comes on.

KENNETH Robin would've turned this video saga into something, wouldn't he?

ELAINE Mm.

KENNETH Posters. Magazines. Songs. Flyers.

ELAINE Mm hmm.

KENNETH I mean. It's been, what, two weeks now? It's all over the Internet. Yesterday, it was on Huffington Post. And we're just sitting at home pretending it's not happening. The least we could do. Go public, right? Put a face to it.

ELAINE No.

KENNETH Yeah Liam said the same thing.

ELAINE Liam's right as usual. What for? Find trouble for yourself. Attention isn't what it used to be, you know.

KENNETH You know. I'm almost 50. What have I ever done to help someone else?

ELAINE You adopted Jayden.

KENNETH Yah, and only after years of being interrogated by social workers. It shouldn't have to be so hard. And that's the UK. Can't even imagine what it's like here.

ELAINE *(turning off the music)* Let me tell you what's going to happen if you go public.

KENNETH Yeah.

ELAINE And by public, by the way, you mean, what? Set up a Facebook page?

KENNETH Maybe.

ELAINE	Give interviews?
KENNETH	Maybe.

ELAINE Best case scenario: you get harassed daily. Worst case scenario: you get harassed daily and doors start closing. Bam, bam, bam. You have that visa interview coming up, right? Bam.

KENNETH But it makes me so angry to think it's just gonna fizzle out. Right? Admit that at least.

ELAINE	Possibly.
KENNETH	So that's the end of that?
ELAINE	We don't know that.

KENNETH Don't see any local media covering the story in a big way. 'Cuz there is no story if it's just a stupid / old woman, right?

ELAINE So what? Let it slip by. You get used to it.

\\ **RICHARD** You ever learn how to fight, in the UK? English boxing, top-notch.

\\ **JAYDEN** No. We don't even have contact sports in school. And I have two gay dads.

\\ **RICHARD** All the more.

ELAINE Every month something like this happens. Some idiot writes into the *Straits Times* forum. Some fundie nutjob goes viral. You get by knowing that most intelligent people think it's all fucking stupid. Then you move on to important things. Like your kids. And not getting harassed.

KENNETH Why do you keep saying harassed like it's actually...

ELAINE	...
KENNETH	What happened?

\\ **RICHARD** *(suddenly sprightly)* Okay, no, come, on your feet. Your Grandpa gonna teach you some self defence.

\\ **JAYDEN** What?

\\ **RICHARD** You want this David 'fler to stop bothering you? You really frighten him a bit. Just enough to scare him off.

\\ **JAYDEN** You mean hit him?

\\ **RICHARD** *(demonstrating)* Punch, one, two, block. Punch, one, two, block. Problem with everyone nowadays, they don't know how to fight for themselves.

Richard and Jayden get into a fighting stance.

ELAINE   Two years ago. Roxy left her old firm 'cuz her bosses were getting prank calls and emails every day from some Hardware Zone trolls. And you know all she did to piss them off was write an Op-Ed about some sexist Army Ad. They were flaming her online. 'Never serve NS just shut the fuck up or we will hunt down your daughter and let her have it.' Every day, without fail, some kind of stupid phone call. Eventually hate mail to our doorstep.

\\ **RICHARD**   To the face. To the chest. To the stomach. Light taps.

ELAINE   Then they found out about me, hacked into her company email and put 'lesbian cunt' next to everything with Roxy's name on it. Her email signature for a whole day was 'Regards, Roxy Chan, Lesbian Cunt.' They found out which nursery we sent Chloe to. We had to move her.

KENNETH   Did you call the police?

ELAINE   Yeah. Did fuck all.

\\ **JAYDEN**   To the face. To the chest. To the stomach. Light taps.

KENNETH   Can't believe it. Awful.

ELAINE   Died down like most things do. But it stays here, you know? Under your skin. A lot has changed since you guys left. It feels more free, but that means it's more free for these assholes too.

KENNETH *(picking up the photo of the three of them)* Can I keep the photo?

Jayden hits Richard a little too hard, and it winds him. The two end up laughing on the floor.

SCENE SIX

Days later.

Zul and Benmin in Zul's room, watching anime on Zul's desktop.

ZUL   So in this form he can only use his fire jutsu.

BENMIN   Orh.

Beat.

BENMIN   Aren't you a bit old to be watching cartoons.

ZUL   Eh it's anime okay, not just cartoon. It's not like for kids, so violent you see.

BENMIN   Boring leh, all they do is shoot fire.

ZUL	You very cute lah.
BENMIN	Really what.

Zul leans in to kiss Benmin, but Benmin pulls back slightly, and Zul kisses his cheek instead.

Pause.

ZUL	Sorry, too much, too soon?
BENMIN	It's okay lah. Thought we were just / watching cartoons.
ZUL	Yah, but you said you were bored what.
BENMIN	Yeah. Bored so watch something else lah.
ZUL	You very funny. Okay lah, you go choose what you want to watch. *(Closing the window)* Got cat videos, cooking videos, shit Singapore meenahs[12] say...

//SPLIT SCENE//

Richard's home. Jayden in his school uniform. Jayden is helping Richard set up a Facebook account.

JAYDEN	Need a picture now, Grandpa.
RICHARD	For what.
JAYDEN	It's called Facebook, you need to put a face there.
RICHARD	I don't have a—
JAYDEN	Smile.

Snap.

RICHARD	So ugly.
JAYDEN	You can change it later.
RICHARD	Okay, so how do I...
JAYDEN	Okay, you look for people here. See that's me. *(Beat)* That's Dad.

Enter Liam.

LIAM	Morning, Dad.
RICHARD	It's almost one.
LIAM	Is it.

---

12. Meenahs – (Malay) Derogatory term for working class Malay girls

JAYDEN	We got a half day today.
LIAM	I know. What're you up to?
JAYDEN	Facebook for Grandpa.
LIAM	That's sweet of you.
RICHARD	You always sleep in this late back home?
LIAM	No, I took some anti-histamines for my…
RICHARD	Must be nice not to work.
LIAM	Well.
RICHARD	Sorry. Tactless. Working on it.
LIAM	It's alright.
JAYDEN	I've added all of us.
RICHARD	Do I just go around adding people?
JAYDEN	No, Grandpa, that's creepy.
RICHARD	Liam, want some breakfast? Or lunch?
LIAM	I'm fine, I can't eat first thing. I get the runs.
RICHARD	The runs?
JAYDEN	Diarrhea. He's awful.
LIAM	Thank you, Jayden.
JAYDEN	Dad, did you see, the video made it to Buzzfeed.
LIAM	Buzzfeed, what's that…?
JAYDEN	Buzzfeed, Dad. It means it's gone / crazy viral.
RICHARD	This that video of the stupid old woman?
LIAM	Dad, do you mind if we don't.
JAYDEN	Yeah Grandpa, see, it's on your newsfeed.
RICHARD	Why are people so interested to watch her? Crazy women dime a dozen in this country.
LIAM	Well, it's controversial.
RICHARD	Yeah, anything that makes Singapore look bad is good business for the liberal Western media.
LIAM	…
RICHARD	I mean, you know what they say, was it Kipling, said you can't make a cat understand a dog.
LIAM	No, I don't / think so.

RICHARD   That Harry Lee, god rest his soul, crazy 'fler, you foreigners never really understand, but he knew what he was doing.

LIAM   That's great, Dad.

\\ **BENMIN** *(seeing a video)* What's this one?

\\ **ZUL**   Oh man, you haven't seen this before? *(Clicking on the video)* Eh you living under what rock.

\\ **BENMIN**   Been with you all the time.

\\ **ZUL**   Basically this crazy waitress is like shouting at this gay couple 'cuz they have a kid and she's like, 'Oh my god, I cannot accept that!'

\\ **BENMIN**   Shit.

\\ **ZUL**   What?

\\ **BENMIN** *(peering)* I think this is my workplace.

\\ **ZUL**   No fucking way.

RICHARD   What's the big deal? You think life is bad for… you know, for you people? Old woman like that going to make life very bad for you?

LIAM   Dad, I'm not sure where this is / coming from.

RICHARD   Don't look so frightened, just like a robust discussion. Gentlemanly discussion.

LIAM   Right. Well. If you were there, you'd know it was actually / very upsetting.

RICHARD   If I was there, I would have walloped the woman in the face.

JAYDEN *(laughing)* Oh man, Dad, he's amazing.

//SPLIT SCENE//

Kenneth is at work, speaking to his HR manager.

LIAM   I mean, Dad, it's easy to laugh about it, but…

RICHARD   Just having a laugh, don't take it seriously.

LIAM   Jayden, have you got any homework to do?

JAYDEN   Yeah.

LIAM   Go on up to your bedroom and do it then, please.

RICHARD   Yes, go ahead.

Jayden exits.

LIAM No, sorry, Dad I need to address it.

\\ **KENNETH** Uh huh. No, I was... no, they had made certain assurances, yes.

RICHARD Okay.

LIAM No disrespect, but... you know. Some of the things that woman said.

Called us perverts, do you know that?

RICHARD Stupid woman.

LIAM Yes, but lots of people say stupid things, you know, and if enough people repeat them, things have been known to happen. We worked so hard to adopt Jayden / so bloody hard, you really have no idea...

\\ **KENNETH** No, he's our son legally, both of us, just here I have the employment pass and... I'm sorry, can we speak more directly? Sorry. Thank you.

Is this about the visa?

LIAM I mean, think about that, and how some people still get away thinking we're perverts and child molesters. You see how that can be upsetting, right?

RICHARD Mm. Of course.

LIAM When we first moved in together sixteen years ago, we had a place in Joo Chiat.

\\ **KENNETH** No, the interview went very well. Liam cracked some jokes, the officer laughed. Like I said, assurances / were made.

LIAM After a while, we noticed the neighbours started giving us these funny looks all the time.

\\ **KENNETH** What do you mean in the current climate? What's changed?

LIAM Then they started slipping letters under our door. Horrible letters.

And some of the things that waitress said, you know, perverts... and it was like the same thing all over again.

\\ **KENNETH** That video? I didn't post it – what's that got to do with anything?

\\ **BENMIN** Shit, shit, shit, shit, shit, shit.

\\ **ZUL**   Oh my god, are you in the video?

\\ **BENMIN** *(almost in tears)* Shit, shit, shit, how long has this been… how many… shit, shit, shit.

\\ **ZUL**   Oi, you okay? Hey.

LIAM   One day, they called the police on us. Two men in uniform turned up at our door. Said they had to investigate. Asked us all kinds of humiliating questions: what's the nature of your relationship? Do you have visitors often? Would you be willing to take a drugs test? They thought we were running some kind of sex club.

RICHARD   Stupid idiots.

\\ **KENNETH** *(beat)* Okay. So what? What? So no gay couples are getting through? At all? Because of this stupid video? For how long?

\\ **ZUL**   What's wrong?

\\ **BENMIN**   Where's my phone? Pass me my phone!

\\ **ZUL**   Okay! Fuck.

LIAM   It takes one stupid idiot to make life very difficult, Dad. After the police, that's when we decided we had to leave. *(Beat)* We've been here little over a month and it's like nothing's changed. So I'm sorry if we're taking this a little too seriously.

RICHARD   Sorry.

Silence.

\\ **KENNETH**   Can we appeal? *(Beat)* / I better speak to my husband.

LIAM   Sorry, killed the mood, didn't I?

// **ZUL**   Babe what's going on?

// **BENMIN**   Wait.

Beat.

Kenneth dials Liam, Liam's phone rings.

//SPLIT SCENE//

The restaurant. Poh Lin is wiping down the tables. Her phone rings. Over the ringing of the phone, someone comes into the restaurant.

POH LIN   Eh, sorry，我们还没开门，你十一点才回来。 [Eh, sorry we haven't open yet, come back at eleven o'clock.]

(Beat) 什么？ [What?]

(Beat) 不知道你在说什么。我说我们还没有开门。 [I don't know what you're talking about. I said we're closed.]

(Beat) 你怎么知道？ [How did you know?]

(Beat) Eh，不关你的事。我是 – [Eh anyway it's none of your business. I was–]

// **BENMIN** *(dialing)* 听电话，听电话。 [Pick up, pick up.]

Poh Lin's phone starts ringing.

POH LIN   Eh！你以为你是谁？你以为全世界的人都要跟你们 – eh，不要进来， 我报警。 [Eh! Who do you think you are! You think everyone in the world got to follow you all and – eh, don't come in, I will call the police.]

阿朝！报警！ [Chew! Call the police!]

Phones ringing.

SCENE SEVEN

Overlapping snatches of dialogue and internet chatter:

DJ ONE   Eh Prata...
DJ TWO   What lah, Kosong...
DJ ONE   You got see the petition anot? To fire the Palace Kitchen Waitress...?
DJ TWO   Mixed feelings man, mixed feelings...
DJ ONE   Eh but ten thousand 'flers have signed lah, Prata...

... (Clickbait) 10 Things You Need to Know About Palace Kitchen Gate...

NEWSCASTER ONE The petition is started by a group of local LGBT activists and straight allies...

... (YouTube) For more info on the Purple Heart Rally, click on our Facebook page at www...

NEWSCASTER TWO The counter-petition, created anonymously but widely circulated through email chains, has received almost as many signatories...

DJ TWO Kosong, there's a rally summore dei...

DJ ONE Wahlau, means now every year got two gay rallies? This one what colour, Prata...

DJ TWO Purple la dei, hard to find purple tees, man...

NEWSCASTER THREE On News 5 Tonight, responding to the ongoing saga, dubbed, Palace Kitchen Gate by netizens, Minister for Home Affairs Ng Chew Seng has said on Facebook that the situation is 'turning into a witch-hunt'...

NEWSCASTER FOUR Some ten thousand supporters are expected to attend... including counter-protestors from the Wear White Campaign...

SCENE EIGHT

Lights up on a beach. East Coast Park. The horizon is hemmed in by ships, but it is a beautiful day. The sound of dogs barking, children. If there is an idyllic life in Singapore, it is family Sundays on East Coast Park. Kenneth and Liam spread out on a mat.

LIAM Jayden's getting tanned.

KENNETH He is.

LIAM So are you. I've missed the sun. Missed the east coast. You know people think in a place as small as Singapore there's no real difference between East and West, but there really is.

KENNETH Not really.

LIAM No. The air smells sweeter in the East. Time moves slower. The trees actually sway. You ever think about our Joo Chiat place.

KENNETH We could go visit later. Jayden might like to see it.

LIAM I miss the curry bush outside. The neighbours's frangipani. They were assholes but they had beautiful flowers.

KENNETH   In the foreground is a dustbin filled with last night's barbecue remains. A pigeon pecks cautiously at rotting corn kernels. Just behind it is a rat, sneaking up. Does the rat want to eat the pigeon?

Perhaps. In the background is the armada of ships that surrounds the whole island like it's on siege. East, west, it's all the same view.

LIAM   What're you going on about?

KENNETH   In school, for English, we used to have oral exams. We'd have to describe pictures. In the background, in the foreground, in the middle. Since you're going back to work.

LIAM   Don't jinx it. Paperwork isn't done.

KENNETH   No?

LIAM   No. There's some clearance pending 'from upstairs'. Sounds like the Vatican, doesn't it. 'From upstairs'. You think the schools are being extra careful now? Because of the... There's that petition now. And a rally.

KENNETH   The Purple Heart rally.

LIAM   Silly little name isn't it?

KENNETH   Worrying about the job isn't going to help you get it. And it's not the end of the world. We could always do a visa run. Johor's nice this time of year.

LIAM   No, I just really want that job. Not getting that visa, it's a blessing, really. It feels right. It's been almost eight years now that I've been out of it. Beginning to feel rusty, almost. Being back here, seeing our old stomping grounds, our old friends, it feels right. To be working again. *(Mock-seriously, mostly to himself)* Telling me not to worry doesn't help. Enjoy the beach. Hold my hand. It'll be okay. Let's just enjoy the moment.

//SPLIT SCENE//

Elaine sitting at Palace Kitchen. In the background, soft singing, church hymns, guitar. Enter Poh Lin with a broom.

POH LIN *(in English)* I say already, you all go away! You all stand here sing song is very nuisance! I don't like it. You don't use me to – *(in Mandarin Chinese)* 你们最好跟我滚，不然我像昨天报警你们才知道！

The singing grows more enthusiastic. Poh Lin lumbers away, frustrated, and then sees Elaine. It takes a while for her to recognize Elaine, but when she does:

ELAINE Excuse me.

POH LIN 哎呀你也是来找麻烦 啊？   [Aiya you also come and find trouble ah?] *(Beat, realizing Elaine doesn't comprehend)* Oh you also another trouble-maker come and find me for WHAT. You come here for WHAT?

ELAINE I'm here to eat.

POH LIN You're the one, that day with the…

ELAINE Yah, with the two guys. And the…

POH LIN The two, is it they tell these people to come everyday? Everyday either come here scold me or sing song for me.

ELAINE No, auntie it really isn't them.

POH LIN You here to…

ELAINE To eat. I like the fried rice.

POH LIN You go eat shit.

ELAINE Poh Lin…

POH LIN *(calling off)* Ah Chew.

ELAINE Poh Lin, can we talk for a while?

POH LIN Talk what.

ELAINE Not here to cause trouble. Sit down, please? I'll buy you a–

POH LIN You tell them to go away first.

ELAINE Tell…

POH LIN Those outside people tell them…

ELAINE *(getting up and yelling)* Hey you guys listen up! I'm Poh Lin's lawyer. This is technically an illegal assembly, and if the police come I will testify that you are creating a nuisance. Can? If you understand, please go, thanks.

The group clears.

POH LIN You really lawyer?

ELAINE No, I work in PR. Sit down, please. How are you, Auntie?

POH LIN Everyday like that lor. I hear outside got people not happy with me. People put things on the Internet. My boss not happy. Is it your…

ELAINE No, they've got nothing to do with–

POH LIN Then you come here for…?

ELAINE I think auntie, you know, it might be good for you to issue an apology, make this stop, I can help you with that, it might–

POH LIN What issue? Issue what?

ELAINE An – is there someone here who can translate…

POH LIN Say sorry? To who?

ELAINE To the–

POH LIN Say sorry for what?

ELAINE For. You know. You treated them very–

POH LIN *(getting up)* It's my right. It's really I don't think that two men can–

ELAINE Well, they can, they take very good care of–

POH LIN And now they send all their people come after me–

ELAINE No, they haven't–

POH LIN You all think attack me very – you all rich people, can speak English, can use the, the, Internet all this, come and, I don't know how to, I everything also, I very simple.

ELAINE Poh Lin, you know you were the one who started this, I was there, I was–

POH LIN Ah you also come and scold me, see, I know one. All of you are the same one. I see you short hair, like that, you also like them, right? Take their side.

ELAINE I'm their friend.

POH LIN You better go, or I call police also.

ELAINE Poh Lin, please.

POH LIN Go away. Go away!

An impasse. Elaine exits.

Lights down.

//SPLIT SCENE//

The beach. Enter Richard with Jayden, eating chips.

LIAM Your dad's given up. *(Calling out)* You weren't gone very long. Nice chips, Jayden?

JAYDEN Soggy, and the ketchup here tastes weird.

RICHARD That's chili. *(Extending his wrist to Kenneth)* This thing stopped working halfway.

JAYDEN Papa, what's that?

KENNETH *(to Richard)* It's a Fitbit darling, your Grandpa needs to get more exercise after his stroke. Pa, you didn't turn it on.

JAYDEN We saw these huge rocks at the other side of the beach, Dad.

LIAM Bulwarks.

JAYDEN Sounds like a bad word, Dad.

LIAM They're called bulwarks.

KENNETH Jayden, did your Grandpa smoke a cigarette?

JAYDEN Two.

KENNETH Pa, not in front of...

RICHARD I was standing away when he went to buy a snack lah.

LIAM Jayden did you scrape your knee?

RICHARD Oh that, yah, he climbed up the...

JAYDEN The bulwark.

LIAM We'd better go wash that out. Come on.

JAYDEN Do you wanna go see the bulwark, Dad? Climb up? The view is nice.

KENNETH *(as they exit)* Jayden, don't make your Dad climb at his age.

Jayden and Liam exit. Richard and Kenneth on the mat, quiet, but not hostile.

KENNETH *(turning on Richard's Fitbit)* You've got to try and hit two hundred today, okay?

RICHARD Is that metres or kilometres or...?

KENNETH Calories.

Comfortable silence.

RICHARD *(looking out)* You ever been on a ship? No? I worked my way back from the UK on one of those. Travelling days are long over.

KENNETH You travelled plenty when I was a boy.

RICHARD That was for work.

KENNETH Yeah.

RICHARD Hardly around. Least you can watch him grow up. *(Beat)* Were you there, for his first day of school? Jayden?

KENNETH ...

RICHARD I was never around for all your first days at school. Except primary one. You remember?

KENNETH No, you were in China.

RICHARD Oh.

KENNETH I was in Dubai. On Jayden's first day.

Silence.

RICHARD Doesn't mean anything. Life is busy.

KENNETH Maybe I do take after you.

RICHARD No. You're not.

KENNETH I mean. Nowhere near as bad as you. You were a tyrant. Always shouting. At me and Ma. Remember you'd whack me with the belt sometimes?

RICHARD My father did that to me.

KENNETH I–

RICHARD That's long over.

Silence.

RICHARD When I was growing up, the neighbourhood boys, we would play football and all that jazz, at this field, right. There was this other boy from the neighbourhood. Scrawny 'fler, skinny, pale skin, you know, a bit soft. He would sit around the field and watch us. Did I ever tell you this story, Ken?

KENNETH ...

RICHARD No? One day, we got fed up with the bugger staring at us, so we asked him if he wanted to come join us for a drink. And he followed. Then we dragged him to an alley and we walloped the bastard. He disappeared after that. I'm not proud of it, but it was a different time.

Silence.

KENNETH   That's horrible.

RICHARD   Never saw the bugger again. Until one day, I was starting up the company. I had to take a loan from the bank, major loan, and guess what? Sitting across the table is that same scrawny pale 'fler. I thought habis[13] over, but I wasn't sure if he remembered me, everything seemed okay. Until he's about to sign off the contract, then he suddenly stops, and the bugger, he says, "You know, I remember you." Stares at me a good one minute. Then he signs the thing, and it's over.

KENNETH   …

RICHARD   I'll never forget how the bugger toyed with me. Doesn't matter what you are, if you're weak, you're weak. Strong, you're strong. In life, you just need to find a way to have power over people. So what if you're gay? A rich banker can do whatever he wants. Life turned out okay for you, didn't it?

You think about it, why I was the kind of father I was. Saw you as a boy, soft and girly. Why do you think I pushed you so hard?

KENNETH   …

RICHARD   You think you're like me, but you're not. Because, you know, when you are old, he's going to look after you because he loves you, not out of guilt.

Silence.

SCENE NINE

Zul and Benmin shopping for clothes.

ZUL   You sure you don't want to wait for me at the Ya Kun.[14]

BENMIN   No, I'll be bored.

ZUL   Yah but you just stand here with your black face, it's like killing the H&M vibe lah. *(Brandishing a shirt)* You should get this.

BENMIN   It's a bit–

ZUL   V-neck doesn't mean gay. It's sexy. Also blue is a good colour.

BENMIN   What are you looking for?

---

13. Habis – (Malay) Done
14. Ya Kun – A popular chain of cafés

ZUL Nothing lah, just look look. Can you just go wait in the Ya Kun, please?

BENMIN Why?

ZUL It's faster if I'm on my own lah.

BENMIN I thought you're just looking around.

As Zul ambles through the store, Benmin realizes what's going on.

BENMIN Are you looking for a purple t-shirt?

ZUL ...

BENMIN You know if you want I can lend you.

ZUL ...

BENMIN I thought you said you're not going to the rally.

ZUL Yah obviously I lied 'cuz I'm dating the nephew of Palace Kitchen bitch, okay?

BENMIN How can you even think of going?

ZUL I don't want to talk about this now.

BENMIN I already said, she's more than just my auntie, how can you – you know they want her to get fired or what. You know that affects me also right?

ZUL Yah and how many times I got to say it's not just about your auntie.

BENMIN Yah then what is it about? You got sign the form also?

ZUL The petition.

BENMIN Yah whatever, you also got sign right.

ZUL That's my business, not yours.

BENMIN Really? I'm your boyfriend right?

ZUL *(beat)* I dunno, are you?

Beat.

ZUL *(pulling Benmin aside)* Look, this is weird, okay. I don't know how to deal with it.

BENMIN Just don't go.

ZUL But I want to. I believe in it. Your auntie really fucked up okay? She really fucked up.

BENMIN She didn't know what she was doing.

ZUL You're kidding. It's all on video, okay? What you see is what you get. She said all those things. Okay, maybe you're new to this.

Yah now you like to suck cock, now you like to get fucked, but there's more than that okay. You've got to deal with it: people treat us like shit, talk shit about us, and they always get away with it. I'm sick of people always getting away with it. I'm sorry this time it's your auntie, I really wish it wasn't, because I think you should go too.

Beat.

BENMIN You're asking me to–

ZUL No I'm not.

BENMIN You said–

ZUL You should. I said you should. Fucking stand up for something.

BENMIN You're asking me to take sides.

ZUL You're gay, there's only one side.

BENMIN I'm not gay.

Beat.

BENMIN I don't want to be gay.

ZUL …

BENMIN Nowadays right, it's like I also don't know who my auntie is? Who is this woman who since young look after me. I can only see this crazy waitress bitch that everyone hates.

ZUL …

BENMIN Last week, we were eating breakfast. Suddenly I felt. I hated her. Like really fucking hate her. She was sitting down, eating her soft boil egg, and I just wanted to scream at her. 'WHY ARE YOU SO STUPID?! WHY ARE YOU SO RETARDED?! WHY ARE YOU SO OLD-FASHIONED?! WHY CAN'T YOU JUST LEAVE PEOPLE ALONE?!'

ZUL Did you?

BENMIN No. 'Cuz then I looked at her and felt bad. Because, wah, she's become so old. Her hands are so wrinkled, got these brown spots and thick veins from carrying plates every day.

ZUL I'm not asking you to take / sides lah, Ben.

BENMIN You're taking their side.

ZUL Taking my own side.

BENMIN Ever think about the two guys? Seriously. What the fuck do I care about these two guys? These married guys? They've got everything, and they want to take everything away from her.

ZUL If you weren't gay, think you would be on the other side.

Silence.

BENMIN Can't I just live quietly?

ZUL ...

BENMIN Just be with you, stay happy?

ZUL ...

BENMIN People are always going to hate us. Why give a shit.

Silence.

ZUL Can you just go wait at the Ya Kun please?

SCENE TEN

Day of the rally.

Hong Lim Park.[15] *Kenneth, Liam, Richard and Jayden are at the fringes of the rally. There's a festive atmosphere, whistling, cheering, music. Zul has volunteered, is giving out flyers and directions.*

JAYDEN Why can't we go in, that's where the drag queens are, Papa, I want to see them.

KENNETH Darling, if you're not Singaporean you gotta stay here, darling.

JAYDEN You're Singaporean.

KENNETH I gave that up a long time ago.

RICHARD Should never have opened this bloody Speaker's Corner, look at all these hooligans.

KENNETH Pa.

RICHARD In Harry Lee's heyday all these 'flers would be locked up.

LIAM Well, thank god he's dead then.

JAYDEN You've got issues Grandpa.

---

15. Hong Lim Park – A park in Chinatown designated as Singapore's Speaker's Corner, the only part of the city where protests and demonstrations are permitted, albeit with strict regulations. Under pain of police action, foreigners are not allowed to participate in demonstrations at the park, with anything from standing at a distance to taking photographs potentially counting as participation

RICHARD All this protest nonsense, this is all Western liberal bias. Waste of a good Saturday.

LIAM Yeah Kenneth, let's not stay too long.

KENNETH We should see it through. It's on our behalf.

LIAM No one knows it's us.

KENNETH Yeah but we do.

LIAM There's police here, and you know we can't even / participate.

KENNETH I know.

LIAM Someone's bound to recognize us, and then what? The last thing we need is that sort of attention.

KENNETH Could we at least stay to hear to speeches?

LIAM That's gonna be the whole thing, Ken.

Zul enters.

ZUL *(giving out flyers)* Hey guys, if you haven't signed the petition yet, take a flyer, this has instructions on how to do it.

KENNETH Thanks.

ZUL *(noticing Liam and Jayden)* Oh, sorry to ask, but are you guys at least PR?[16] 'Cuz foreigners aren't allowed to join the rally, just stay around here is good enough. You know lah.

KENNETH Yah we...

LIAM We were just about to go.

JAYDEN Aw, Dad, Papa, I want to stay!

ZUL Oh, you guys are a family – that's so cute.

KENNETH Thanks.

ZUL How long you been together?

KENNETH About sixteen years.

LIAM Seventeen actually.

ZUL *(to Jayden)* I'm Zul.

JAYDEN I'm Jayden.

RICHARD *(to Zul)* Young man, you with these rally people?

ZUL I'm just a volunteer.

---

16. PR – Permanent residents

RICHARD You not worried these government 'flers gonna come and tangkap[17] you?

ZUL Think they're more scared of us, uncle.

RICHARD Yah, you think that.

ZUL You guys are a beautiful family.

LIAM Thank you.

ZUL All the best. Don't get too close.

Zul parts.

LIAM Even they seem a bit on edge.

KENNETH Pa, can you take Jayden farther away?

JAYDEN Oh come on.

RICHARD Where?

KENNETH There's a café across the street, just wait for us there.

JAYDEN I want to stay.

KENNETH We'd rather you not, Jayden, it might get–

JAYDEN But it's like a carnival!

RICHARD Yah with police. You ever see police at a carnival? Come boy, I'll get you a coffee.

JAYDEN *(as they exit)* I don't drink coffee.

LIAM So many angry, sweaty bodies, it's like a club, but everyone's pissed off.

KENNETH Sorry, I know you're nervous.

LIAM Not nervous, just – you never know with this place anymore, do you? You think you've got a visa, the next day you're hunting for a job. You think you've got the job, and then they tell you the position's closed. Feels like a carnival now, but give one man a gun and he says he'll fire on the crowd.

KENNETH That was just a Facebook troll.

LIAM But he thought it. That's bad enough *(Beat)* What?

KENNETH Nothing. I used to cruise here. Ages ago.

LIAM Tell me something new.

KENNETH It was furtive then, bushes and newspapers, darkness. Now this. In broad daylight. Purple everywhere. Balloons.

LIAM Police.

---

17. Tangkap – (Malay) Catch.

KENNETH	Police. *(Beat)*
KENNETH	If he was alive, Robin would've been right at the centre.
LIAM	Robin your ex?
KENNETH	Right in the middle with a loud-hailer. Screaming.
LIAM	And where would you be?
KENNETH	Next to him, telling him to tone it down?
LIAM	Maybe we wouldn't have met, then.
KENNETH	Well if we had, then I'd be right here, holding your hand. *(Beat)* Just wish, looking at this… you know, wish I could put my name to it, my face. Say something, anything, instead of running away again, and again. Take ownership for once. I'd hand deliver the petition to that bloody waitress myself.
LIAM	Don't you think you've done enough?

Liam kisses Kenneth's head as they watch the proceedings.

//SPLIT SCENE//

Lights on Poh Lin's home. Poh Lin is lying down on the sofa, staring blankly ahead.

Benmin enters the living room from his bedroom. Exchange in Chinese.

BENMIN	姨妈。 [Yi Ma.]
POH LIN	…
BENMIN	雨停了。去楼下啦。走一下。 [Rain stop already. Go downstairs lah. Walk a bit.]
POH LIN	…
BENMIN	你不可以每天躲在屋里。 [You cannot hide inside forever.]
POH LIN	你不要管我。 [Leave me alone]
BENMIN	…
POH LIN	我看早报说，今天有人在牛车水集合。 [Read in Zhao Bao today got people gathering in Chinatown.]
BENMIN	Mm.
POH LIN	阿 Chew 说叫他们去死。 [Ah Chew said tell them go and die.]

BENMIN 不要担心 lor。 [Yah, so don't worry lor]

POH LIN 在那里做了三十年，没有功劳也有苦劳，对不对？ [30 years working there, must mean something right?]
(Beat) 我是不是真的做错了？ [You think I really did something so bad?]

BENMIN ...

POH LIN Hmm? Ben?

BENMIN 时代变了。 [Things have changed.]

POH LIN ...

BENMIN 我觉得⋯ 我觉得你应该尊重别人的生活。 [I think... I think you need to respect how people want to live.]
他们没有讲你，你为什么要讲他们？ [They never say you, what for you say them?]

POH LIN ...

BENMIN But hor，你是我的姨妈。 [But you're my Yi Ma.] 你做什么都好，对我来说你不是坏人 [Whatever you do, to me you're not a bad person.]

POH LIN Okay.

Silence.

Enter Elaine. She appears at the door. Exchange in English.

ELAINE Hello. Excuse me.

BENMIN *(going to the door)* Yes?

ELAINE Hi, I'm sorry. I'm looking for Poh Lin.

BENMIN Who are you?

ELAINE Uh... my name is Elaine. Hi. Are you her son? Is she... I just wanted to check on her.

POH LIN *(walking over)* 哎呀，是谁⋯ [Aiya, who is it...]

Poh Lin recognizes Elaine. A long pause.

ELAINE Poh Lin?

POH LIN *(to Benmin)* 她是那两个人的朋友。 [She's the friend of the couple.]

BENMIN *(to Elaine)* You're the couple's friend? You here to cause trouble?

ELAINE No, no, no trouble. I...

BENMIN	Why are you here? Don't you all have the rally?
ELAINE	Auntie, it's not too late to make an apology.

Poh Lin makes to walk off.

ELAINE	No. *(To Poh Lin)* Auntie, please.
POH LIN *(to Benmin)*	关门。 [Close the door.]
ELAINE	I can help...

Silence.

Elaine exits.

Poh Lin goes back onto the sofa. Benmin goes to comfort her.

//SPLIT SCENE//

A bench in the park on the fringes of the rally. Richard and Jayden observing from afar. There are distant strains of a speech made by the lead activist.

RICHARD   Okay, that's enough. These communists getting on my nerves.

JAYDEN   Just a bit longer. My dads think I don't know what's going on, but this is about us, isn't it?

RICHARD   Suppose.

JAYDEN   That's a lot of people.

RICHARD   Yah, it's just going to be the same thing for the next hour, so much talking, and you can't even hear anything. Waste of a good Saturday. We better go now. Bound to be trouble where people are stirring shit.

JAYDEN   Stirring shit. That's a good one.

RICHARD   Yah, don't stir shit and tell your parents I taught you that.

JAYDEN   One, two, punch. To the face, to the chest, to the stomach. Light taps.

RICHARD   What?

JAYDEN   If there's trouble.

RICHARD   One, two, punch. Guard. To the face, to the chest, to the stomach. Hard jabs.

A roaring cheer in the distance.

Elaine, who has arrived at the rally, finds Kenneth and Liam.

ELAINE	Hey.
LIAM	Where were you?
ELAINE	Got held up.

Another cheer.

KENNETH	They're starting.
LIAM	We better go and get Jayden.
KENNETH	He'll be fine.

//SPLIT SCENE//

Zul, thick in the crowd, listens to the speech.

The strains of the speech grow clearer.

ACTIVIST Faggots, countrymen, lesbos and queers! *(A cheer)* You know why we're here! *(A cheer)*

JAYDEN You can hear the speech fine, Grandpa.

\\ *Zul picks up his phone. Dials it. Back home, Benmin, sitting by Poh Lin, picks up.*

\\ **ZUL** *(on the phone)* Ben. Listen.

\\ *Zul holds his phone up in the air.*

Richard has noticed a small group of counter-protestors on the fringes of the rally, near them.

RICHARD Come, Jayden, time to go.

JAYDEN Let him finish first, Grandpa.

ACTIVIST You know what's up! We're angry! We're pissed off! *(A cheer)* And it's about time, so we're here to do something about it! *(A cheer)*

Galvanised, the counter-protestors suddenly retort.

COUNTER	Perverts! Perverts! Perverts!
RICHARD	Jayden.
JAYDEN	Troublemakers?
RICHARD	Bloody idiot fundies. Come on, let's go.

ACTIVIST To the people from the other camp here to stir shit today, we say 'GO AWAY!' *(Cheers)*
COUNTER Bloody perverts!

Liam moves away.

RICHARD Jayden I said we are going now.
JAYDEN Do you hear them?
RICHARD Don't bother with that, come on.
JAYDEN Grandpa. Do you hear them?
RICHARD It's not safe, come on.
ACTIVIST To same-sex parents in our midst who struggle just to make it through each day, we say, 'HANG IN THERE!' *(A cheer)*
COUNTER Pedophiles!
JAYDEN *(to the counter-protestors)* Hey!
RICHARD Jayden, don't–
JAYDEN I said HEY!

Jayden is distressed, galvanized.

ACTIVIST To the establishment, laws and values that have stood for so long before Palace Kitchen, we say, 'IT'S TIME FOR A HEART TO HEART TALK.' *(A cheer)*
JAYDEN Oi! Asshole!
RICHARD Don't antagonize them.
JAYDEN One, two, punch, Grandpa. *(To the counter-protest)* Oi! My parents are not pedophiles!
RICHARD Jayden!
JAYDEN Oi! Leave my parents alone!

The counter-protestors advance on Jayden.

ACTIVIST To Minister Ng Chew Seng whose comments have no place in the 21st century *(a cheer)*, / we say 'LISTEN TO THIS!' *(A cheer)*
JAYDEN *(overlapping with the speech)* You have no idea who we are! You know nothing about us!
RICHARD Oi! You leave him alone you bloody fucking fundie idiots!

Lights down on Jayden and Richard.

//SPLIT SCENE//

Poh Lin's home. Poh Lin and Benmin on the sofa. Her landline starts to ring.

\\ **ACTIVIST**   And to the waitress, Chew Poh Lin, who had no idea that her little act of hate could spark off this massive movement across our island, we say THANK YOU! *(A cheer)*

Benmin listens to the speech over his phone.

ACT TWO
SCENE ONE

Disorientation.

Auburn. Late afternoon.

KENNETH	Show's at eight.
LIAM	And?
KENNETH	Elaine has our tickets.
LIAM	I wanna nap.
KENNETH	You can nap during the show. It's modern dance.
LIAM	No…
KENNETH	Elaine's girlfriend is in it.
LIAM	Do we have to? It's only six.
KENNETH	Already six. Anyway after that we can go out with Tommy and the boys and get some drinks.
LIAM	I need a disco nap, I've been on my feet all day.
KENNETH	Fine, I'll wake you up in fifteen.
LIAM	No, come lie down with me.
KENNETH	Such a pig.

Kenneth joins Liam on the couch, rather he sits on the floor and leans against it as Liam lays back.

LIAM	Do you like my flower arrangement? On the dining table. I stole some frangipani from the fuckers next door.
KENNETH	They're beautiful.
LIAM	I love that tree. Do you think we might grow one too?

KENNETH   Could find out.
LIAM   Yeah.
KENNETH   You know the tree is full of hantu right?
LIAM   Ghosts?
KENNETH   Pontianaks.
LIAM   You think they'll flourish in the UK?
KENNETH   Pontianaks?
LIAM   Frangipanis.
KENNETH   Why?
LIAM   Nothing. Would miss it that's all. If we ever left. That tree. The smell of it.
KENNETH   ...
LIAM   Not that we are leaving.
KENNETH   Why are we talking about leaving?
LIAM   Moving is good, keeps you nimble.
KENNETH   To the UK?
LIAM   Might be good. You think?
KENNETH   What difference would it make.
LIAM   We could get a really nice place in the suburbs for what we're paying here. Grow rhododendrons. Be domestic.
KENNETH   I like it here.
LIAM   You're used to here. What do you have here? Your parents are twenty minutes away, but you never–
KENNETH   It's not–
LIAM   I miss my parents. *(Beat)* I miss lots of things. I love it here, but there's – you know, do I want to grow old here?
KENNETH   Grow old?
LIAM   Yah, become proper adults. Get married.
KENNETH   Married.
LIAM   My mate in the public service back home says there's a bill. Civil Partnership. Might be passed as soon as next year.

Beat.

KENNETH   Mr Liam Butler, are you proposing?
LIAM *(beat)* I think so?

KENNETH   Proposing over a bill? That's very Singaporean.

Beat.

KENNETH   Civil partnership.
LIAM   And who knows. Wedding bells, baby showers.
KENNETH   Baby showers.
LIAM   It's a boy. It's a girl.
KENNETH   But not here.
LIAM   No, not here. Not where the neighbours slip us hate mail.
KENNETH   What about the frangipani?
LIAM   Well what about the frangipani? If those assholes next door can grow them, maybe they aren't that beautiful after all.

Beat. A kiss.

A gradual shift.

LIAM   Is that a maybe-yes?
KENNETH   I'll ask. HR.
LIAM   Can't sleep now.
KENNETH   Me too.
LIAM *(getting up)* Or think, really.
KENNETH   Me too.
LIAM   Or breathe.
KENNETH   Me too.

A knock at the door. Beat. Liam goes to get it.

LIAM   It's the police.

A shift. A hospital. Rapidfire.

RICHARD   Son, the police are here. They're done with me, wanna talk to one of you.
LIAM   I'll talk to them.

Liam exits.

KENNETH   We shouldn't have been there. Shouldn't have been there, fuck.
RICHARD   It's okay, those bastards are going to get it.

Silence.

KENNETH   Why was he there? Wasn't he at the–
RICHARD   He wanted to see.
KENNETH   Why was he there at all? I told you to–
RICHARD   I tried to–
KENNETH   No you didn't try hard enough. And when he starts fighting with grown men, you–
RICHARD   I got too angry, they were yelling, he was–
KENNETH   Pa, you were just supposed to take him to the fucking café.
RICHARD   I know! What's the point of talking about it now?
KENNETH   And because of that you also got hurt.
RICHARD   It's nothing.

Richard exits.

Silence. Enter Liam and Elaine.

LIAM   The police are leaving. *(Hugs Kenneth)* It's okay, Ken. He'll be up soon.
KENNETH   You okay?
LIAM   Not really.
ELAINE   *(beat)* Well. Roxy's worried, I'm going to head home.
LIAM   *(aside)* Thanks Elaine.
ELAINE   Call me when he's up. *(Beat)* If, uh, it's any consolation, the waitress got fired.
KENNETH   It is.
LIAM   Poor thing.
KENNETH   Poor thing?
ELAINE   None of this should ever have happened.
KENNETH   No, she should've kept her fucking mouth shut then maybe none of this would have happened. Is her son lying in a hospital bed? Is she sitting in a hospital wing worried sick?
ELAINE   Her name is Poh Lin– Nevermind. Call me.
LIAM   Say hi to Roxy, Elaine.

Elaine exits.

LIAM   You didn't have to snap at her.
KENNETH   I'm sorry.

LIAM   She'll understand.
KENNETH   I feel sick. You remember that day the police came to Joo Chiat. My god, I spent years running from that feeling, and now it's back here again, right here. Except now our son...
LIAM   I did say not to go.
KENNETH   I know.
LIAM   I did.
KENNETH   I'm sorry.
LIAM   Your dad doesn't have very good judgment.

Enter Richard.

RICHARD   Boy's up.
LIAM   Thank god.

They move to Jayden's hospital room.

//SPLIT SCENE//

Zul and Benmin at the kopitiam at Toa Payoh. Benmin is wordlessly drinking green tea.

// ZUL   He bought me a gin and tonic. And we talked and talked.

The hospital.

JAYDEN   My face feels like crap.
RICHARD   Bet it does.
JAYDEN   I forgot to guard, Grandpa.
LIAM   What's he talking about?
RICHARD   Aiya.
JAYDEN   Am I in trouble?
KENNETH   No, but the people who hurt you are, so it's fine. You hurting anywhere else?
JAYDEN   Not really, just my face I guess. I had the best dream though, Dad. Remember Kara from Form One? She was in it, and we snogged like crazy Dad.
LIAM   That's lovely darling.
KENNETH   Don't ever pick a fight again, Jayden, you understand? You know how worried we were?

JAYDEN	I was just, they called you–
LIAM	It's alright.
JAYDEN	It's not, they called you pedophiles so I fought them.
// **ZUL**	He bought me another gin and tonic. Introduced me to his friends.
KENNETH	We're a family, so we do things together. So next time–
LIAM	Hopefully no more next times.
KENNETH	Next time you come find us.
// **ZUL**	And I liked it. He was hot. He asked me over.
KENNETH	Okay, Jayden?
JAYDEN	Okay.

The family embrace, lights down on them.

ZUL	But that's it. I didn't go. We didn't do anything.
BENMIN	…
ZUL	Can you say something?
BENMIN	My auntie got fired.
ZUL	I know.
BENMIN	Means I don't really give a shit about this.
ZUL	…
BENMIN	You happy?
ZUL	What?
BENMIN	My auntie got fired. It's what you all wanted, right?
ZUL	No. Yes. I dunno.
BENMIN	Was he one of the–
ZUL	Yeah.
BENMIN	The people who–
ZUL	Organised, yeah.
BENMIN	Slut.

Beat.

ZUL	We didn't do anything, it's just–
BENMIN	Why?
ZUL	I was lonely.
BENMIN	Then you can come find me what, for–

ZUL	I didn't want to see you–
BENMIN	Because–
ZUL	Because I was having a good time.
BENMIN	With–
ZUL	Not with him, that's not what I meant. With the people there, after the rally, they were cool people, I could talk to them and–
BENMIN	Cannot talk to me.
ZUL	That's not–
BENMIN	Okay, I understand. I'm not smart enough, not–
ZUL	No!
BENMIN	Not whatever enough, not hot enough?
ZUL	No!
BENMIN	Not cool enough?
ZUL	Maybe.
BENMIN	Not cool…
ZUL	I… For the past few weeks. We just keep fighting about you and your auntie. I – it's, tell me how am I supposed to deal with this correctly?
BENMIN	Listen to me maybe? I told you not to go for the rally but–
ZUL	Yah, but I had a great time. I had a fucking great time, Ben. You heard it. It was amazing. There were so many people there, all–
BENMIN	All?
ZUL	I wish we could've been there together. 'Cuz you're my boyfriend, and I wanted you to hold my hand, listen to the speeches. Instead, here we are stuck.

Silence.

BENMIN	Don't blame me.
ZUL	No I'm not–
BENMIN	Don't blame me.

Silence.

ZUL	I saw a family at the rally. Two dads, one son, with the grandfather.
BENMIN	So.
ZUL	I dunno. Reminded me of my ex boyfriend.

BENMIN	He cheated on you.
ZUL	Yah. He did. With some Canadian guy he met at Tantric. Because he said he didn't see a future with me. He said I didn't have dreams.
BENMIN	You want–
ZUL	I don't know. Maybe I do. I didn't even really think about it until today. What do you want?
BENMIN	I don't know.
ZUL	I can see what my ex means. I think you... don't even talk about dreams, you never even started dreaming. I let that guy flirt with me 'cuz he's everything you're not. I can't bring you out to meet my friends, 'cuz you're scared they'll post pictures of you. I can't come to your place, obviously. When we're out, you act like we're just friends. We're hiding all the time. I'm 30, I don't want to hide anymore–
BENMIN	My auntie is the most important thing in my life.
ZUL	You can have your own life you know.
BENMIN	My auntie is the most important thing in my life.
ZUL	Okay.
BENMIN	I don't have time for anything else now.
ZUL	Okay.

Beat.

BENMIN	I can't be gay anymore.
ZUL	You can't just switch it off.
BENMIN	Actually yah I think I can. Before I met you, I never had to think about these things. Now I just want it to stop. Just everything, stop. Shut up, go away.

Beat.

ZUL	Okay.
BENMIN	No, not you.

They sit in silence for a while. Then Zul gets up and leaves.

SCENE TWO

A week passes. Richard's home. Late at night, Richard is alone at his computer.

YouTube videos play. He watches distractedly.

Snatches of news coverage play:

CHORUS ... In other news...
... In other news...

As the following passage plays, Richard gets increasingly frustrated.

BBC NEWSCASTER The waitress at the centre of a discrimination scandal that has rocked the island state for the past six weeks is finally given the sack, but controversy continues as reports of violence, unusual for the highly regulated city state, emerge...

NEWSCASTER TWO *(in Malay)* Para pasukan polis Negara masih belum dapat mengenal pasti suspek yang bertanggungjawab diatas keganasan yang berlaku semasa perhimpunan Purple Heart di Hong Lim Park seminggu yang lalu... [After a week of investigation, the Singapore Police have yet to find the men responsible for the violence at last week's Purple Heart Rally at Hong Lim Park...]

NEWSCASTER THREE Issuing a stern warning to interest groups, Home Affairs Minister Ng Chew Seng had this to say:

MINISTER An elderly woman has lost her job. People have been injured. This is not the way we do things in Singapore. This is urgent cause for a re-evaluation of public assembly policies...

NEWSCASTER FOUR *(in Mandarin)* 他形容这场暴力事件必然推翻了同性恋议题，并呼吁无限期的暂停 在洪林公园举行的示威游行。[He describes the violence as inevitable pushback to the 'gay agenda' and has called for a moratorium on demonstrations at Hong Lim Park for the indefinite future...]

CHORUS ... In other news...
... Turbulent times ahead for local businesses looking to secure late-night licenses along Arab Street...

... In other news...

... Nicki Minaj today broke the Internet with a scandalous Tweet about her Grammy snub, more news after the...

... In other news...

... Fresh 92 FM DJs, Prata and Kosong, rebuked yet again for a racist segment on their morning drive talk-show...

... In other news...

Incensed, Richard fiddles about until he finds his Facebook profile, and uploads a picture.

RICHARD *(his Facebook post)* Look at how you right wing idiots brutalized my grandson. Three grown men attacked a twelve year old boy. These are the bruises on his face. He got three stitches. Multiple bruises. Barbaric. And you call who perverts? Will you let the bastards who did this get away scot free?

Post.

CHORUS ... Share...

... Share...

... Fucking hell, they attacked a kid...

... Share...

... Share...

... Trigger Warning: disturbing images. A man claiming to be the boy's grandfather has posted photos of the teenager's injuries on We Are Against Pink Dot in Singapore's Facebook group last night...

... Share...

... The photo is obviously Photoshopped, plus if the boy is white, why is the grandfather Chinese...

... Share...

... This is the face of homophobia and intolerance...

... Share...

... Don't let these assholes get away with...

The Chorus becomes a garble of voices and fades away.

SCENE THREE

The next morning. Kenneth and Jayden in the kitchen.

JAYDEN	I can eat solid food now, the doctor said.
KENNETH	Not until the swelling goes down, and your cheeks are still–
JAYDEN	But I'm so sick of all this gross mush.
KENNETH	I made it.
JAYDEN	It's still mush.
KENNETH	It's porridge.
JAYDEN	It's not porridge, it's–
KENNETH	It's only 'cuz you've been hurt that I'm putting up with all your sass.
JAYDEN	I should get hurt more often then.
KENNETH	Don't even joke about that.

Beat.

JAYDEN	Sorry.
KENNETH	Papa isn't scolding you, just don't say silly things like that.
JAYDEN	I know.
KENNETH	Okay, good. *(Beat)* You okay to go back to school next week?
JAYDEN	I don't want to.
KENNETH	Why? Everything okay with school?
JAYDEN	Yeah. Everything's fine.
KENNETH	Your classmates, are they–
JAYDEN	Yeah I like 'em. 'Cept this one kid who was always messing around with me, so I roughed him up a lil' bit / and he…
KENNETH	What?
JAYDEN	Yeah, not like, I didn't hit him, I just pretended like I would.
KENNETH	What was he–
JAYDEN	Papa it's nothing, he was just calling me sissy and shit, because he knew about you guys, and I–
KENNETH	So you hit him? Who taught you how to–

JAYDEN	Papa I want you to listen to me very carefully.
KENNETH	Okay.
JAYDEN	It's fine. I stood up to him, he backed off, no one got hurt.
KENNETH	Okay. Don't tell Dad.

Enter Richard.

RICHARD	Where's Liam?
KENNETH	Another job interview. Pa, I made some porridge.

//SPLIT SCENE//

Lights up on Poh Lin's flat. Poh Lin is morosely flipping through the TV. Moments pass. Elaine appears at the door.

ELAINE	Hello Auntie.
POH LIN	What you want?
ELAINE	Just checking in on you again.
POH LIN	No job, no money. You tell me lor.
ELAINE	…
POH LIN	Your friends happy now? Feel safe now, one waitress no more job?
ELAINE	Not really.
POH LIN	Not really? Means they want some more is it?
ELAINE	No. At uh… At the park, their son got beaten up.

Beat.

POH LIN   Must be those people who support me lah. Nowadays everyday they come here also. Sing song lah, pray for me lah, come here to check in on me. Cannot stand them. They all bluff one lah. "Oh Auntie, how are you doing… come let me massage…" They even collect money for me. They want video me crying ah, I chase them away. So your friends… the boy, he okay?

ELAINE	Yeah. He's okay, back on his feet. Minor injuries lah.
POH LIN	Eh, outside so hot. Come in lah, I give you a drink.
ELAINE	Oh no lah, it's okay.

POH LIN *(opening the gate)* Come in, come in.

Elaine comes into the flat.

POH LIN   You sit down first.

Poh Lin, house-proud, exits to fetch a soda.

She returns in a more presentable top. They sit on the sofa.

ELAINE   Nice house.

POH LIN   Where got nice. Nowadays I got more time to clean, maybe that's why.

ELAINE   You know they're looking for a coffee lady at my old office. Maybe I ask for you?

POH LIN   Hah, is it.

ELAINE   I can't guarantee anything, 'cuz I don't work there anymore lah, but... can try.

POH LIN   Good lah. The god answer my prayer.

ELAINE   Oh, you're Christian?

POH LIN   No. See... *(bringing Elaine to her home altar)* I pray to a lot of god. *(Removing a picture of Christ from her altar)* Buddha, Guanyinma, Da Tok Kong, the Indian one Ganesha you know, Jesus. Like that got more chance of getting what you want. You pray to who?

ELAINE   I used to be Catholic, but not anymore.

POH LIN *(retrieving a picture)*   Mother Mary. Give you.

ELAINE   Thank you.

POH LIN   You got children?

ELAINE   Oh, yes. *(Retrieving a picture)* There. Girl.

POH LIN   Cute ah. How old?

ELAINE   Five.

POH LIN   Naughty face.

ELAINE   Oh very naughty.

POH LIN   Mixed ah? Your husband is what?

ELAINE   My wife.

POH LIN   Wife.

ELAINE   I had her. We went to a clinic in Thailand.

POH LIN   Oh. *(Beat)* So two mothers.

ELAINE   Yeah.

POH LIN Like my Benmin lah. He's my sister's son, at first he stay with her in Malaysia. Then when he nine years old, he come stay with me until now. His mother is useless one. His father also, useless bum. All men are useless bum.

ELAINE You're not married.

POH LIN Divorced long ago. *(Beat)* Five years old a lot of trouble right. Start to talk back, everything also "No, no, no".

ELAINE "Why mummy, why?"

POH LIN Yeah, yeah.

ELAINE You have your own child?

POH LIN Yeah one girl. Passed away in Malaysia long time ago before I come to Singapore.

ELAINE I'm so sorry.

POH LIN It's okay. The god take away, but now I have Benmin, like my own son. He look after me. *(She retrieves a photo album from under the coffee table)* Eh I give you see holiday photos.

\\ **RICHARD** You fry the shallots yourself?

\\ **KENNETH** Yeah.

\\ **RICHARD** The rice you mixed...

\\ **KENNETH** With glutinous rice.

POH LIN This one Bangkok last year.

\\ **RICHARD** The texture is good.

POH LIN Ben take me one, he paid for everything. My first time in Thailand.

ELAINE You liked it?

POH LIN Oh yes. Hot. Colourful. Smelly. Food very good. Spicy. I like. People very friendly. Shopping very good.

\\ **RICHARD** Where'd you learn to do that?

\\ **KENNETH** Ma taught me. Before I left for UK. Good?

\\ **RICHARD** Yeah.

\\ **KENNETH** Got more if you want.

\\ **RICHARD** You want?

\\ **JAYDEN** No thanks.

Elaine finishes her drink.

POH LIN You want one more drink?

ELAINE   No, it's alright, I didn't mean to stay long, I should get going. Got to fetch my daughter from school. I'll let you know about the coffee lady job soon, okay?

POH LIN   Okay lah.

As Elaine makes to leave, Benmin arrives at the door with bags of groceries.

ELAINE   Oh hi.

BENMIN   …

ELAINE   Was just going. Bye.

BENMIN   Bye.

ELAINE   Thanks Poh Lin, you take care.

Elaine exits.

BENMIN *(unpacking the groceries)* 她来做么？ [What did she want?]

POH LIN   没有啦。她说可能可以帮我找到工作。 [Nothing lah. Said she might be able to find me a job.]

BENMIN   那么好？ [So good ah?]

POH LIN   看怎样啦，这些人什么都可以答应的。这些多少钱？ [See how lah, these people can promise a lot one. How much for the groceries?]

BENMIN   不用啦。 [Don't need lah.]

POH LIN *(picking up a bottle of oyster sauce)* 你买错牌子了。 [You got the wrong brand.]

BENMIN   Orh.

POH LIN   不要紧。 [It's okay.]

BENMIN   你几时要出去啊？下楼 leh。 [When are you going to get out of the house, huh? Go walk downstairs lah.] 怕什么人家不会认出你的啦，每个 Auntie 看起来都一样的。 [You scared what? People won't recognise you one lah, all old auntie look the same one.]

POH LIN   谁说我怕？ [Who said I'm afraid?]

BENMIN *(passing her a stack)* 信。 [Letters.]

POH LIN   全部都是账单。 [All bills.]

BENMIN *(exiting to the kitchen)* 账单我来。放一边。 [Bills I handle. Leave them one side.]

Poh Lin takes the letters, sifting through them. She picks a few out. Opens them and tries to read them. Benmin enters.

POH LIN 这个不是账单啦，手写的，英文，你帮我看。
[This one not bill lah, Handwritten one. In English. Eh, help me see.]

Benmin takes the letters and reads them. Long pause.

POH LIN 什么来的？ [What is it?]

BENMIN 没有。问我们要不要卖房子。 [Nothing. Asking if we want to sell the house.]

POH LIN Chey。Eh，可能卖掉也好。 [Chey. Eh maybe sell also good.]

BENMIN Mm. *(Reading the other letters)* 很迟了，你不用煮饭 meh？ [Late already, you don't need to cook dinner meh?]

POH LIN Yah, yah.

Poh Lin exits to the kitchen, leaving Benmin alone with the letters, a pained look on his face. Lights down on Poh Lin's home.

In the kitchen of Richard's home.

RICHARD You should enrol him in Judo.

JAYDEN Judo?

KENNETH You've already tried that with me.

RICHARD Yeah. Bet he'll have to fight again some day, what with the two of you.

KENNETH Two of us?

RICHARD I'm just saying. People like you, easy targets.

KENNETH Okay, Pa, I'll think about it.

RICHARD You know last night, I was on Facebook.

KENNETH When did you get Facebook?

JAYDEN I set it up, Papa.

KENNETH That's nice of you.

RICHARD And anyway, there's this group there, these We Are Against the Pinkdot buggers, full of these 'flers saying all kinds of–

KENNETH Yah, you shouldn't go and–

RICHARD I got so angry, you know, I just... you see the things they post anot?
All that kind of stupid...

KENNETH	Stupid things not worth raising your BP over.
RICHARD	I shot off something. Just let them have it.
KENNETH	What? Like a post?
JAYDEN	Oh I wanna see! *(Goes on Facebook on his phone)*
KENNETH	What did you post?

JAYDEN *(he sees the post)* This it? *(Beat)* Papa...

KENNETH	What's the matter?

Kenneth takes a look. A long silence.

KENNETH	Jayden, take your breakfast upstairs.
JAYDEN	What...
KENNETH	Go now.

Jayden leaves.

Long horrified silence.

RICHARD	They don't realise, you know, until they–
KENNETH	Shit.
RICHARD	What?
KENNETH	Why would you do–
RICHARD	'Cuz one week and these buggers still not caught, I just wanted to show them–
KENNETH	You uploaded a picture of Jayden on Facebook.
RICHARD	Yes!
KENNETH	With his face all purple and swollen.
RICHARD	Yes!
KENNETH	What the fuck is wrong with you?

Pause.

RICHARD	What's wrong, I don't–
KENNETH	You don't understand, Pa, it's all over the–
RICHARD	I just posted in one group!
KENNETH	No, it's all over, it's all over–
RICHARD	What do you mean it's–
KENNETH	You – you have no idea how these things, you should have, it's not as simple, you, oh my god.
RICHARD	What do you mean it's everywhere?

KENNETH   Oh my god. Just look, it's even on these stupid news blogs.
RICHARD   Yeah, how would / I know that...
KENNETH   Just ask, just ask, just ask, just ask...
RICHARD   It was a spur of the–
KENNETH   Fuck lah, Pa, what were you trying to–
RICHARD   Why are you angry with me?
KENNETH   You know we've been trying to lay low here, with all this tension out there, we're already having enough trouble as it is, and now–
RICHARD   People should see–
KENNETH   No! People should–
RICHARD   I was just so angry. People should see–
KENNETH   He's my son, Pa! He's my son. Not yours. *(Beat)* You think I haven't wanted to go public? Think I haven't wanted to go find these assholes myself? Think I'm not fucking furious? But you go put his face out in public like that, you know how easy it is for these people to find out who we are? And you go and aggravate them? They already beat him up once, what more do you – what kind of trouble they can – you think Jayden is going to be happy, his fucked up face all over the Internet like that for the whole world to see? His friends, his classmates, his teachers. You even think about that?
RICHARD   I was just trying to help.
KENNETH   What is wrong with you? Why do you keep making these fucking stupid mistakes?
RICHARD   He's my grandson what!
KENNETH   No you're not listening, you don't even – you had your chance, Pa, with me, your own fucking son, and you did a shit job at that.

Silence.

RICHARD   Like I said. I was just trying to help.
KENNETH   Oh my god, you have no idea. / I need to call Liam.
RICHARD   I can delete it?
KENNETH   No, you can't–
RICHARD   I can–
KENNETH   No, just don't do anything anymore.
RICHARD   I can, tell them it was–
KENNETH   No.

RICHARD Then what. What the hell, tell me what I can do to help!

KENNETH Just don't! Don't help. You've always been like this Pa. You think you're helping but you just fuck things up.

Silence.

RICHARD This is my house. You do not talk to me like that in my house.

KENNETH What?

RICHARD You are not the man of this house.

KENNETH Are you fucking serious.

RICHARD I open my house to you and your family, I try and protect you and your–

KENNETH Don't you dare even start with that.

RICHARD And this is how you talk to–

KENNETH Don't you even dare use that kind of tone with–

RICHARD Like I'm some kind of senile old–

KENNETH Pa, seriously, I've been very patient.

RICHARD Like suddenly you're a big man, can talk to his father like–

KENNETH Oh my god, shut up.

Silence.

RICHARD It'll be fine. It'll be fine.

KENNETH You don't know. What it's like. To deal with these people.

RICHARD They're cowards, they just hide on the Internet and… what's the worst they can…

KENNETH Pa, just don't act like you know. Please. You always talk like you know. But you don't. And when it comes to this, please don't talk like you know. Okay? You cannot throw your son out and then years later talk like you know anything.

RICHARD I thought we're over that.

KENNETH Why? Because we don't talk about it? Because you have good intentions? It's not that easy, Pa.

Silence.

RICHARD That was so long ago.

KENNETH   That night you got so angry you threw me out. Me and the guy in my bed. Right there. Down that staircase, out that door, without a shirt on my back. You remember that? His name was Robin. He got so traumatized by that, he broke up with me. Then later, these policemen, they raided a gay bar he was at, arrested him. Threatened to publish his face in the papers. He got depressed.

RICHARD   I didn't know.

KENNETH   Threw himself off the 25th floor at his Ang Mo Kio flat.

Silence.

KENNETH   So don't act like you know anything.

Silence.

KENNETH   I have to call my husband. And I think we need to move to another place.

RICHARD   You don't have to do that.

KENNETH   I... I think it's for the best. They're going to find your address and...

RICHARD   You don't have to leave like that. I'm sorry. Where are you going to stay? The boy's already used to this place.

KENNETH   I dunno. I dunno. *(On the phone)* Liam.

RICHARD   I'm sorry.

KENNETH   Liam, come home soon. I'll explain later. Just don't check anything online till you get back. No, he's fine. *(Hangs up)*

Silence.

RICHARD   Don't go.

KENNETH   ...

RICHARD   Please.

KENNETH   ...

RICHARD   I've got nothing left.

Silence.

SCENE FOUR

Internet chatter:

CHORUS   ... with that kind of CB[18] face, boy had it coming...
... why were foreigners at the rally anyway. @SPF[19] please investigate...
... violence begets violence, he must have provoked...
... don't feed the troll, don't feed the troll...
... you guys are all fucking pigs...
... ang moh meddling in SG affairs...
... found the family's address, PM for details...
... one of the 'fathers' is a banker, UK citizen... the other a teacher... any idea if he's teaching in local school...
... boy is attending local international school, PM for details...
... is the school aware that there are students with same-sex parents? Should the other kids be allowed to mix...
... I want to leave this country so badly...

The chatter bleeds into:

SCENE FIVE

Poh Lin and Benmin at home, having dinner.

BENMIN   那个女人有跟你说工作的事吗？ [That woman got back to you about the job yet?]

POH LIN   Elaine ah？没有 leh。[Elaine? No.]

BENMIN   Mm. *(Beat)* 我的朋友说 Ang Mo Kio Hub MOS Burger 在请人。[My friend says Ang Mo Kio hub the MOS Burger looking for staff.]

POH LIN   哦。薪水多少钱？ [Oh. Pay how much?]

BENMIN   一个小时八块钱。 [$8 an hour.]

POH LIN   那么少。*(Beat)* 想想啦。酒楼怎样？ [So low. *(Beat)* Think about it. How's the restaurant?]

---

18. CB – (Singlish) Acronym for 'cheebye,' a Hokkien expletive equivalent to 'cunt'
19. SPF (acronym) – Singapore Police Force

BENMIN 还好。*(Beat)* 我跟阿 Chew 说我不做了。 [Okay. *(Beat)* Ah Yi I told Chew I'm going to quit.]

POH LIN Huh，什么意思？ [Huh, what you mean?]

BENMIN 他炒你，我告诉他我也不要做 lor。 [He fired you, so I told him I will also quit.]

POH LIN 不要笨啦。你怎么养自己？ [Don't be stupid. How are you going to support yourself?]

BENMIN 我还年轻，我可以 – [I'm young, I can–]

POH LIN – 我等一下打电话给阿朝，叫他算了。你休想辞职。 [–I'll call Chew later tell him to forget what you said. Don't you dare do that.]
你不用为我做什么，不用为我伤害自己。明白吗？ [You don't have to do anything on my behalf, especially don't need to hurt yourself for me. Understand anot?]

BENMIN 但是我怎么在那里做工 – [But how can I work there–]

POH LIN –不要再说了。 [–enough.]
(Pause) 我现在 Okay 了。刚才去楼下走走了。 [I am okay now. Went downstairs just now. Took a walk.]

BENMIN 好。 [Good.]

Beat.

POH LIN 拿了信。还有那些卖屋子的信。 [Picked up the mail. Got more of those real estate agent letters.]

//SPLIT SCENE//

Liam and Kenneth in Richard's home. They're going through a small stack of letters.

KENNETH Shit.

LIAM How'd they even find our address?

KENNETH These photos are...

LIAM The school Facebook page.

Beat.

LIAM Letters in the mail again. Can we make a police report?

KENNETH We could.
LIAM Where do you even start with this?

Beat.

\\ **POH LIN** 我应该知道是讲什么的。你不用假假。 [I think I know what they are. Don't need to pretend.]
\\ **BENMIN** 我只是不要你… [Just didn't want you to…]
\\ **POH LIN** 帮我看，可以吗？ [Help me read. Can?]
\\ **BENMIN** 不要啦。读了只会让你害怕。 [Don't want lah. Make you scared only.]
\\ **POH LIN** 就是说他们有我们的地址 lor？他们会不会来找麻烦？ [Means they have our address is it? Will they come make trouble?]
\\ **BENMIN** 不会啦。他们来，我们可以报警。信在哪里？ [No lah. If they come, we can report police. Where are the letters?]
\\ **POH LIN** *(producing them)* Ben，我要你翻译给我听。Please. [Ben, I want you to translate for me. Please.]

Silence. Benmin opens the letters. Scans them.

\\ **BENMIN** 垃圾而已。 [It's just trash.]
\\ **POH LIN** …
\\ **BENMIN** 废话而已啦。 [It's nonsense only lah.]
\\ **POH LIN** …
\\ **BENMIN** 这个说… [This one says…]

Silence.

\\ **POH LIN** 说什么？ [Says what?]
\\ **BENMIN** "你是…" ["You are…"]

Silence. Benmin gets up, finds a box of matches and a metal tin.

\\ **POH LIN** 你做么？ [What are you doing?]
\\ **BENMIN** 这些都不关你的事。你都已经知道错了。 [I don't want you to hear. You've already been punished.]
\\ **POH LIN** …
\\ **BENMIN** 我不管你做了什么。我不管别人说什么。 [I don't care what you did. I don't care what people say.] 你要找工作一定有的。你要往前看。You will find another job. You've got to move on.

你不可以一直怕这个，怕那个。You can't keep being afraid.

KENNETH   There was more of this shit on my dad's Facebook before I shut it down. I thought they were joking.

LIAM   Your fucking dad.

Enter Richard.

RICHARD   What's wrong?

He sees the letters. Walks over.

RICHARD   Let me see.
KENNETH   It's okay.
RICHARD   Let me see.

He takes the letters. Looks through them. A long silence.

KENNETH   We're going to make a police report.
RICHARD   This is my fault.
KENNETH   No use talking about that now.

Silence.

RICHARD   I think you should go.
LIAM   Go...
RICHARD   Not safe here for the boy anymore.
LIAM   We could move to Elaine's.
KENNETH   He means go back to London.

Benmin finishes burning the letters. A bowl of ashes.

\\ **POH LIN**   Ben.

Silence across the stage.

\\ **BENMIN**   Yi Ma.
\\ **POH LIN**   Mm?
\\ **BENMIN**   你做错了，你知道吗？ [You know you were wrong, right?]
\\ **POH LIN**   我知道。 [Yes.]

Long silence.

\\ **BENMIN**   姨妈，我喜欢男人。 [I'm gay, Yi Ma.]

SCENE SIX

Except for Benmin's passages, which are delivered on the phone, these are Facebook posts. The internet chatters around them.

ELAINE Her face is in my face. I can see the flecks of spit flick off her teeth, that's how close she is to me. I'm picking Chloe up from school, and she pushes herself into me, goes "Are you this girl's mum? I've always noticed there are two ladies who come and pick Chloe up, sometimes you, sometimes the other lady, I always assumed you were sisters. But I put two and two together."

CHORUS ... Like ... Like ... Share ...

KENNETH Tomorrow we leave Singapore, so in light of all the chaos, I've allowed myself this one post. My name is Kenneth Woon-Butler, and I am the man in the Palace Kitchen video. My family and I came to live in Singapore with the best intentions, but no longer think it's wise to remain in this country.

CHORUS ... Like ... Share ...

BENMIN When I was maybe twelve, I used to go Balestier market there to help my uncle with his toy shop. There was a toilet there. There'd always be one uncle there, about fifty years old, hanging around at the urinal. We called him Crocodile Ah Pek,[20] 'cuz he always wore this green Crocodile polo. He would just stand in the toilet urinal all day, watching guys pee.

CHORUS ... Like ... Share ...

KENNETH Since we've been back, I keep going back to this weird memory from my ACS[21] Days. I was twelve. It was a rainy day, and I'd gone home with a note stuck to my backpack which read FAT FAGGOT. My dad saw it. He yelled at me, and made me squat outside the main door as punishment. Naturally, I was confused.

CHORUS ... Like ... Anger ...

ELAINE She then began to lecture me. Like really just rant at me for a good five minutes. Says we'll confuse the other kids. Says they won't understand why or how Chloe has two mothers.

CHORUS ... Like ... Laughter ...

---

20. Ah Pek – (Hokkien) Old man
21. ACS (Acronym) – Anglo Chinese School, a prestigious boys's school in Singapore

KENNETH I squatted, crying. No one had ever called me faggot before, and now I was being punished for it. My father had thrown the note in a pool of water, and as I squatted there, I watched the foolscap paper slowly soak up the water for what must have been hours. The pen marks slowly dissolved away, soon the lines did too. And then the whole thing became this sodden piece of pulp.

CHORUS ... Like ...

ELAINE My nails are biting into the flesh of my palm, my teeth into my lip, I'm about to start crying. I looked at this bitch square in the face, and I thought, fuck, I'm going to punch her right now. And my fists were ready.

CHORUS ... Like ...

KENNETH Since Liam and I have been back, I keep thinking about it. Not the words or the feelings. Just the paper in the puddle. The way when I poked it with my finger, it just broke apart. The past few weeks, I've felt like I'm dissolving in rainwater.

BENMIN One day I was peeing, then some shuai beng[22] came into the toilet. He was the first guy I ever found cute. I couldn't help staring at his dick.

Then I noticed Crocodile Ah Pek was on the other end looking also.

The shuai beng after a while noticed too, quickly put his dick back inside his pants, and grabbed the uncle, started to hantam him, whack whack until he himself was crying.

ELAINE But I didn't punch her. I'm writing this post instead. Every night, I take stock of my life's with-held punches. Some nights they keep up, some nights they don't. I recently learned there are some people you can't change. Not with all the punches in the world. You sleep at night knowing they'll get left behind in the end.

KENNETH Just pulp. Like if something comes and nudges me, I can fight and scream and kick all I want, but I'll just end up breaking apart, floating away, little bits of lint in a muddy puddle.

Lights fade on Kenneth and Elaine.

Benmin is on the phone, Zul on the other line.

BENMIN I remember thinking since then. There's something wrong about looking at guys, but I liked it. I thought I would never be happy. As if because I like men, somehow, it would always feel wrong. One day, I'll become some ah pek staring at young men in a toilet. I

---

22. Shuai Beng – (Hokkien) Handsome guy

kept seeing these ah peks everywhere, floating around all the toilets like ghosts lidat. So I thought, okay, you can play first, but after a while you have to settle down, marry a woman, have children.

ZUL   Yeah, then I sucked your dick.

They laugh.

BENMIN   You asked me to pick one side. But there's too many. Pick which one? I only have my auntie, and you. I want both. I miss listening to you talk. Get angry. I was afraid you were trying to change me. But I want you to change me. I like that feeling.

Silence.

BENMIN   Are you there?
ZUL   Yeah.
BENMIN   So how?
ZUL   Why do gay men always have to be so messy. Messy, messy.
BENMIN   Huh?
ZUL   I got a green tea craving. *(Beat)* See you tonight?

SCENE SEVEN

A soundscape. A mass of reports, interviews, some related, others not. Tensions rising, conflicts looming, demagoguery, arguments, anger, desperation.

Lights up on Richard's home. A bunch of large suitcases in the living room. Richard comes in, looks at the suitcases. Sits on the couch. A feeling comes over him. He takes out a pack of cigarettes and starts to smoke.

Enter Kenneth.

KENNETH   Pa, don't smoke, please.

Long silence.

Enter Liam.

LIAM   Elaine's on the way with the car. I'll go fetch Jayden.
RICHARD   Maybe I should go to the airport?

Liam exits.

KENNETH   No need Pa, it's late.

Silence.

RICHARD Son. I'm sorry about...
KENNETH I know.
RICHARD The past few months. They've been... very happy for me.
KENNETH ...
RICHARD Not everyone gets a second chance. I hope you forgive me.
KENNETH ...

Enter Liam and Jayden.

JAYDEN Grandpa.
RICHARD Eh, my young man.
JAYDEN We can Skype.
RICHARD You teach me how.
JAYDEN I hate this.

They hug.

RICHARD The two of you look after him. And you look after them, young man.
JAYDEN Can't you come with us?
RICHARD I... you know, my whole life is here.
JAYDEN They have good doctors in the UK.
LIAM They do, darling.
KENNETH We'll think about it, alright? *(Beat)* Pa.
RICHARD Don't worry about me. I won't chase away the new maid.

A brief hug. Liam and Richard share a handshake.

LIAM Thanks for everything Dad.

Beat.

KENNETH Pa, you know...

Beat.

KENNETH Call you when we get there.
RICHARD Okay.
LIAM Alright, that must be Elaine. Don't want to keep her waiting. Jayden, got your stuff ready?

They gather their bags and make to leave. The doorbell rings. Richard goes to answer it. Enter Elaine, Poh Lin, and Benmin in tow.

A long silence.

They all share a long look in silence.

The end.

THE FU MANCHU COMPLEX

The Fu Manchu Complex was produced a year on from 2012 which had a been a tumultuous one for British East Asians in the theatre with the furore over the Royal Shakespeare Company's decision to cast the Chinese classic *The Orphan of Zhao* with barely any East Asian Actors at all besides some very young ones playing minor roles. We're used to mass social media protests at race casting decisions now. Then, I think it was more or less unprecedented and its repercussions have been felt ever since in the shape of astronomically improved opportunities for East Asians in the theatre, not least from the RSC themselves who more than made amends with a highly successful 2017 production of *Snow In Midsummer*.

The Fu Manchu Complex pastiches stereotyping by subverting Sax Rohmer's legendary orientalised super-villain, Fu Manchu, a character so pervasive and compelling his shadow is still felt to this day in Western media's view of the 'East'. Interestingly, Fu Manchu, despite myriad screen adaptations, has never to this day been portrayed by an actor of East Asian heritage. It is in many ways the archetypal 'yellowface' role.

I was also pastiching the British period drama, very much the staple of our entertainment industry which launches more illustrious careers than any other genre. It almost entirely excludes actors of colour too, of course, unless there's a period racial curio such as a dodgy opium dealer.

The play got a battering from some critics. It's not perfect of course but I was also sent another review after the play closed where the reviewer finished with this: 'I laughed lots, and also found myself examining the prejudices that lurk in my own mind.' I can remember thinking at the time what a truly honest statement that was and therefore how rare in its honesty.

Daniel York Loh is an award-winning writer and filmmaker who is one of 21 writers of colour featured in the best-selling essay collection *The Good Immigrant*. His short plays have been staged at the Royal Court, Orange Tree, Theatre Royal Stratford East and The Bush. Along with composer Craig Adams he was the winner of the 2016 Perfect Pitch award to create an original stage musical, *Sinking Water*, based on events around the 2004 Morecambe Bay Chinese cockle-pickers' disaster. His play about the World War One Chinese Labour Corps, *Forgotten* 遗忘, is being produced by Moongate and Yellow Earth. He is also one-third of alt-folk band Wondermare whose self-titled debut album is available on iTunes and Spotify.

THE FU MANCHU COMPLEX

DANIEL YORK LOH

Based on characters and scenarios from Sax Rohmer's *Fu Manchu* novels.

The Fu Manchu Complex was produced by Moongate Productions and Ovalhouse from October 1st–19th 2013 at Ovalhouse.

The production was generously supported by Arts Council England, Ovalhouse, Singapore International Foundation and via Kickstarter.

Characters
DR PETRIE
NAYLAND SMITH
MRS MCTAGGERT / O'REILLY / 'CHINAMAN'
FAH LO SUEE / THE ASSASSIN
FU MANCHU

Cast
Paul Chan	Nayland Smith
Chipo Chung	Fu Manchu
Andrew Koji	Dr Petrie
Jennifer Lim	Fah Lo Suee / Assassin
Moj Taylor	Mrs McTaggert / O'Reilly / 'Chinaman'

Moj Taylor was too sick to perform for a series of performances and his line of parts was played on consecutive nights by Paul Hyu, Gabby Wong and Stephen Hoo.

Production Team
Director	Justin Audibert
Producer	Mark Cartwright
Creative Producer	Jennifer Lim
Designer	Lily Arnold
Design Assistant	Anna Reid

Lighting Designer	Richard Williamson
Sound Designer / Composer	Aleah Morrison
Musical Director	Benjamin Woodgates
Movement Director	Andrea Pelaez
Assistant Producer	Emma Yap
Production Manager	Dan Carr
Stage Manager	Hannah Boustred
Assistant Stage Manager	Bethany Roberts

Scene

A stylised black and white film version of Victorian / Edwardian London.

Time

A stylised black and white film version of Victorian / Edwardian period drama.

PROLOGUE

As the lights fade the stage fills with smoke (a recurring theme) and the cast of five enter all wearing 'whiteface' – half masks that indicate that the (East Asian) actors are at present playing 'white people'.

And now we hear the music reminiscent of Stephen Sondheim's 'The Ballad of Sweeney Todd' but arranged in an odd combination of Victorian music hall (plinky piano) with jarring 'oriental' overtones (garish cymbal crashes etc.)

And now the cast sing, the more obviously 'colonial-looking' whitefaces taking the more aggressive lyrics–

COMPANY   Attend the tale of Fu Manchu
   His skin is yellow, his eyes are skewed
   He wants to beat colonials
   But he doesn't play by Queensbury rules
   These orientals are very odd
   We pray to God
   We should never let them act in Shake… speare!
   He's set up shop in London town

To infiltrate and drag us down
These orientals are everywhere, they're clever and cunning and utterly strange
We fear them
We fear they'll change... us
The yellow peril should never be seen!
Swing your chopsticks high, ching chong
Stay indoors and fry
We don't want to see your slanty eeeeeeyyyyyyeeeeees...

And now we see rolling captions as the music blasts away. Perhaps there is a voice over as well in the style of old fashioned weekly cinema...

> SINISTER ORIENTALS... WITH EPICANTHIC EYELIDS... AND YELLOWY SKIN... HATCH DASTARDLY SCHEMES... WITH SINISTER DRUGS... COMPLEX STRATAGEMS... AND IMPENETRABLE INSCRUTABILITY... LADIES AND GENTLEMEN PREPARE TO WITNESS, BUT PRAY YOU DO NOT SUCCUMB TO...
> THE FU MANCHU COMPLEX!!!

And now the lights come up on the one actor who has remained who now removes his 'whiteface' mask to reveal his East Asian features. He is dressed in vaguely Edwardian / Victorian costume.

He looks at the audience for a while before speaking—

NAYLAND SMITH   You see me now. Not as I was. But as I have become. As he has... made me. Pray to the only God the civilised world recognises that the same fate does not befall you. Because I fear it may already be too late. His devious oriental wiles have already forced great men to succumb to his sinister and horribly ingenious designs.

What you are about to witness is a salutary tale. So horrible and macabre it hardly bears telling. It begins with myself. But not as I am now. My original self. My true self. Before...

(And now Nayland Smith whips out a 'whiteface' mask and places it on his face) Before he... or should I say she... but first—

It began with a surprise visit to an old friend...

SCENE ONE

Lights up on a full stage. We are now in Dr Petrie's lodgings. The screen shows the image of a peaceful-looking (yet of course foggy) London mews street.

Another Chinese-looking man enters. Like Dr Petrie he too is in Edwardian costume and he too is wearing 'whiteface'. He carries a pipe which he smokes incessantly.

DR PETRIE   Nayland Smith of Burma! My dear chap. But I was just thinking of you as I watered my primroses and pruned my lavenders–

NAYLAND SMITH   Never mind the horticulture, Petrie my dear fellow, there is not a moment to lose!

DR PETRIE   Not a moment to lose, old cock?

NAYLAND SMITH   Indeed no, Petrie, the entire western world, the entire world order, all of civilisation as we know it in fact... is in mortal danger!

DR PETRIE   I say, Smith, that sounds rather alarming!

NAYLAND SMITH   Alarming?? Petrie, old hound, as we speak the Yellow Peril is spreading across the Enlightened World at the speed of a very fast carrier pigeon.

DR PETRIE   But what in the name of The Empire is this Yellow Peril?? Tell me, Smith, for the love of conkers, tell me!

NAYLAND SMITH   Very well, Petrie, but know that you are entering into a world quite outside your relaxed and convivial English heritage utopia and into one where dark, malevolent creatures from dusky places with barely pronounceable names hatch dastardly plans to infiltrate our magnificent sceptered isle...

DR PETRIE   Golly gosh!

NAYLAND SMITH   I am here, Petrie, to avert a disaster. But I fear it may already be too late.

You see here– *(Perhaps Smith unfurls a map, perhaps there is a spinning atlas but we see a map of the world which Smith now points to)* Four weeks ago, just outside Berlin in a neo-Brechtian German cabaret club awash with placards and discordant singing Baron Wilhelm Ferdinand Sax Saxonby von Wolfenheimer das Streinberg vanished without trace.

DR PETRIE   I say, Smith old bean! The alienation effect?

NAYLAND SMITH   Whatever, Petrie, old dungheap, but he hasn't been seen since. And it gets worse. Two weeks later. In Da Nederlandssssccch. Knight Commander Johann-Vincent Remy van der Kierkangander-Schleuss vanished into thin air.

DR PETRIE   Jumping apple pie, Smith, we're quite certain he hasn't just passed out somewhere after imbibing too much of the whacky Dutch baccy?

NAYLAND SMITH   Hardly, Petrie old gladhand, he was last seen practicing water colours on the north bank of the Oosterschelde outside the quiet town of Westenschouwen.

DR PETRIE   Indeed, Smith, old lionheart, such serene and sedate surroundings surely indicate foul play.

NAYLAND SMITH   Calamity piles on calamity, Petrie. Only five days ago Le Marquis de Rouennant Les Revenants De Castille De Betrand vanished from a can-can club in the Bastille.

DR PETRIE   But, Smith old bounder, this is simply every single one of the architects of the established world order. Every single one of the great men who designed that clever system whereby all those little ethnic chaps in places we've never heard of work for a pittance to make things which we then sell to each other at exorbitant prices.

NAYLAND SMITH   Every single one, Petrie old charm. Every last man jack of the engineers of economic exploitation gone. Except for...

DR PETRIE   Except for...

NAYLAND SMITH   Sir Crichton Colonial, Petrie. Our own Sir Crichton Colonial, former governor of the fragrant port of Hong Kong.

DR PETRIE   Sir Crichton Colonial? The man who single-handedly established the entire sub-continent as one gi-normous free trade entity? Who put down a civil rights protest in the only diplomatic and responsible way there is, by setting the dogs on the upstarts after first teargassing and beating them with batons?

But don't tell me he's vanished as well?

NAYLAND SMITH   Not just yet, Petrie old yawn, but it can only be a matter of time. We must alert Sir Crichton immediately to this imminent Yellow Peril danger to his resplendent person. We must tell him at once!

DR PETRIE   But... Smith! This is too horrible to contemplate. If what you're saying is true–

NAYLAND SMITH   The entire Western World is in mortal danger of subjugation to the economic might of the powers of The Orient.

There is a blast of melodramatic music as both characters react.

DR PETRIE   Oh my giddy aunt, what to do? I still have a hangover from last night and I woke up late and I haven't even taken high tea yet and and and and and… this just ISN'T FAIR!

NAYLAND SMITH   Fair?? Good gracious, man, there's a reason cricket wasn't invented in the Third World you know! You think these cunning little devils in strange attire are going to come out and fight us fair and square so we can mow them down with our gunboats and muskets? For the love of Betsy, man, but you're naive!

DR PETRIE   Oh this is too terrible, Smith old ponce. In fact it's so truly and appallingly and dashedly traumatic that… it calls for sustenance!

(He takes a bell and rings it vigorously and calls offstage) Mrs McTaggert, you endearingly lazy and inept little underling! Do get your rather large and misshapen posterior up here with some tiffin and refreshments for Mr Nayland Smith of Burma and myself, would you? Thanks awfully, old pig!

Mrs McTaggert calls from offstage. She speaks in a Scottish accent that gets ludicrously exaggerated throughout the following scene.

MRS MCTAGGERT *(off)* Aye, I'm comin' as fast as ah can, sir!

DR PETRIE *(to Nayland Smith)* A chap can't battle a malevolent criminal master plan on an empty stomach, you know.

NAYLAND SMITH   Quite right, Petrie old mucker, quite right. No sense taking on the evil of Old Cathay without first imbibing some tiffin.

Enter Mrs McTaggert. An actor in a grey wig and 'whiteface' carrying a large tray of tea and food.

MRS MCTAGGERT   Here's yer wee afternoon tea fer yerself and yer wee friend there, Dr Petrie. An' it just so happens that ah've got a wee letter here fer bonny wee Mr Nayland an' all, so ah have…

Mrs McTaggert places the tray on the table and hands the letter to Nayland Smith who studies her suspiciously.

NAYLAND SMITH   Now tell me, my good woman. Are you by any chance… Celtic?

MRS MCTAGGERT *(aside)* Oh crikey, here we go! *(To Nayland Smith in a ridiculously exaggerated accent)* Och aye the noo, that ah am. Once upon a wee time ah was a rounded oot three dimensional human being.

But now ah'm just a wee colonised caricature cliché of a comedy Scots woman (that ah am).

NAYLAND SMITH Yes, well, as long as you red haired freckly caber tosser people bally well remember who's won all the wars and don't go getting all *Braveheart* on us we'll all be just fine, won't we?

MRS MCTAGGERT Ooooh, that ah will, fine sir, never you worry yer wee warlike little mind.

Dr Petrie has been examining the food on the tray and now holds up a rather soggy looking 'spring roll' with his fork.

DR PETRIE Mrs McTaggert, you lumpen and rather archaic looking McNugget Neanderthal, might I enquire what the blazes is this food you've deigned to serve we two fine servants of the realm?

MRS MCTAGGERT *(so enthused by the food she forgets her 'act')* Oooh, that! It's dead good! Ah believe it's known as a spring roll.

NAYLAND SMITH Spring roll?? What in the name of the Queen is a spring roll, you asinine little porridge wog?

MRS MCTAGGERT Oh, they're like these wee tasty round things those lovely wee Chinese folk like tae partake of. Basically tubes of batter filled wi' bean sprouts an'–

NAYLAND SMITH *(interrupting)* You ridiculous thistle arse of an excuse for a woman, did you say 'wee Chinese folk'?

MRS MCTAGGERT Oh aye, that ah did, fine sir, that ah did. There's a wee crood of them set up a wee stall doon in the market. They're from auld Hong Kong so they are–

(During the following speech the general stage lights grow darker as the light on Mrs McTaggert grows bright and brighter) A place ah believe was ceded to you colonising Sassenach ruling classes 'cos you managed tae addict the entire population o' Southern China tae opium. An' then ye went an' won a wee war when they had the temerity to take exception tae the fact tha' ye were peddlin' a highly addictive an' destructive class A substance which causes misery, destruction an' death on a grand scale. An all fa' the profit an' furtherment o' the interests o' the British Empire, the single biggest drug runnin' cartel in the entire history o' the world.

Now the stage lights snap back to their normal state.

DR PETRIE Mrs McTaggert, your impudence is quite extraordinary! Might I remind you that you're hired to be my general lackey not lecture my friend and I on global geo-politics!

Mrs McTaggert has quite forgotten herself but now snaps back into her 'stereotype Scottish'.

MRS MCTAGGERT Och, right y'are, sir, ah'm that sorry, so ah am. Anyhoo, suffice tae say ah thought the wee Chinese folk's greasy wee scran would make a nice wee change fro' the usual stodgy diet that ah did.

NAYLAND SMITH Shiver the tree trunks and let England shake! This confirms all my very worst suspicions, Petrie. Chinese! In the market!!! *(To Mrs McTaggert)* Ye gods, Mrs McCretin, you have brought the seductive culinary poison of those filthy alien orientals into our very midst! Damn you, you moronic haggistani, don't you know an Englishman's home is his castle?!?

(Nayland Smith takes the tray and throws it out of the window, then stands triumphantly for a moment before realising what he's done. He gives a start) Oh fiddlesticks, damn and blast! I was so incensed I threw that filthy deep fried ching ching slop out of the window when it could contain valuable clues! And it was all your fault, you bagpipe blowing imbecile!

MRS MCTAGGERT Och, ah'm that sorry so ah am the noo. I didnae realise, ah didnae ken, ah took the high road, ah took the low road an' ah guess my heart was in the highlands a'chasin' doon a deer–

NAYLAND SMITH *(to Dr Petrie)* Petrie, may I?

DR PETRIE Why, be my guest, old bean, be my guest.

Nayland Smith promptly floors Mrs McTaggert with a sharp uppercut.

NAYLAND SMITH That'll teach you, you crass little kilt wearer! Now get down there and gather the evidence before I decide to practice more of my famed Queensbury boxing prowess on your astonishingly ugly Gorbals fishwife countenance!

MRS MCTAGGERT Och aye the noo, Mr Wee Nayland, that ah will, thankin' you kindly wee sir thankin' you kindly, there's an ending o' the dance, and fair Morag's safe in France, and the Clans they hae paid the lawing...

Mrs McTaggert crawls off.

NAYLAND SMITH Of all the brazen effrontery... in the market, Petrie old faithful! Where honest servants of Her Majesty go to replenish their meat n' two veg! They're selling spring rolls in the market! Those little yellow blighters will be wanting to play themselves on the stage next!

DR PETRIE It hardly seems conceivable but... come to think of it, Smith my dear fellow, I have seen far more yellow faces of late...

NAYLAND SMITH They're everywhere, Petrie old chap! Like a plague of locusts swarming out of the Orient!

DR PETRIE Indeed! But Smith, old bean, what to do?? And shouldn't you read that letter Mrs McHaggisface brought?

NAYLAND SMITH What? Oh my giddy aunt how right you are, Petrie, old egg, how right you are! Now, let me see... *(He opens the letter and reads for a split second)* Adlardikins and spank me hard the way my form master did at Eton!!! But this is too terrible!

DR PETRIE What is it, Smith old bean? In the name of St. George, what on earth is it?

NAYLAND SMITH We're too late, Petrie old noodle, we're too late!

DR PETRIE You don't mean to say–

NAYLAND SMITH Sir Crichton Colonial, Petrie, he's... vanished!

DR PETRIE Vanished??

NAYLAND SMITH And his man-servant suspects foul play. And this– *(Smith holds out a card which perhaps we see is a clichéd oriental looking dragon, perhaps giving the finger)* –was left at the scene of the crime.

DR PETRIE But what on earth can it mean, Smith old toenail?

NAYLAND SMITH It means that, as I suspected, the perpetrator of these truly terrible crimes that threaten our very way of life is a fiendish Oriental. We must investigate, Petrie, and not a moment is to be wasted. One cannot indulge one's natural imperial suaveness when the evil of Old Cathay is at work. Come, Petrie!

Smith and Petrie exit only to enter again–

SCENE TWO

–Outside a far more palatial looking mansion in London at night bathed of course in omnipresent fog as the stage itself fills with smoke.

As the music fades Smith and Petrie, now in overcoats, enter doing exaggerated 'cold' acting, stamping feet, breathing into hands etc.

Silence.

An owl hoots.

DR PETRIE   Smith, old mucker...

NAYLAND SMITH   Yes, Petrie old flip flop?

DR PETRIE   Are we quite sure there's been foul play? I mean to say... Sir Crichton Colonial's house adjoins the park.

The parks of London are frequented by young men who... rather seek the er... company of other... members... of the male... species. *(Hurriedly)* So I'm told.

NAYLAND SMITH   Petrie, you naive young pup! A gentleman of Sir Crichton Colonial's calibre knows there is a time and a place for sexual proclivities. No, Petrie old sausage (no pun intended) I sense his hand in this. His foul, yellow, long fingernailed, tapering talon of pure celestial evil. I feel a discomfort deep in my soul, Petrie. Deep! Deep!

Oh Petrie, I fear! I fear!

He weeps.

DR PETRIE   My poor poor courageous friend!

A 'twinky twonk' semi music hall / semi oriental version of 'Bring Him Home' from Les Miserables *begins to play:*

DR PETRIE *(sings)* He is brave

But overwhelmed

He will save

He will fight for the realm

He loves ethnics

Duskies and poofs

But only if

They're sub-ser-vi-ent

Help him fight

With all his might

And not be blight-ed

By immigrant and upstart gooks

He is strong

Manly and virile–

NAYLAND SMITH *(interrupting)* That's enough, Petrie, you're making me uncomfortable!

DR PETRIE   Sorry, I... found myself strangely inspired by you.

NAYLAND SMITH   If there's one thing in this world I despise and loathe even more than pesky orientals and foreigners it's sickly sentimental show-tunes, do you hear me?

DR PETRIE   Of course. My apologies.

NAYLAND SMITH   Accepted.

DR PETRIE   It's just... I find myself drawn to you, Nayland old cock. It's like a yearning. A most curious... stirring. I first felt it when we shared a dorm together at Charterhouse. I would often flagellate myself over it, knowing it to be wrong but then at the same time rebelling, thinking, oh to blazes with it, why should I not unleash the love that dare not speak its name! It gave rise to some most tempestuous dreams, I can tell you. Many's the time I awoke to find myself covered in–

NAYLAND SMITH   Petrie, if you ever so much as dare to mention this again I shall break your jaw, do you hear me?

DR PETRIE   Yes, of course. I'm terribly sorry, old fox.

NAYLAND SMITH   Pull yourself together man!

DR PETRIE   Yes, yes. It's not as if one isn't attracted to the ladies. One most certainly is. But they're dashed terrifying creatures, Smith, one doesn't quite know what to do with 'em.

NAYLAND SMITH   Get it over with as quickly as possible and remember you're not there for her pleasure.

DR PETRIE   Oh absolutely, Smith old brick, you're such a resolute and strong chap, it's why I admire you so much.

NAYLAND SMITH   Yes, but enough of the Uranian pavilion end leanings, eh?

DR PETRIE   Quite. Don't know what came over me.

NAYLAND SMITH   He did, Petrie old dog, he came all over you.

DR PETRIE   I say! Literally?

NAYLAND SMITH   For goodness sake, man, you've got man sex on the brain! Don't you see? This is his malign and decadent Eastern influence pervading our consciousness like an invisible yellow virus infecting you with all the sensual decadence of the The Orient. He's trying to turn you into a bloody ladyboy woofter, the odious yellow fiend that he is–

DR PETRIE   But you still haven't told me who he is yet, Smith old puff!

NAYLAND SMITH   I daren't, Petrie old juice, I daren't! I daren't utter the foul celestial demi-villain's name. You just be on your guard, do you hear?

DR PETRIE   Yes, yes, Smith old stalwart, I shall! I shall remain on guard. There's no way I'm letting any cunning Chinaman in through my back passage!

NAYLAND SMITH   Quite.

At that point they are interrupted by O'Reilly, Sir Crichton Colonial's manservant, again in 'whiteface'.

O'REILLY   Gordon Bennett, fine sirs, thankin' you kindly for comin' out on this parky old evenin' to investigate the fact 'is nibs, the right 'onourable and splendid old gentleman, Sir Crighton Eloysius Peregrin Montefurie Colonial, who paid me the princely and generous sum of two an' six a week to be 'is all purpose dogsbody 'as been taken orf somewhere. Thankin' you kindly, your eminences, Gord bless the Queen an' all 'oo sail in 'er, Honest John O'Reilly at your service, your worships.

NAYLAND SMITH   O'Reilly? You're not an Irishman are you?

O'REILLY   Oh good lord be praised, fine sir, I'm not sure I would describe myself as such, though I believe my great-great-grandfather did indeed hail from somewhere in County Kildare.

NAYLAND SMITH   Don't you mince words with me you lugubrious peasant. You're a little green munchkin and that's that!

O'REILLY   If you say so, good sir, of course, that I am, fine sir.

NAYLAND SMITH   There's a good potato-nosher. Now then, clover face, you said you heard a strange cry?

O'REILLY   That I did, oh well endowed sir.

NAYLAND SMITH   From whence, pray tell me, you Fenian oaf?

O'REILLY   Over that back wall on your left is the back lane from whence the cry came.

NAYLAND SMITH   *(to O'Reilly)* Now then, Paddy Potato Breath. This cry. Was it like… this? *(Smith does an exaggerated and drawn out version of a Bruce Lee 'kung fu' noise, high pitched and quavering)* OOOOOEEEEEEAAAAARRRREEEEEGGGGHHHH!

Beat.

O'REILLY   Beggin' your pardon oh fine, fine sir, an' not wishin' to cause you no offence or umbrage, sir, but I would say it was more like this, sir: *(O'Reilly makes the same noise but with a slightly different 'quaver')* OOOOOEEEEEEAAAAARRRREEEEEOOOGGGHHHH!

Beat.

DR PETRIE   Oh I see, yes, a subtle difference but a marked one nonetheless, yes, so like this– *(Petrie imitates O'Reilly perfectly)* OOOOOEEEEEEAAAAARRRREEEEEOOOGGGHHHH!

O'REILLY   Oh, that'll be it, good sir, stone the crows an' Gord bless the Royal corgis an' all but you're a dashed fine mimic if you don't mind me sayin' so, fine handsome young sir.

DR PETRIE   Oh indeed, yes, it was a talent oft remarked upon when I was a small boy enjoying an idyllic and happy childhood in finest Kent. I was able to perfectly imitate the mating calls of both the Great Spotted Woodpecker and Long-tailed Tit purely from hearing them.

O'REILLY   Most remarkable, oh strapping young sir, you clearly 'ave a gift. Someone should put you on the stage, sir, if you don't mind me sayin'.

DR PETRIE   Do you really think so? Gosh, how flattering, yes, the thespian arts have always held great appeal–

NAYLAND SMITH *(interrupting)* Yes, well, if we can just cease for a moment pulling each other's Long Tail Peckers or whatever could we return ourselves once again to the gravity of the situation? The man who now single-handedly holds the entire international monetary system in conjunction has vanished without trace!

DR PETRIE   Yes, of course, Smith old steadfast, terribly sorry!

O'REILLY   Quite right, oh fine and upright gentleman, beggin' your pardon and lickin' your boot soles an' all that, yessir.

NAYLAND SMITH   Right. So can we establish that the noise you heard was like this: *(Repeats his original noise)* OOOOOEEEEEEAAAAARRRREEEEEGGGHHHH!

Beat.

O'REILLY   Well... no, sir. As I believe 'as been established by myself and the fine young master 'ere the noise was more like– *(repeats HIS noise)* OOOOOEEEEEEAAAAARRRREEEEEOOOGGGHHHH!

Beat.

NAYLAND SMITH   You see, this is what I despise so much about you riff raff working class poor people. You're all so leadenly pedantic! This sort of analistic attention to minutiae comes from all that penny-pinching, doesn't it? Here you are, O'Reilly McGuinness Bollocks, take a shilling for your troubles. *(Tosses him a coin which O'Reilly instantly catches)*

And here's something else too. It's called a Bullingdon kiss! *(Smith headbutts O'Reilly in the face)*

Now be off with you, you revolting little munchkin pleb!

O'Reilly staggers towards the exit.

O'REILLY   Oh yes, of course, thankin' you kindly, fine sir, Gord bless you an' yours an' all who shit-sit in 'er, indeed indeedidoo, tippin' the old forelock an' strokin' the old cock, oh yes oh yes oh yes…

Exits.

NAYLAND SMITH   The situation is grave indeed, Petrie old jiz. Grave to the point of graveness. That cry that you and O'Spudface were able to so perfectly imitate has confirmed all my very worst fears about who has taken Sir Crichton Colonial of Bombay. I can reveal to you who our foe is.

DR PETRIE   Who, Smith? Who??

NAYLAND SMITH   Who??

DR PETRIE   Yes, who??

NAYLAND SMITH   Why, Dr Fu Manchu!

There is a blast of melodramatic music as both characters react.

NAYLAND SMITH   Come along, Petrie, there's not a moment to lose! CAB!!!

SCENE THREE

And they are instantly in a horse- (or motor-) drawn hackney carriage.

DR PETRIE   But Smith, old larynx. Who is Dr Fu Manchu?

NAYLAND SMITH   Ah, Petrie… imagine a person, tall, lean and feline. High shouldered, with a brow like Shakespeare and a face like Satan. Invest him with all the cruel cunning of an entire Eastern race, able to outdo us in business, cook at lightning speed, single-handedly destroy the environment so they can sell us wind turbines, manipulate global currency and genetically modify swimmers to win gold medals. All this accumulated in one giant intellect, with all the resources of a wealthy government. Imagine that awful being, and you have a mental picture of Dr Fu Manchu, the yellow peril incarnate!

DR PETRIE   Goodness gracious me, what a terrifying prospect!

NAYLAND SMITH   And it gets worse, Petrie, believe me.

DR PETRIE   In what way worse, Smith old pole?

NAYLAND SMITH   For starters if you look behind us you'll see that someone has got into another cab...

Petrie looks. He and we can see lights though the omnipresent fog in the very far distance.

DR PETRIE   I say! They appear to be following us!

NAYLAND SMITH   As I knew they surely would!

DR PETRIE   Bless my cotton socks and gentleman's underwear. If I escape alive and untainted from this horrifying business I shall know I bear a truly charmed life.

NAYLAND SMITH   Indeed, Petrie old jam jar, indeed. There is little to fear until we arrive. Afterwards there is much.

DR PETRIE   Dear God, Smith old ball, what perverted intelligence is at work here! Quite extraordinary and really too much for a chap who simply wants a quiet roast dinner followed by port and cigars on a Sunday afternoon!

Now the cab has stopped and Smith and Petrie walk seamlessly into Petrie's lodgings.

SCENE FOUR

DR PETRIE   Smith, am I correct in assuming we have been followed all the way here?

NAYLAND SMITH   An attempt is to be made upon my life. I see it as a trap, Petrie old queen. With myself as bait.

DR PETRIE   Most alluring, Smith old rake!

NAYLAND SMITH   If we can capture one of his creatures they could lead us straight to Dr Fu Manchu himself! *(Runs to the window and shakes his fists at it)* The villain! The fiendishly clever villain! I suspected Sir Crichton Colonial was next and I was right. But I came too late, Petrie! That hits me hard, old man.

DR PETRIE   But you mustn't be hard on yourself, Nayland, old bean. This after all is a criminal mind of unparallelled acumen we're up against.

NAYLAND SMITH   Quite right, Petrie, quite right. We can only pray it's not too late. We must find Sir Crichton, Petrie, we must!

DR PETRIE   And we will, Smith old toilet seat, we will. Now come. Let me tuck you in and let us dream of jam roly poly and cricket on the village green and a lovely posh filly with buttocks the size of the North York Moors.

No sense worrying ourselves. It just wouldn't be English!

NAYLAND SMITH   You're quite right, Petrie. When the moment arrives and England expects, we shall be ready!

Petrie tucks Smith up in a blanket and gazes lovingly at him as the 'twinky twonk' version of Bring Him Home plays again.

DR PETRIE *(sings) Let him rest*

And sleep tight

So he may best

Fight the yellow blight...

Petrie too falls into a slumber.

Silence.

And now the window opens. Through it comes The Assassin clad entirely in black and with a silk 'balaclava' that masks his face. He creeps balletically up to Smith's sleeping form before striking an elaborate martial arts pose as if poised to strike...

Suddenly with a start, Smith awakens and in one swift movement strikes The Assassin with a swift roundhouse whilst Petrie too awakens and bundles the staggering Assassin down with a perfectly-executed rugby tackle.

NAYLAND SMITH   I say, Petrie, that was a fine tackle you executed there!

DR PETRIE   Why, thank you, Smith, I was in the Harrow first fifteen, you know. I played fly half.

Smith bundles the stunned Assassin into a chair.

NAYLAND SMITH   Stay back, Petrie, this type knows every single pressure point in the human body. One touch could either kill you or force you to ejaculate on the spot!

DR PETRIE   I say! This is a brand new Persian carpet. But... what is he?

NAYLAND SMITH   As I suspected, Petrie old pug, he's a dacoit.

DR PETRIE   A dacoit??

NAYLAND SMITH   That or a thuggee.

DR PETRIE   I beg your pardon?

NAYLAND SMITH   Arch bandits and assassins of India and... the East... wherever... vicious little blighters trained in all forms of combat.

DR PETRIE   Looks more like a ninja to me...

NAYLAND SMITH   A what?

DR PETRIE   A ninja.

NAYLAND SMITH   What in the name of the Prince's soiled jockstrap is a ninja??

DR PETRIE   A covert agent or mercenary in feudal Japan who specialised in unorthodox warfare. They appeared in the Sengoku or 'warring states' period, in the 15th century, but antecedents may have existed in the 14th century, and possibly even in the 12th century.

Contrasting very much with the samurai, who observe strict rules of honour and combat, the ninjas are crafty underhand little buggers who throw pointy star things at people...

Read about them in *Boys Own Adventures*.

NAYLAND SMITH   I'm not sure I approve of your choice of literature, Petrie. Japanese, you say?

DR PETRIE   Indeed.

NAYLAND SMITH   Yes, well, all of these orientals have interchangeable cultures. One slanty eyed little yellowface is very much like another.

DR PETRIE   Like indistinguishable sunny-sided peas in a pod, dear Nayland.

He studies the Assassin.

NAYLAND SMITH   Now then. I'm going have to speak the little savage's lingo. Forgive me Petrie.

(He now addresses The Assassin in an exaggerated 'sing song' Chinese accent. The following conversation is conducted with the Assassin speaking in dumbshow 'mime') Who-is-your... mastaaaaahhhhhhhh?

ASSASSIN *(mimes)*   You what?

NAYLAND SMITH   Who-is-your... mastaaaaahhhhhhhh?

ASSASSIN *(mimes)* Are you some kind of idiot?

NAYLAND SMITH   Don't play dumb with me you little yellow pipe cleaner!

ASSASSIN *(mimes)* Wanker!

NAYLAND SMITH   What on earth's he saying?

DR PETRIE   I think I get his drift…

ASSASSIN *(mimes)* I can't talk, you fucking imbecile!

NAYLAND SMITH   What the Dickens?

ASSASSIN *(mimes)* I can't talk, you cockbangle arsehole. They cut my tongue out.

NAYLAND SMITH   Speak, damn you, speak, you wok frying wassock!

ASSASSIN *(mimes)* I cannot TALK, you moron.

DR PETRIE   Oh, I see! He can't talk, Smith.

ASSASSIN *(mimes)* Yes, that's right! Hallelujah!

DR PETRIE   Yes, I see, most clever the way he 'physicalises' what he wishes to say…

ASSASSIN *(mimes)* At least one of you's got a brain!

NAYLAND SMITH   Yes, my favourite kind of Chinaman. Silent.

DR PETRIE   Right, now. Let me see if I can…

And now Petrie 'mimes' at The Assassin as we see subtitles on the screen.

DR PETRIE *(mimes)* Who is your boss?

ASSASSIN *(mimes)* Fu Manchu.

DR PETRIE   Oh, Fu Manchu! Yes, dashed clever, I say!

NAYLAND SMITH   Ask him where Fu Manchu is, Petrie!

ASSASSIN *(mimes)* If you think I'm telling you where he is you're even more fucked up than I thought!

DR PETRIE *(mimes)* Oh, be a good chap and tell us!

ASSASSIN *(mimes)* Bollocks to the pair of you. With bells on. Pair of peanut face gammons. Go on. Fuck right off!

Smith suddenly produces his revolver and points it at the Assassin.

NAYLAND SMITH   Tell us where Fu Manchu is or I'll shoot you in the face, you stinking slant eyed sot!

ASSASSIN *(mimes)* Alright alright! Keep your fucking hair on! Bloody hell!

DR PETRIE   Wait, Smith, he's going to tell us!
ASSASSIN *(mimes)* Fu Manchu is at Singapore Charlie's.
DR PETRIE   Fu Manchu is... singing... for his supper? No I don't quite follow–
NAYLAND SMITH   Crafty little chink's taking the piss! Let me shoot the little bastard!
DR PETRIE   No wait, Smith, he's trying, look!
ASSASSIN *(mimes)* It's in the East End.
The Assassin points frantically to the east.
DR PETRIE   Yes, yes, we know, you're from the East, you're a slippery oriental, we know!
ASSASSIN *(mimes)* No, you ball-sack, I mean, it's where the cockneys live.
DR PETRIE   Yes, yes, you have a penis... I'm sure it's very large and therefore completely subverts the stereotype of Asiatic males having small–
NAYLAND SMITH   Petrie, I'm beginning to think the chap's a bit simple.
ASSASSIN *(mimes)* No, no, you fucking pair of blockheads. Cockneys! Cockneys! For fuck's sake! Knees up mother brown, I'm forever blowing bubbles!
DR PETRIE   Knees up... oh my word! Yes! I see! Cockneys! Yes! Cockneys!!!
ASSASSIN *(mimes)* Thank the fucking stars!
DR PETRIE   What about them?
ASSASSIN *(mimes)* Oh smell the fucking coffee, bitch! Fu Manchu is where the cockneys are!!!
DR PETRIE   Wha-? Oh! I get it! Fu Manchu is in the East End!
ASSASSIN *(mimes)* YES! YES!!!
Petrie and the Assassin 'high five' each other.
NAYLAND SMITH   But where?? Where in the East End?? Where, you bloody Chinese bastard, where?
DR PETRIE   Yes, good point. *(Mimes)* Whereabouts in the East End, old bean?
ASSASSIN *(mimes)* Oh for heaven's sake. It's like a brothel... gay and straight... all tastes catered for... but more of an opium den than anything else. Where people go to smoke opium and get stoned.

DR PETRIE   Shagging... smoking... falling asleep... it's not a gentleman's club is it?

NAYLAND SMITH   I have it, I have it! It's in Shadwell. A notorious opium den called Shen-Yan's, otherwise known as Singapore Charlie's, which in typically cunning Byzantine manner, fronts as an innocent barber shop.

ASSASSIN *(mimes)* Yes, yes, you're right, that's the one, come here and let me hug you, brother.

Smith shoots him dead.

NAYLAND SMITH   Come along, Petrie old cock. There may still be time to save Sir Crichton. To Shadwell and Singapore Charlie's!

DR PETRIE   But, Smith old chum, should a gentleman visit such an establishment?

NAYLAND SMITH   Your fortitude does you proud, Petrie old mucker, but in the service of Queen and country even the most nefarious of activities is permissible. But we must disguise ourselves as cockerney ruffians. Come, Petrie!

They exit.

SCENE FIVE

Sinister black and white film music plays as the stage floods with smoke, more and more of it, noticeably too much.

And now there is coughing at the back of the stage as Nayland Smith and Dr Petrie enter waving smoke away and coughing. They are dressed in rough overcoats and flat caps.

DR PETRIE   That smell, Smith... so... intoxicating... overpowering...

NAYLAND SMITH   Opium laudanum, Petrie. Deceptively seductive but ultimately deadly. The yellow scum peddle it shamelessly, the slanty little fiends.

DR PETRIE   But, Smith...

NAYLAND SMITH   Yes, Petrie?

DR PETRIE   Wasn't it we Brits who peddled it to them, as Mrs McTaggert attested?

NAYLAND SMITH   Of for heaven's sake, man! The Great British Empire has to generate revenue somehow! Do you suppose that caviar and finest brandy and cigars come cheap in the modern global economy?

DR PETRIE   No, I suppose not.

NAYLAND SMITH   If the dastardly little yellow tykes want to smoke the stuff then it's only proper to exploit that. It's their own fault anyway. Little bastards wouldn't buy our pianos.

DR PETRIE   We were trying to sell them pianos? What on earth would a predominantly peasant nation want with pianos?

NAYLAND SMITH   We had to sell them something, Petrie. It's the law of free trade! We were spending a bloody fortune on their tea and silk and rhubarb.

DR PETRIE   Rhubarb?? You mean to say we were buying rhubarb off the yellow cadgers?

NAYLAND SMITH   Afraid so, Petrie, old feckless. All that rhubarb crumble in public school halls up and down the land. I'm afraid to say demand long ago outstripped supply.

DR PETRIE   I say. Doesn't seem very fair somehow, does it?

NAYLAND SMITH   But enough of this post colonial angst, Petrie. Now, do you think that you can cleverly disguise your voice to sound like a cockerney working class oik?

DR PETRIE   The bastards denied us rhubarb crumble. You just watch me, Smith old sweetheart!

(He calls out loudly in a ludicrous B movie 'cockney' accent) Oi!!! Oi!!! Wakee wakee, yer li'l yellow blighters, me an' me ole China 'ere (no pun intended) was 'opin' you might oblige us wiv some of your 'ighly addictive smoky chinky nectar so, c'mon, Bruce, knees up Mother Brown an' all that, let's be 'avin' yer!

For a moment there is nothing but silence. Then, entering stage left, we see another actor dressed in a dank greasy wig, thick spectacles and tatty 'chinoiserie' robe, shuffling like an old man.

When he speaks it's in an exaggerated B movie Chinese accent in chattering 'simian' fashion that should sound notably 'false'.

'CHINAMAN'   No shavee, no shavee, too latee, I shutee shop aleddee! Go away, go away!

NAYLAND SMITH *(to Dr Petrie)* He's bluffing, Petrie! The slippery little slope's bluffing!

DR PETRIE   Apples an' pears me ole China, don't you try an' get all crafty wiv me, you clever little sing-song ching-chong ming-mong! I knows your game. Nah be a good chinky an' get inside an' gimme an' my matey a couple o' pipee, savvy?

'CHINAMAN'   But no habe pipee.

NAYLAND SMITH *(to Dr Petrie)* Money! The greedy little blighters love money!

DR PETRIE   'Ere, kop 'old o' that fer yer pains, ting-tong.

He gives the Chinaman a coin.

'CHINAMAN'   Oh. Thankee thankee, mastahhhh. But me no habe pipee!

NAYLAND SMITH *(to Dr Petrie)* After the carrot, give the little gimp the stick, Petrie!

DR PETRIE *(as himself)* The stick? Oh, let me see... *(As the 'Cockerney')* Naaaah, listen 'ere, sunshine features, I'm warnin' ya. You keep me waitin' an' I'll... I'll... pull the 'ole gaff dahn, Charlie! So 'elp me I will! Apples an' pears, I'm forever blowin' bubbles an' all that.

'CHINAMAN'   No habe got pipee. I samee tellee. Fucking deaf cuntee!

NAYLAND SMITH *(to Dr Petrie)* Threaten him, Petrie, threaten him, man!

Dr Petrie raises his fist at the 'Chinaman'.

NAYLAND SMITH   'Ow dare you, ya little egg foo yong noshin' Barclays banker! I ain't mutton jeff an' I'll plant one right on yer fancy yellow boat race if you don't go an' get me an' my mate two pipee double quickee chop chopee! Understand me talkee talkee?

'CHINAMAN'   Yes, boss, no boss, whippee my arsee an' callee me kinkee, boss. I go quick quick chop chopee chinkee chonkee. *('Chinaman' exits, calling as he goes)* Missee, missee, come quickee, two pipee!

NAYLAND SMITH   You see, Petrie, the oriental race only understands brutal colonial authority. I think of them as akin to dogs that constantly need to be kept in hand with a good firm boot up their hideously yellow backsides.

DR PETRIE   Well, I did my best, Smith. But what did you make of my performance? The way I altered my voice there?

NAYLAND SMITH   Oh yes. Very good, Petrie, old drop, most convincing.

DR PETRIE   Why thank you, Smith, I was a notable Othello for the Purley Light Operatic Society before I took the old Hippocratic Oath.

NAYLAND SMITH Really, Petrie. How fascinating.
DR PETRIE I smeared myself with chocolate cake, you know.
NAYLAND SMITH Petrie, this is neither the time nor the place to discuss your sexual practices–
DR PETRIE No I meant to impersonate a negro.
NAYLAND SMITH Most inventive, I'm sure–
DR PETRIE 'Oooooooh, my Des-dee-monah...'
NAYLAND SMITH Yes, well, I'd thank you not to reprise what I'm sure was a very well nuanced and observed blackface performance at the present moment, Petrie, because... I say...
DR PETRIE That smell, Smith... a new smell, so... overpowering, one feels quite light headed and...
NAYLAND SMITH Careful, Petrie resist it! Fu Manchu is a master poisoner to whom the Borgias are but children. This new odour is... oh, now I see... Petrie, beware! The female of the yellow species!

Slinky 'Chinese' music plays – all keening erhus sighing wistful heart tugging melodies – as a shape appears through the fog of smoke and now we see... an actress appears, her face done up like a cliché 'China doll', dressed in an impossibly tight red cheongsam and carrying two ridiculously phallic looking opium pipes. She doesn't walk so much as dance towards the two whiteface men, all flowing curves and seductive wiggles as they stare on, hopelessly entranced.

Finally she stops in front of them and does a kind of curtsey all the time radiating coyness and breathy sensuality.

FAH LO SUEE My name is Fah Lo Suee. Lady Of The Fan. Sweet Perfume.
I am oriental damsel. Delicate, subservient... obedient.
At the same time imminently untrustworthy, shallow and sly. Created from the lurid imaginings of noble white master who I exist to worship and serve. *(She giggles coyly)*
Especially handsome one like you two and... *(As her eyes meet Dr Petrie she visibly swoons)* ... especially... you...
(Dr Petrie is hypnotised as Fah Lo Suee exaggeratedly struggles to regain her composure)
You are most handsome and virile man I ever see.

So... strong. Make Fah Lo Suee feel... weak. Not like puny man from my country with pigeon chest and needle stick. If you allow Fah Lo Suee... I will pleasure you in ways you have never even dare imagine...

Dr Petrie is in a state of some helplessness.

DR PETRIE *(his voice cracked)* Yes... well... gosh! Erm... later, perhaps.

She giggles coyly.

FAH LO SUEE Yes, for now, you must smoke pipee. Pipee make you... relaxee. Less prone to be... premature... improve... stamina. Later, Fah Lo Suee return. Then love you... long time... all night... take you to very peak of ecstasy with ancient sutra of love, practice in my land since very dawn of creation. At same time make you feel masterful and powerful in order to preserve and massage delicate masculine pride.

(She hands them both a smoking pipe)

Now. I go.

(Giving a last longing glance at Dr Petrie she starts to disappear, then stops) What is your name, oh potent one?

DR PETRIE Um... it's Petrie er... William.

FAH LO SUEE Wi-li-am. Ooooh, so pretty! Remember, Wi-li-am... I am your slave.

And she is gone.

The two men are silent for a moment.

DR PETRIE Who... was... she?

NAYLAND SMITH The fiend! The cunning yellow fiend! But the outrageous genius of the cunning yellow fiend. She was a big card to play but he played it anyway!

DR PETRIE I don't understand. You know that girl?

NAYLAND SMITH His daughter, Petrie, his daughter!

DR PETRIE But she's so... lovely.

NAYLAND SMITH Oh genetically modified I'd imagine. Injected with all manner of cunning Eastern hormones and pheromones to render her irresistible to all but the most stoic of English lionhearts. Believe me, Petrie old spunk, one brush of her fingernail could leave you in a rather nasty mess.

(Unbeknownst to himself Nayland Smith is puffing on the opium pipe distractedly as he speaks) She is one of the finest weapons in the enemy's armoury, Petrie. But a woman is a two edged sword.

Treacherous. To our great good fortune she has formed a sudden predilection, curiously Oriental, for yourself.

DR PETRIE *(flattered)* Oh! Surely not!

NAYLAND SMITH   Oh you may scoff, Petrie, but it is evident. Love in the East is like the conjurer's mango tree; it is born, grows and flowers at the touch of a hand. But why do I feel so curiously light headed?

(Suddenly realises he's been smoking the opium pipe) Good God, I quite forgot myself! I am quite literally mashed up dread style! I feel 'mellow' and loving. I wish to wear something called tie dye. And flowers in my hair. And dance to rhythmic music played on steel drums and psychedelic guitars. And wave my backside in concentric circles while a blonde haired girl with gem stone eyes dances with me by the moonlight... no... no... this cannot be!

(Throws the pipe away in disgust, finds a jug of water and throws it in his face) This won't do at all, Petrie! I'm off my face and you've got an Eastern engendered boner. We need assistance to find Sir Crichton!

(He reaches into his pocket, produces an old fashioned looking whistle and blows into it but there is no sound) In true Tory fashion, I've resorted to the dog whistle.

Within twenty minutes there'll be a squadron of Scotland Yard's finest here. But I fear to wait, Petrie. I can sense that fiendish enemy of the white race is close to the fulfilment of his devilish plan.

We must act. Call him, Petrie.

DR PETRIE   Oh, right! *('Cockney' accent)* Oi, China! Get your little yellow posterior aht 'ere now! Chop chop, scrunch face!

Enter 'Chinaman'.

'CHINAMAN'   Yes, yes, I come quickee. Whatee wantee, cockernee?

Nayland Smith suddenly rips off his 'disguise' revealing himself in perfect Edwardian dress.

NAYLAND SMITH   I'm no cockerney, you yellow imbecile, I'm Commissioner Denis Nayland Smith of Scotland Yard formerly of Burma and I may be stoned out of my tiny mind and ready to skip the light fandango and kiss the sky and jammin' in the name of Jah but I demand you take me to the leader of your foul movement that spells the end of our glorious global ascendency!

'CHINAMAN'   You fuck offee!

The 'Chinaman' goes into an elaborate martial arts 'move' complete with squawks and high pitched whoops.

NAYLAND SMITH   Oh, fisticuffs, is it, Charlie? Come along then!

Nayland Smith squares up in a 'straight up' 'Queensbury rules' type fashion.

DR PETRIE   Careful, Smith, he looks dangerous!

NAYLAND SMITH   Oh, be assured, Petrie, I know how to handle his oriental thuggery! *(The 'Chinaman' finally screams in bloodthirsty fashion and leaps at Nayland who whips out his gun and shoots him dead)* Hah! That showed you, you little yellow jigger! Thought you could try your fancy Eastern chop socky on an Englishman? Come along, Petrie, there's not a moment to lose!

They exit as we hear Fu Manchu leering and cackling softly as the stage lights go green and yellowy in a hazy opium blur...

SCENE SIX

Enter Dr Petrie alone.

DR PETRIE   Smith?? Where are you? Smith?

He exits. Fu Manchu's laughter now echoes around the theatre as Nayland Smith enters...

NAYLAND SMITH   Petrie! What the devil's become of you? Petrie?

He exits. Fu Manchu's laughter continues as Dr Petrie enters...

DR PETRIE   Smith? Smith?? Oh my goodness, this place is like a maze, built with all the ball-tampering circularity of the oriental mind! It's really too much for a strait laced stiff upper lip fair play chap who always walks when he's given out to comprehend. But... that smell...

And now we hear a familiar musical theme and a familiar shape appears through the smoke, the undulating red cheongsam of Fah Lo Suee. As soon as she sees Petrie she is all soft coyness.

FAH LO SUEE   Wi-li-am, thank the heaven it is you. I have been longing for you. My whole body is aching for your touch. I am like delicate flower you can cup in your manly hand. With merest caress I will bloom for you.

Ooooh, Wi-li-am, take me, please!

DR PETRIE   Fa Lo Sweet.

FAH LO SUEE *(correcting him)* Suee, oh masterful one, Fa Lo Suee.

DR PETRIE *(attempting)* Sss...oil.

FAH LO SUEE *(correcting him)* Suee. Suee. Oh never mind, silly Englishman. The way my lovely name sounds harsh and ugly in your crude tongue makes me even more enraptured with you. I long we make beast of two back together, my ardent Western conqueror. Take me! Take me, Wi-li-am! Shatter my impuissant primitive defences with your forceful patriotic weapon. Conquer me mercilessly and ruthlessly plunder my natural resources! Take me now!!!

DR PETRIE Fa Lo... Soot, I, I... want to... I do. Your mere presence has induced in me a state of sensual thrall that a chap who used to be a boy scout and go fishing for tiddlers simply isn't accustomed to. I desire with every fibre of my genteel and unruffled being to ravish you endlessly for hours on end but... you are the daughter of my mortal enemy, indeed the enemy of all Britannia, how can I trust you?

FAH LO SUEE Oooh, Wi-li-am, I have been bad girl. It's true. But now I want to be good girl. Help me be good girl, Wi-li-am. Convert me to your western ways. Be my missonary in the missionary position. Please, Wi-li-am, pleeeeaaaasse...

Fah Lo Suee has now got to a position where their lips are inches apart.

DR PETRIE You are too lovely a creature... devilishly intoxicating... a man could lose his mind to such a woman as you... I mustn't, I mustn't... God help me but I must succumb!

(And now they kiss. A moment of sensual stillness. As they part, Fah Lo has a cunning smile as Petrie begins to tremble and convulse...)

What's... happening...to me... what have you done... what...

(And now Petrie begins to spasm uncontrollably in great shuddering bursts as Fah Lo (and Fu Manchu on the screen) laugh hysterically...)

No! No! God help me!

(One last scream as Petrie hunches over so his face is concealed to the audience. Then he straightens up with a start and the audience see that his 'whiteface' mask has vanished and his own (East Asian) features are revealed)

I feel... different, what's... happened? *(He pulls out a cigarette case and stares at his reflection in it.)*

No... no... but how can this be? It's a fate worse than death! I'm... I'm... God help me, I'm CHINESE!!!

Enter Nayland Smith.

NAYLAND SMITH   Petrie! My God! You're CHINESE!!!

DR PETRIE   Smith... she... I... I don't feel well, Smith, I need... I need... I need I need I need I need... to EAT! I need to EAT! I need beef brisket noodles, choi sam vegetables, braised pig knuckles, mapo doufu, RICE, I need RICE, give me RICE!

NAYLAND SMITH   Get back, man! Get back, I'm warning you!

(Nayland Smith shoots Petrie, killing him instantly.)

Oh, Petrie, old mongrel. My steadfast boon companion of male bondery and platonic masculine loyalty. Many's the time you fagged for me at Marlborough and I yearned for us to consummate our forbidden passion for each other. You lantern jawed specimen of male perfection! You're gone. Gone! And I'm left with nothing but aching regret and bitter loneliness borne of lost opportunity and timid conformity.

(He turns to confront Fah Lo Suee) It was you who did this to him, wasn't it, you cunning yellow she vixen!?

FAH LO SUEE   I did! But... now I will confound and beguile you completely by appealing to the largest thing about you.

Certainly larger than your rather flaccid and inept little post colonial penis. In short, the weakest and most vulnerable aspect of your stolidly aggressive imperialist psyche. Even weaker than the aim and direction of the early morning piss you take after a night of gin-sodden sing songs. Even more vulnerable than your waistline is to expanding from eating too many steak and kidney pies once you get past the ripe old age of 23. I did indeed turn your erstwhile bosom beau and soul mate into a slavering stereotypical Chinaman but... I did it *(She suddenly changes tack)* ...for you.

NAYLAND SMITH   For me??

FAH LO SUEE   I only pretend to like Wi-li-am. It you I really love, oh small but perfect form one. I yearn to pleasure every one of your carnal sense until you have enter the seventh realm of tantric ecstasy and are screaming with erotic pleasure. I will make every fibre in your tiny body sing with the sweetest of sensual harmony. I will teach you to make love to me for days on end until we both levitate in sheer unbridle extended orgasm. I turn your friend Chinese because I was jealous and want you all for myself. Oooooh, please, Nay-land, pleeeaaase...

Nayland Smith is transfixed as Fah Lo draws nearer and nearer until... at the very last moment he produces a revolver and shoots her straight in the face.

NAYLAND SMITH Hah! You twisted oriental floozie, did you think I would fall for a story like that? We English believe in fair play, you know!

(On the screen the image of Fu Manchu continues to chuckle softly)

Where are you, you yellow devil? Come out and face me like a man so I can shoot you in the head with my gun, you degenerate squint eyed monster! You foul Eastern bounder! You oriental blackguard! I shall shoot you dead, you hear!

Suddenly there is an almighty crash of a cymbal that seems to make the whole theatre shake. As Nayland Smith staggers, dazed by the noise, from the smoke emerges the yellow robed figure of Fu Manchu...

A moment. Silence. Fu Manchu smiles demonically.

FU MANCHU Inspector Nayland Smith of Burma. At long last we meet.

NAYLAND SMITH And at long last you die, you foul yellow toad!

He raises his gun and shoots at Fu Manchu who raises one hand in the air and casually 'catches' the bullet which he then allows to drop to the floor as Nayland Smith looks on stunned. Fu Manchu chuckles softly.

FU MANCHU You English are so leadenly predictable.

NAYLAND SMITH Oh yes? Well, how about this, squinty?

He fires off four more shots which Fu Manchu variously dodges and catches with elegant, sweeping and elaborate moves until in the end Nayland Smith is left frantically clicking away at the trigger of a gun that has no more bullets left.

Again Fu Manchu chuckles softly.

FU MANCHU You pathetic little occidental. So imbued with an innate yet utterly deluded sense of your own fast fading superiority. Did you imagine that I, as one of the foremost experts in martial combat, could be struck by mere bullets? How crude your methods are, Mr Smith.

You have an imagination that befits your country's weather. Dank and dull. Grey and overcast. How I loathe guns with all their harsh noise and jarring commotion.

How they offend my heightened and stylized sense of celestial Eastern subtlety. How easily you conform to the time honoured stereotype of your countrymen.

Perhaps you would like to drink some real ale and parade around in your union jack underpants singing the theme tune to *The Dambusters*, you obnoxious little rosy cheeked oik?

NAYLAND SMITH   Insult me all you like, you terrible offspring of the quickening of Eastern wombs. It'll soon be curtains for you and your diabolical epicanthic schemes. You may be able to dodge four bullets with your dastardly and ingenious oriental wiles but can you dodge 60? This despicable and disgusting den of vice is currently surrounded by a whole squadron of Scotland Yard's finest!

Fu Manchu produces some form of archaic and oriental-looking remote control from within his robe and points it at the screen.

FU MANCHU   Ah, your fine boys in blue! Your pride and joy. Sir Robert Peel's finest! Do you mean… these by any chance, Mr Smith?

On 'these', Fu Manchu presses a button and we see 'Victorian' style police in tunics and helmets, all wearing 'whiteface' and marching towards some sort of camera.

NAYLAND SMITH   But… of all the ingenious criminal… how?

FU MANCHU   I believe one day it will be known as C.C.T.V., Mr Smith. As with paper money, we Chinese are centuries ahead of you primitive potato mouths. A race of pirates, all you can do is appropriate other cultures for your own. Tell me, what is uniquely 'English'? What great and unique gifts to world culture has your puny and pathetic little nation imparted? Fish, chips, beer and football hooliganism (as I have foreseen in the future). Even your renowned gift for situation comedy will desert you sometime around the beginning of the 21st Century. And as for your football itself… I have one word for you: Iceland.

NAYLAND SMITH   Very well, you despicable yellow fiend, I concede, as we English with our renowned sense of fair play are wont to do, that we are no match for the confoundedly clever conceits of you cunning Cathayans. But all you've done is show me that you can see your downfall approaching.

FU MANCHU   Not so, Mr Nay-land Smith of Burma, not so. You are about to enjoy a unique opportunity to study the meditative art of fungology. To witness the *sui generis* transformative properties of the *ah chong lyco perdon.*

Or in plainer parlance: the Ching Chong Chinaman Puff-ball. By a process of my own I have greatly enhanced this Ching Chong Chinaman Puff-ball. Observe, Mr Nay-land Smith, observe:

(On the screen now a mist seems to descend over the policemen who begin to cough and choke) Note the cloud you now see. It is a thick variety of odour from my peregrine, inscrutable and most mystical culture that shall forever remain obscure to you and your kind and is the order *empusa*. You in fair old dreary England will be familiar with the transformative progress of caterpillars into butterflies. I have developed this evolution drawn from the *hellinsia albidactylus* herb only found in a remote corner of Jiangxi province at the top of a cliff which must be assailed by the most skilled and fearless of naked lascars drawn from the *hweh hwan hwuk* ethnic tribe from inner Hubei region, many of whom die on the journey there and back, in order to reach the crop at the top of a cliff guarded by the fiercest amoyensis South China Tigers that can strip a man's flesh to the bone with one lick of their granular tongue and where swarms of deadly *tritaeniorhynchus* mosquitos, from whom one bite can cause a man's testicles to turn bright purple and swell to the size of large party balloons, gather and mate. But enough orienteering information, if you will pardon the pun. Observe the piquant effect of my manipulation of the concentrated source of this herb...

During the above the men on the screen have begun to convulse and shudder, bend double and violently tremble. Now they all start coming up having removed their 'whiteface' masks, looking at each other in bafflement and confusion...

NAYLAND SMITH This is appalling... diabolical... oh you merciless yellow devil, I do believe you are Satan incarnate you despicable Far Eastern demi dragon! You epicanthic enactment of evil! You garlic-guzzling celestial Gorgon!

FU MANCHU Observe the immediate conclusion of the germination, Mr Smith.

(Fu Manchu closes his eyes and begins to sigh orgasmically) Aaaaaaaaahhh so! It is a triumph! This process is the scientific triumph of my life! Is it not... magnificent?

Now the men on the screen are chattering and gurning. They have found bowls of noodles and rice and are eating ten to the dozen with chop sticks while they chatter excitedly in exaggerated 'Chinese' fashion.

NAYLAND SMITH Despicable, despicable Chinaman!

FU MANCHU You see, Nay-land, we devious transmundane and otherworldly Chinese do not conquer other races in the crude and clumsy way your staggeringly uncouth Empire, with its gunboats and cannon and enforced religious indoctrination, does. We Chinese loathe this unaesthetically blunt and leadenly unpleasant straightforward confrontation. It lacks all elegance, nuance and finesse. We celestial and magical Chinese will assimilate rather than conquer. Absorb rather than dominate. Subsume rather than repel. Receive as opposed to... penetrate. In short, you will become like US, Mr Smith. During the unadept boxer uprising we had a saying. 'You can never conquer all of the Chinese'.

Very soon, the entire world will be Chinese!

NAYLAND SMITH   No! No!

FU MANCHU   Oh yes, Mr Smith. They have transformed like butterflies. This is my chrysalis. My becoming. I AM THE GOD OF ASSIMILATION!!

At this point Fu Manchu throws back his head and begins to chuckle loudly in exaggerated 'Dr Doom' style.

NAYLAND SMITH   You vile dynastic behemoth! I suppose this is what you did to Sir Crichton Colonial and the rest?

FU MANCHU   Sir Crichton Colonial is at present running a Chinese take away in the village of Wapping where I hear his prawn toast is extremely popular with the locals. Baron Wilhelm on the other hand is serving pu-er tea somewhere in the Rhine. The Dutchman, Johan-Vincent, meanwhile, is demonstrating calligraphy in one of the racier areas in Amsterdam whilst the French Marquis is giving florid and acrobatic martial art circus exhibitions in Le Moulin Rouge as we speak. Every conceivable cliché and trope catered for.

NAYLAND SMITH   You despicable yellow devil! We may never be able to conquer all of the Chinese but you can never turn all of our fair and pleasant isle into pesky orientals. Do you hear me, you sinister sloe eyed savage? There'll always be an England, and England will be free! You just try turning me into one of your noodle noshing nincompoops! I believe your devilishly tempting seductress of a Suzy Wong daughter tried that with me and look at her now. *(Smith stands back to reveal the body of Fa Loh Suee.)*

If her fiendish yellow feminine wiles couldn't extract a kiss from me, what chance do you think a bald minger like yourself has? Hmmm?

FU MANCHU *(dissembling rather obviously)* My daughter!! You have slain my daughter!! NOOOOO!!!

The offspring of my eighteenth (and favourite) concubine. Oh, Nayland, you colonial oppressors are a brutal people indeed. No nonsense brooked. The same way you sailed your gunboats up our river, and sacked our Summer Palace of artefacts to be exhibited in your museums, whilst pooing in the Celestial Emperor's bed, you have murdered my slippery, seductive and slinkily sensual scion. Perhaps you are right, Nay-land. Perhaps my low Confucian cunning really is no match for your upright stiff upper lip and boot in the bollocks. I concede to your steadfast Brittanic obduracy which has quite confounded my watery cosmological circularity. I surrender to your laissez-faire free market ethos and will humbly sign an Unequal Treaty with you ceding yet more territory to your great and mighty commonwealth for you to regain your sovereign status as a great trading nation-state once more.

NAYLAND SMITH   Very well. In the spirit of decent Christian mercy, I accept your total and unconditional surrender and look forward to your paying reparations for your ignominious and humiliating defeat at the hands of a superior civilisation.

Fu Manchu produces a small 'exotic' looking box from his robes.

FU MANCHU   In that case would you care for a chocolate? Scented Turkish Delight from the heart of the old Orient.

NAYLAND SMITH   Seeing as you've admitted defeat and are behaving like something resembling a gentleman, then don't mind if I do, ching chong– *(He reaches for a chocolate)*

FU MANCHU   Here, take the whole box. *(Nayland Smith greedily takes the box, but as he opens it a puff of smoke explodes upwards causing him to cough and retch violently)* Ha! Fooled you, you rubicund cheeked imbecile! My inscrutable countenance gave nothing away and you fell for my Sun Tzu stratagem like the gulled half wit you undoubtedly are! Not so much taking candy from a baby as giving it. Ha ha ha!

NAYLAND SMITH   Oh, you monster! You foul yellow tyrant! What's... happening... to meeeeeee?

FU MANCHU   First comes the trance-like state followed by... assimilation, Mr Smith. Relatively painless but you may find the experience... disturbing, nonetheless *(Nayland Smith has frozen, eyes staring outwards)*

And now I have you in a pliant and neutral state, there is one question I must ask you, Mr Nay-land Smith.

Precisely why is it that you despise and fear we orientals so much?

Nayland Smith begins to talk in a staccato drone which becomes gradually more pronounced and impassioned as he goes on...

NAYLAND SMITH   Why... why... well... because... sinister looking... hooded slant eyes... horrible jaundice skin... so many of you... like a herd of ants... yellow ants... swarming... everywhere... impassive... impossible to tell what you bastards are thinking... giving nothing away... smiling like Cheshire cats, only not Cheshire cats because Cheshire is in ENGLAND, oh yes... your food's too spicy, too rich for a palate bred on stodge... your music's too twangy and twongy... you sound like robots when you speak... up and down all the time, up and down... you don't call a spade a spade... you go round and round the fucking houses in a maddeningly indirect way as if you're trying to play some ancient game of Chinese chequers... you're... UGLY... my God, but you're UGLY... horrible, efficient, relentless, resourceful little bastards, you've started winning at sports, you'll be good at football next! You're becoming like black people! And you're too bloody clever! It's not fair! We used to be able to conquer you. Make you subservient. Have one token oriental in the play who didn't say much, but now you want to be everywhere! Now you're buying all our houses and driving the property prices up. You're waiting for the January sales at one minute past midnight. You even bought the House of bloody Fraser! It'll be the House of Windsor next. And we need a villain! My word, how we need a villain! And you fit the bill, you argumentative, uppity little yellow upstarts, we put on make-up and taped our eyelids to play you, what MORE do you want you little yellow tykes? You you you...

And now Nayland Smith screams and goes into a spasm, bending double as Fu Manchu chuckles.

FU MANCHU   You were saying, Mr Smith?

Nayland Smith suddenly lurches up and we see that his whiteface mask has gone and his Chinese features are now visible as he hops around in exaggerated oriental fashion.

NAYLAND SMITH   You wanna buy fakee lolex watchee flom meeee, misssta?

Aaaah so, harro harro harro, I go quickee quickee chop chopee get you bowlee noodlee, velly tastee, soy saucee, speakee strangeee, kung fu kickee, acrobatee, singee songee, silly danceee, big grineee, toothee toothee, yeseee yeseee, me no sexeee, me a gimpeee yeseee yesee yeseee aaah so–

He freezes abruptly with a silly 'toothy' grin on his face as Fu Manchi snaps his fingers once. He then snaps his fingers again and the rest of the characters – Dr Petrie, Fa Loh Suee, 'Chinaman' – arise and stand facing the audience flashing the same silly 'toothy' grins.

DR PETRIE / FA LOH SUEE / 'CHINAMAN' / NAYLAND SMITH
MASTAAAHHHHH!!!

FU MANCHU   And now my cunning and intricately conceived master plan begins to reach fruition. We will subsume you. All of you. First we take Limehouse. Then... we take... THE WORLD!!!

Fu Manchu cackles maniacally as a large cymbal crashes loudly and...

Suddenly Nayland Smith is alone–

NAYLAND SMITH   So I awaken from the dream...

Except *(Nayland touches his face as he speaks)* it was no dream... As a result of my encounter with Fu Manchu I find myself in multi-cultural limbo. Has the fiend triumphed? Am I on the diversity express for all time? Am I to be... replaced??

(Under the following speech the sound of the global Far Right movement seeps in: chants, speeches, marching, marching...)

No. No! I will not!

We are... taking... back... control...

The invading hordes will not swamp us. They won't make us eat their food and adopt their customs and serve us in restaurants and take care of us in hospitals and pick fruit in our fields and make us our coffee and wipe the poo from our backsides never never never–

WE WILL NEVER SURRENDER!

Silence.

Nayland Smith laughs.

He laughs and laughs.

Somewhere else someone else laughs.

Nayland Smith stops laughing.

The sound of Fu Manchu laughing.

Nayland Smith smiles.

The lights fade.

The end.

Aurora Metro Books

some of our other play collections

SOUTHEAST ASIAN PLAYS
eds. Cheryl Robson and Aubrey Mellor
ISBN 978-1-906582-86-9   £16.99

BLACK AND ASIAN PLAYS ANTHOLOGY
introduced by Afia Nkrumah
ISBN 978-0-9536757-4-6   £12.99

SIX PLAYS BY BLACK AND ASIAN WOMEN WRITERS
ed. Kadija George
ISBN 978-0-9515877-2-0   £7.50

DURBAN DIALOGUES, INDIAN VOICE
by Ashwin Singh
ISBN 978-1-906582-42-5   £15.99

DURBAN DIALOGUES, THEN AND NOW
by Ashwin Singh
ISBN 978-1-911501-93-0   £14.99

NEW SOUTH AFRICAN PLAYS
edited and introduced by Charles J. Fourie
ISBN 978-0-9536757-4-6   £12.99

www.aurorametro.com